A SHORT HISTORY OF

INDONESIA

Short History of Asia Series

Series Editor: Milton Osborne
Milton Osborne has had an association with the Asian region for over 40 years as an academic, public servant and independent writer. He is the author of eight books on Asian topics, including *Southeast Asia: An Introductory History*, first published in 1979 and now in its eighth edition, and, most recently, *The Mekong: Turbulent Past, Uncertain Future*, published in 2000.

A SHORT HISTORY OF
INDONESIA

THE UNLIKELY NATION?

Colin Brown

ALLEN&UNWIN

First published in 2003

Copyright © Colin Brown 2003

Allen & Unwin
83 Alexander Street
Crows Nest NSW 2065
Australia
Phone: (61 2) 8425 0100
Fax: (61 2) 9906 2218
Email: info@allenandunwin.com
Web: www.allenandunwin.com

National Library of Australia
Cataloguing-in-Publication entry:

Brown, Colin,
 A short history of Indonesia : the unlikely nation?

 Bibliography.
 Includes index.
 ISBN 1 86508 838 2

 1. Indonesia—History.
 I. Title. (Series : Short histories of Asia).

959.4

Index compiled by Russell Brooks.
Set in 11/14 pt Goudy by Midland Typesetters, Maryborough, Victoria
Printed by South Wind Productions, Singapore

10 9 8 7 6 5 4 3 2 1

For Christopher and Meily.
This is their story, more than it is mine.

CONTENTS

Acknowledgements

The author of any book acquires a mountain of debts, both academic and social. I am no exception.

The first draft of this book was written in the second half of 2000, while I was on study leave from Flinders University. For part of this time, I was a Visiting Fellow at the International Institute for Asian Studies in Leiden, the Netherlands. I gratefully acknowledge the warm collegial support I received during my stay there, from the Director Professor W. A. L. Stokhof and all his colleagues.

I also spent several weeks in the Faculty of Social and Political Sciences at Parahyangan University, Bandung, Indonesia. I have been visiting Parahyangan regularly for some years now; once again, staff and students there made me feel most welcome. I thank in particular the Rector of the University, Professor B. Suprapto Brotosiswojo, the Deputy Rector for Academic Affairs, Mr Johannes Gunawan, the Deputy Rector for International Cooperation, Dr R. W. Triweko, and the then Dean of the Faculty, Dr Pius Suratman Kartasasmita.

Griffith University, where I first taught Indonesian history, provided me with office and library facilities for the final part of my leave. I thank Professor Nick Knight, Dean of the Faculty of Asian and International Studies, and Professor Colin Mackerras.

At Flinders University, I have had the good fortune to work with a number of very talented scholars. I must single out Dr Jim Schiller, with whom I have co-taught courses and co-supervised postgraduate students, for his willingness to discuss almost any aspect of Indonesia, and his deep knowledge of and feeling for the country. We have not always agreed on interpretation of events, but I have always admired and respected the persuasive ways in which he makes his points.

I also acknowledge the students I have taught, and debated with, at Griffith University, the University of Tasmania, Parahyangan University and Flinders University. It is almost a cliché to say so, but I have learned as much from these students as I have taught them. I have also enjoyed many debates and discussions about their country with Indonesian students in Adelaide, testing their patience at times, I know, by my inability to see things in quite the same way they do. I thank them.

Outside the academic world, I thank colleagues in the Australia Indonesia Business Council for making me think and re-think my understandings of Indonesia in response to their questions and challenges. I am grateful, also, to the Grey Hounds for their probing queries about matters Indonesian.

And finally, of course, I acknowledge the enormous debt I owe to my wife Iem, who started me on the long road to learning Indonesian, and who has shared with me so freely her knowledge of Indonesia, and her commitment to it. Like many others in similar positions, she has sacrificed her own academic career to support me in mine, and done so without demur.

Needless to say, however, while I am grateful for all that the people mentioned above have taught me, responsibility for errors and omissions in this book rests with me alone.

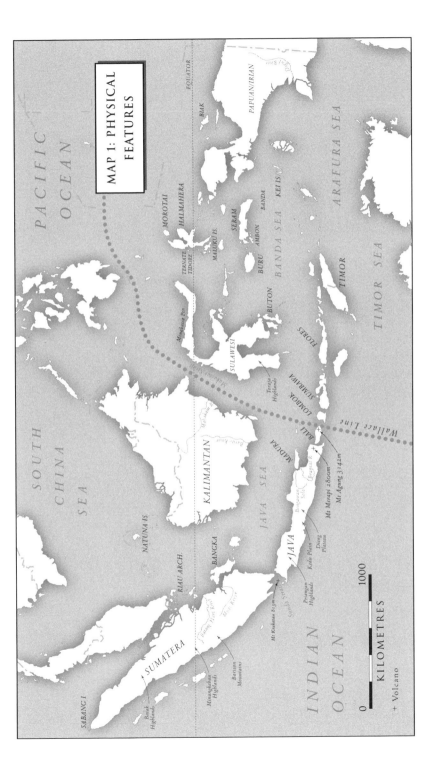

MAP 1: PHYSICAL FEATURES

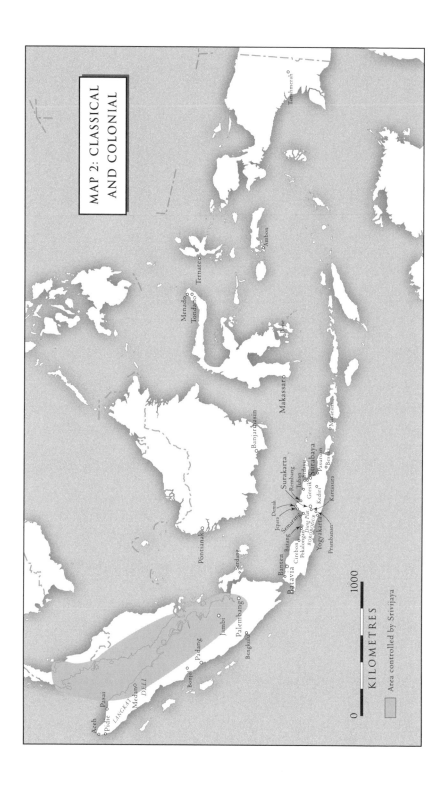

MAP 2: CLASSICAL
AND COLONIAL

Aceh
Pidie
Pasai
Medano
LANGKAT
DELI
Bonjol
Padang
Bengkulu
Jambi
Palembang

Pontianak

Banjarmasin

Menado
Tondano
Ternate

Ambon

Makassar

Sedan

Banten
Batavia
Cirebon
Pekalongan Plat
Ujung Pang
BOROBODUR
Yogyakarta
Prambanan

Jepara Demak
Kudus
Semarang
Surakarta
Rembang
Tuban
Sidayu
Gresik Surabaya
Kediri
Pasuruan
Besuki
Kartasura
Mataram

Tambmerah

Bone

KILOMETRES

0   1000

Area controlled by Srivijaya

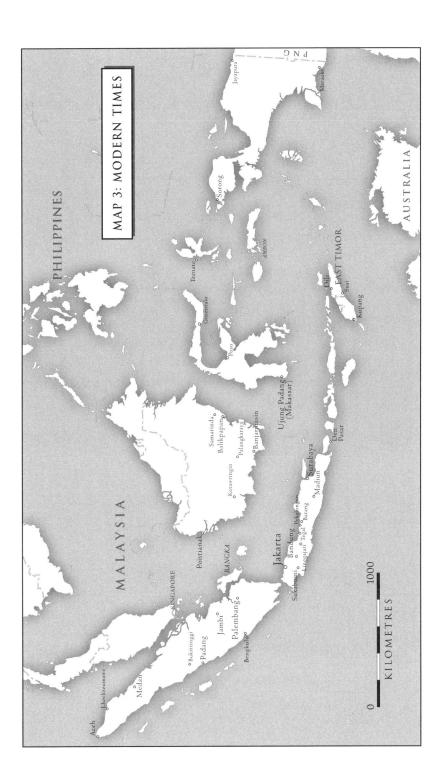

MAP 3: MODERN TIMES

PHILIPPINES

MALAYSIA

AUSTRALIA

EAST TIMOR

P N G

Aceh
Lhokseumawe
Medan
Bukittinggi
Padang
Jambi
Palembang
Bengkulu
BANGKA
SINGAPORE
Pontianak
Jakarta
Bandung
Sukabumi
Linggajati
Tegal
Pekalongan
Batang
Madiun
Surabaya
Den
Pasar
Kotawringin
Palangkaraya
Banjarmasin
Samarinda
Balikpapan
Ujung Padang
(Makassar)
Poso
Gorontalo
Ternate
Sorong
AMBON
Dili
Suai
Kupang
Jayapura
Merauke

KILOMETRES

0   1000

Acronyms

ASEAN	Association of Southeast Asian Nations
BCE	Before Current Era
CE	Current Era
DOM	Daerah Operasi Militer (Military Operations Area)
FDI	Foreign Direct Investment
GAM	Gerakan Aceh Merdaka (Free Aceh Movement)
GAPI	Gabungan Politik Indonesia (Indonesian Political Federation)
Gerindo	Gerakan Rakyat Indonesia (Indonesia People's Movement)
GDP	Gross Domestic Product
Golkar	Golongan Karya (Functional Groups)
ICMI	Ikatan Cendekiawan Muslin Indonesia (League of Indonesian Muslim Intellectuals)
INTERFET	International Force for East Timor
ISDV	Indische Sociaal-Democratische Vereeniging (Indies Social Democratic Association)
KADIN	Kamar Dagang dan Industri (Chamber of Commerce and Industry)
KNIL	Koninklijk Nederlandsch Indisch Leger (Royal Netherlands Indies Army)
KNIP	Komite Nasional Indonesia Pusat (Indonesian Central National Committee)
MIAI	Majelis Islam A'laa Indonesia (All-Indonesian Muslim Congress)
MPR	Majelis Permusyawaratan Rakyat (People's Consultative Assembly)
NHM	Nederlandsche Handel Maatschappij (Netherlands Trading Company)
NU	Nahdatul Ulama (Muslim Scholars Association)
OPM	Organisasi Papua Merdeka (Free Papua Movement)
Partindo	Partai Indonesia (Indonesia Party)

PDI	Partai Demokrasi Indonesia (Indonesian Democratic Party
PDIP	Partai Demokrasi Indonesia–Perjuangan (Indonesian Democratic Party of Struggle)
PI	Perhimpunan Indonesia (Indonesian Association)
PKB	Partai Kebangkitan Bangsa (National Awakening Party)
PKI	Partai Komunis Indonesia (Indonesian Communist Party)
PNI	Partai Nasionalis Indonesia (Indonesian Nationalist Party)
New PNI	Pendidikan Nasional Indonesia (Indonesian National Education)
PPP	Partai Persatuan Pembangunan (United Development Party)
PPPKI	Permufakatan Perhimpunan Politik Kebangsaan Indonesia (Union of Political Organisations of the Indonesian People)
PRRI	Pemerintah Revolusioner Republik Indonesia (Revolutionary Government of the Republic of Indonesia)
PSI	Partai Sosialis Indonesia (Indonesian Socialist Party)
PSII	Partai Sarekat Islam Indonesia (Islamic League Party of Indonesia)
RUSI	Republic of the United States of Indonesia
SI	Sarekat Islam (Islamic League)
SIRA	Sentra Informasi Referendum Aceh (Acehnese Centre for Referendum Information)
STOVIA	School Tot Opleiding Van Inlandsche Artsen (School for the Training of Native Doctors)
TKR	Tentara Keamanan Rakyat (People's Security Army)
UDT	União Democrática Timorense (Timorese Democratic Union)
UNAMET	United Nations Assistance Mission in East Timor
VOC	Vereenigde Oost-Indische Compagnie (United East India Company)
VSTP	Vereeniging Spoor-en Tramweg-Personeel (Rail and Tramways Workers Union)

Glossary

Airlangga	King of east/central Java (991–1046)
Arjunawiwaha	'The Marriage of Arjuna', an epic poem by court poet Mpu Kanwa and loosely based on the Indian tale *The Mahabarata*. Composed during the reign of Airlangga
Borobudur	Buddhist temple in Central Java, construction of which began in the ninth century
bupati	Head of a district (*kabupaten*)
cultuurstelsel	Cultivation System
Gajah Mada	Prime Minister of central Java-based kingdom of Majapahit in the mid-fourteenth century
Hikayat Banjar	'The Story of Banjar', written sometime between the fifteenth and seventeenth centuries
jong	Old-Javanese term for sea-going ship, probably the origin of the word 'junk'
kongsi	Group of people (normally of ethnic Chinese origin) coming together for commercial or business purposes
kris	Traditional dagger with a wavy-edged blade
marhaen	Term coined by Sukarno to define the ordinary, poor Indonesian; it differs from the Marxist idea of 'proletarian' because the *marhaen* does own some income-producing goods, such as farming tools, fishing net or a buffalo
mufukat	Consensus
musyawarah	Deliberation
Negarakrtagama	Epic poem composed by the court poet Prapanca in 1365 during the Majapahit era
Paderi	Reformist Muslims influenced by the Wahhabist movement in Arabia; influential in Minangkabau

	(Sumatera) from early in the nineteenth century
Pancasila	The five principles of the Indonesian state
Pararaton	'The Book of Kings', written in the sixteenth century; a chronology of the kings of Majapahit
pasisir	North coast of Java
pemuda	Young people
peranakan	Ethnic Chinese whose cultural orientation is primarily towards Indonesia rather than China
pesantren	Islamic rural boarding school
Prambanan	Hindu temple in Central Java, construction of which began in the nineteenth century
priyayi	Javanese aristocracy
puputan	Mass suicide (Bali)
totok	Pure, genuine (in racial sense); usually referring to ethnic Chinese whose cultural orientation is towards China rather than Indonesia
ulama	Religious scholar
uleebalang	Regional chief in Aceh
Volksraad	People's Council: quasi-parliament established by the Dutch in 1916 and which first met two years later
walak	Local communities in Minahasa, north Sulawesi
wali songo	The Nine Saints, reputed to have brought Islam to Java in the sixteenth century

Note on transcription

The process of standardising the spelling of Indonesian words, and especially place names, is of relatively recent origin, and still incomplete. Since 1945 there have been two revisions of the spelling system used for Indonesian, the most recent one, in 1972, standardising Indonesian and Malaysian spellings. The main changes which follow from this revision are that the old 'dj' was changed to 'j' (Djakarta to Jakarta), the old 'j' to 'y' (Jogjakarta to Yogyakarta) and the old 'tj' to 'c' (Atjeh to Aceh). The pronunciation of this revised spelling follows the logical pattern for English speakers, except that the 'c' is pronounced as if it were written 'ch'. Words that have been introduced into Indonesian from Arabic, Sanskrit or old Javanese are sometimes found with variant spellings, depending on the original romanisation. Thus, for example, the organisation I have referred to as Nahdatul Ulama is sometimes rendered as Nahdlatul Ulama. The classical kingdom of south Sumatera which I call Srivijaya is sometimes rendered as Sriwijaya (and under an older spelling convention, as Srividjaja or Sriwidjaja). The classical old Javanese text *Negarakrtagama* is sometimes spelled as *Negarakertagama*.

I have not changed the spelling of personal names to conform to contemporary orthography unless the person concerned has done so him or herself. Thus I have retained Tjokroaminto (not changing it to Cokroaminoto) and Sjahrir (not Syahrir). However the names of Indonesia's first two Presidents I have spelled as Sukarno and Suharto even though at the time they were born their names were spelled as Soekarno and Soeharto, because both used the revised forms in official contexts.

I have generally used the spelling of place names currently in use in Indonesia, although this may at times be unfamiliar to the English-speaking reader. Thus, for instance, I have used Aceh rather than Acheh, Sumatera rather than Sumatra, Makasar rather than Makassar. I have also used Indonesian place names in preference to the ones often used by foreigners: thus Kalimantan rather than Borneo, Sulawesi rather than Celebes.

Finally, a number of places have had their names changed, or their spelling altered over the centuries: Jayakarta became Batavia, then Djakarta and then Jakarta; Makasar was once called Ujung Pandang; Yogyakarta has been spelled as Jogjakarta and Djokdjakarta. In all cases, I have used the current terminology and spelling except where quotations are drawn directly from other documents.

1
THE INDONESIAN CONTEXT

The term 'Indonesia' is a problematic one. Since it was coined in the mid-nineteenth century, it has been used in a variety of different, and sometimes contradictory, ways. This chapter starts by considering these different usages, and indicates the ways in which it will be used in the book. This is followed by a consideration of the physical environment within which the history of the archipelago and its peoples is located. It concludes with a brief discussion of the societies that were in existence in the archipelago at the beginning of the Common Era, 2000 years ago.

What's in a name?

One of the problems of thinking and writing about Indonesia at the beginning of the twenty-first century is working out just what 'Indonesia' refers to. Since its coinage in the mid-nineteenth century the word has acquired various geographical, political and social meanings, of which the original geographical meaning is perhaps the least controversial. A British geographer, James Richardson Logan, coined the name to refer to the vast archipelago, with many thousands of islands, off the southeast tip of mainland Asia. A combination of 'India' and *nêsos* (Greek for 'islands'), Indonesia meant 'Indian islands'. In part, the name reflected the fact that for many European writers of the day the Indonesian archipelago was seen as an extension of the Indian subcontinent, especially in cultural terms. The British also used the term 'Further India' to describe the region; the Dutch called their colonial possessions in the islands *Nederlands Indie*, meaning 'Dutch India' or 'Dutch Indies'. More generally, as the name India had not yet taken on the geographically precise meaning it has today, in some senses India meant simply what modern Europeans now refer to as Southeast Asia.

By the early part of the twentieth century, the term 'Indonesia' was taking on political and social connotations, both for the nationalist movement seeking to free the archipelago of its Dutch colonial rulers, and for the Dutch themselves. By the late 1920s, the nationalist movement was using the name to describe both the political entity it was hoping to bring into existence in place of the Dutch colonial state, and the social community, the nation, which was to inhabit that state. The nationalists were using the word in the names of their political parties; calling themselves Indonesians; referring to their language—a modernised form of Malay—as Indonesian. The Dutch authorities, seeking to deny both these meanings, refused to use the word in any official way, and did their best to deny that it had any meaning.

The political entity Indonesia came into existence between 1945, with the proclamation of independence by Sukarno and Hatta, and 1949, when the Dutch acknowledged that independence. The inhabitants of a few parts of the archipelago—most notably in south Maluku—sought to place themselves outside this state, but by the mid-1950s it could be said that the Indonesian state was clearly and firmly established.

However, the struggle to give social meaning to the word Indonesia, to persuade the peoples of the archipelago to identify themselves collectively as Indonesians, proved to be a much more difficult task. Certainly before the twentieth century, none of the inhabitants of the archipelago would have seen themselves in these collective terms, and even after 1945, there were tensions between regional, ethnic and national identities. These tensions were perhaps most marked in the case of people of ethnic Chinese descent: as we will see, the question of whether and under what conditions such people could be counted as Indonesians, in either the political or social sense, is one which has aroused great controversy since 1945. But other groups of people in the archipelago at various times also rejected attempts by the state to define them as Indonesians.

By the later years of the twentieth century, however, a combination of the charismatic nationalism of Sukarno, Indonesia's first President, and the authoritarianism of Suharto, its second, seemed to have cemented-in a sense of belonging to the Indonesian nation across the vast bulk of the archipelago. There were exceptions, East Timor being the most obvious, but generally speaking the concept of 'being Indonesian' seemed established.

At the turn of the next century, though, just a few years on, the social meaning of Indonesia appears to have become more clouded, and less certain, than at any time since 1945. The year 1999 brought the referendum in East Timor, which saw 78 per cent of the population choosing to reject membership of the Indonesian nation and state. This was an exceptional case, in that East Timor had never been part of the Netherlands Indies, and thus had never been part of the original struggle for Indonesian independence. In the aftermath of the fall of Suharto, and in particular of the East Timor vote, breakaway movements in Aceh and Papua[1] have also gained strength in their challenges to the Indonesian state and nation.

At the time of writing, the question of whether Indonesia will survive as a nation and as a state remains unanswered. On balance, as will be argued in Chapter 9, the likelihood is that it will; that the experience of Indonesian-ness shared by inhabitants of the archipelago over the previous half-century or more will prevail over more short-term resentment at the ways in which the Suharto government, in the name of the state, exploited and suppressed the regions. But the possibility remains that in the early years of this century Indonesia will either cease to exist as a political and social entity, or continue to exist only in a severely truncated form.

The various different interpretations of the term Indonesia, and the instability of its political and social meanings, are of considerable relevance to this book. In a sense the book has been written backwards, using the Indonesian nation and state at the end of the twentieth century as its starting or defining point. From this it follows that in geographical terms Indonesia refers to that string of islands which at the end of the twentieth century constituted the state of Indonesia. Thus the western half of the island of New Guinea is included, the eastern half excluded; the southern and eastern two-thirds of the island of Kalimantan are included, the rest left out. Historically, however, this approach presents some problems. The peoples of the east coast of the island of Sumatera, for instance, have firm and long-established links—political, social, economic—with the peoples of the Malay Peninsula: links which are much stronger than those with the peoples of the eastern islands of the archipelago. To define Sumatera as being included within the scope of this book, while excluding consideration of the Malay Peninsula, to some extent at least goes against the historical experience. But the same is true of the histories of many of the countries of Asia and Africa: their contemporary shapes have largely emerged out of the struggle against colonialism, which in turn has meant that it was the colonialists who determined the borders of the post-colonial states, leaving the leaders of the new states with the difficult task of creating a social community within politically defined borders which ignored ties of perhaps great antiquity with communities lying beyond those borders.

With those caveats in mind, I want now to turn to a brief examination of the historical environment of the Indonesian archipelago, and its human environment, up to around the seventh century of the Current Era.[2]

The physical environment

The histories of all peoples are influenced, to greater or lesser extent, by the physical environments they inhabit. This is particularly so of Indonesia. The fact that Indonesia is an archipelago of more than 13 600 islands, and that at least until recently the inland areas of many of its islands were difficult to traverse, has meant that for many of its peoples its waterways have been much more important than roads as transport routes. It was along the seaways and river routes that religions, languages, ideologies—and genes—moved. The South China Sea and the Java Sea, bounded by the islands of Kalimantan, Sumatera and Java, and by the Malay Peninsula, have been compared by some historians to the Mediterranean Sea in terms of the role they have played in the region's history. The peoples living on the littoral of these Indonesian seas did not form a single community any more than did their counterparts in the Mediterranean region. But they have long been linked by ties of trade, religion and language that have helped to create a network of cultures which are related one to another.

The seas separating the islands of the western half of the archipelago—as far east as the eastern coasts of Kalimantan and Bali—are shallow, their beds being submerged portions of the Sunda Shelf. This shelf is the most southerly of a series of great blocs or plates making up the Eurasian landmass. It protrudes from the southeastern tip of the Asian mainland, under the South China and Java Seas, into Kalimantan, Sumatera and Java. Today the submerged parts of the shelf for the most part are less than 50 metres under water. Thus even relatively small changes in sea levels could change dramatically the coastlines of the region. If the sea level dropped by just 20 metres, the Malay Peninsula, Sumatera and Java would be joined together; at 50 metres, Kalimantan would also be joined to the Asian mainland. We know that sea levels here have in fact varied enormously over time: prehistorians tell us, for instance, that the whole of the Sunda Shelf might have been dry land as recently as 18 000 years ago.

These changes in sea levels, and in particular the fact that in quite recent times much of the central and western sections of the Indonesian archipelago were connected by dry land to the Asian mainland, do much to explain the spread of humanity around the region, and in particular the close ethnic and linguistic ties between the peoples of Java, Sumatera and the Southeast Asian mainland. They also explain the fact that these same islands are characterised by mainland Asian flora and fauna: orchids, teak, bamboo, elephants, monkeys, tigers, rhinoceroses and the like.

To the east of the Sunda Shelf, and across what is now a fairly deep sea channel, lies the Sahul Shelf, the plate from which protrude the islands of the eastern end of the archipelago, including New Guinea—and Australia. On the islands of the Sahul Shelf we find Australasian flora and fauna—eucalypt trees, kangaroos, cassowaries and so forth. More importantly, many of the peoples of the islands of the Sahul Shelf have had closer ethnic and cultural ties to the peoples of the Pacific islands than to their nearer neighbours in more westerly parts of the archipelago.

This is not to say that there were no interactions between the peoples of the eastern archipelago and those of the islands to their west;

clearly there were. The complex ethnography of the region from Bali to the Maluku Islands is evidence of the extent to which the peoples of the archipelago blended and mixed. But for most of the period covered by this book, the peoples of New Guinea were largely isolated from political and economic developments in the central and western parts of the archipelago. The factor which brought western New Guinea into closest contact with the rest of the archipelago was colonialism: by the early twentieth century the Dutch had established a series of settlements there, bringing at least parts of the region under the same colonial administration as Java, Sumatera and the other islands, thus ultimately ensuring its inclusion in the future Republic of Indonesia.

The dividing line between the Sunda Shelf and the Sahul Shelf in effect marks the ecological division between Asia and Australasia. On precisely where to draw this line, scholars are not in agreement. Two of the best-known attempts to fix the line were made in the nineteenth century by the British scientists Wallace and Huxley: they agreed that the line lay between Bali and Lombok in the south, and Kalimantan and Sulawesi further north, but whereas Huxley's line continued west of the Philippines, Wallace's went to the east.

That Indonesia straddles this line accounts, at least in part, for its great natural and demographic diversity. Among modern states, probably only Russia—and less certainly China and India—encompass such geographic and cultural diversity within their national boundaries.

The islands of the Indonesian archipelago are for the most part made up of partly drowned mountain arcs. Two main arcs, running in parallel, sweep south and east from the Himalayas, through the Bay of Bengal, and emerge from the seas to form first the island of Sumatera, then Java, Bali and the chain of islands to its east, then Sulawesi. Kalimantan and New Guinea are formed by different arcs, the former an extension of the Malay Peninsula, the latter an extension of the chains which form many of the island archipelagos of the south Pacific Ocean.

For the most part these mountain chains are geologically active; Indonesia lies firmly within the so-called 'Ring of Fire' circling the north Pacific Ocean. Sumatera has no fewer than ten active volcanoes and fifteen dormant ones, Java eighteen and seventeen respectively. In Java, the material ejected by these volcanoes and mixed with the naturally occurring soils produces a very fertile soil, which has contributed greatly to the island's agricultural productivity. The Sumateran volcanoes, on the other hand, throw out material that is different in chemical composition that has led to soils which are generally poorer than those in Java. Thus Java historically has been the agricultural centre of the archipelago.

The other important natural characteristic of the archipelago, which has been of enormous significance in shaping regional histories, is its climate, and in particular the patterns of the winds which blow across it. The dominant feature here is the monsoon, which blows from the south and the east in the northern summer, from the north and west in the winter.

The summer monsoon blows out of the central Australian desert. It picks up a small amount of moisture as it passes over the Timor and Arafura Seas, which is deposited as rain on the southern slopes of the mountains of the central islands of the archipelago, but it is basically a dry wind. For most of Indonesia, summer is the dry season.

The northern monsoon blows in the reverse direction, and before it gets to the archipelago passes over much wider stretches of water in the South China and Java Seas. It is thus a very moist wind, bringing extensive rainfalls to the region. The northern winter is the wet season for most of Indonesia, especially for those regions to the north of the mountain chains.

The monsoons have a major influence on patterns of agriculture across Indonesia, and have helped to concentrate populations in the western part of the archipelago, and along the coasts of the Java Sea. But the monsoons have had another impact on Indonesia, one that has arguably been more important for its history, for they have brought traders to and through the archipelago for at least the past 2000 years.

During the northern summer—the middle months of the year— the monsoon blowing from the south and east enabled Indonesian traders to sail north to China; the winter monsoon brought them home again. For the traders from China, the pattern was reversed, but just as reliable: they came south to Indonesia on the winter monsoon, and returned home on the summer one.

For the trade with India, the summer monsoon permitted travel across the Bay of Bengal towards Sumatera and the Malay Peninsula; the winter monsoon saw travel in the opposite direction.

The monsoon winds thus placed the Indonesian archipelago in a location of enormous strategic significance—at the crossroads of seaborne trade between west and south Asia on the one hand, and northeast Asia on the other. The coasts of the Straits of Melaka, the Java Sea and the South China Sea were ideal locations for the establishment of ports to service trade passing through the region. As we will see, the shores of the Straits of Melaka and the north coast of Java were to be two crucially important focal points for the development and support of this trade and as a consequence were to play leading roles in the development of societies and states in the region, for not only did the monsoons support trade, they carried in their wake philosophies, religions, sciences and political principles.

The ethnographic environment

Where did the peoples of the archipelago come from? Generations of scholars have debated this issue without arriving at any definitive answer, at least in part because it depends on at what point in the evolutionary process we say that 'Indonesian peoples' emerged. However, if we accept that the present-day indigenous Indonesian population consists of two broad ethnic groups, the Melanesian in the east and the Austronesian in the west, we can get a little further in addressing the question. There seems little doubt that the Melanesian-speaking peoples, now to be found chiefly in Papua and a few of its offshore islands, arrived first, probably from the east. They spread westward through the archipelago, possibly as far west as the Andaman Islands in the Bay of Bengal, and north into the Philippines. The Austronesian speakers almost certainly arrived later from southern China via Taiwan and the Philippine Islands. Austronesian speakers had probably settled the Philippines by about 2500 BCE, Kalimantan, Sulawesi and Timor by about 2000 BCE and Halmahera by 1500 BCE. These peoples were hunters and gatherers, but they were also agriculturalists, and brought with them domesticated pigs and dogs. The Melanesian-speaking peoples retreated eastward before them.

By the beginning of the Current Era, a number of sophisticated societies were well established in parts of the Indonesian archipelago, alongside others with perhaps simpler and less complex cultures. The language groups which formed the basis of most of the languages of the archipelago, Austronesian and Melanesian, were in place. Wet-rice farming was being practised in those regions which could support it, with buffalo and oxen providing the traction power. The most sophisticated societies were almost certainly those in Java, but even here there were no states in anything like the modern sense of the term. Rather they were communities, sharing perhaps some cultural characteristics with their neighbours, but not tied to them by political bonds. On the other islands, societies were smaller and more scattered, and at different stages of technological development, consistent with the different natural environments they faced.

The early centuries of the Current Era were to see the emergence of the first real states in the archipelago.

2
THE RISE OF STATES
1–1500 CE

The millennium and a half from the beginning of the Current Era to the end of the fifteenth century represent the golden era of Indonesian history, the period when indigenous states in the archipelago reached their greatest geographic, political, literary and scientific heights, before their slow decline into colonial subjugation began. It was during this period that the great temples and religious monuments, including those of Borobudur and Prambanan, were built; that the romantic hero-figures Gajah Mada and Airlangga performed the feats that earned them immortality; and that epics such as the *Negarakrtagama* and the *Pararaton* were written. And, perhaps most importantly for our story, it was during this period that the first states which variously claimed sovereignty over virtually the whole of present-day Indonesia appeared.

Naturally, not all of the archipelago was equally affected by the developments of this time. Indeed, many societies experienced little or no impact, their histories lying right outside the archipelagic mainstream. The great islands of Sumatera, Kalimantan and Sulawesi were dotted with agricultural societies, such as the Batak, the Dayak and the Toraja, whose horizons—both literal and figurative—did not extend beyond their immediate localities. Other societies located on smaller and remoter islands had even less contact with the world beyond their own communities. This period saw the emergence of the two major locuses of power—social and political, as well as economic—which have dominated much of Indonesia's history since then: the Straits of Melaka in the west of the archipelago, and Java in the centre.

There were two forces driving the histories of most of the states of the Indonesian archipelago during this period. One was religion, the other was trade. This was the time when three of the great world religions, Hinduism, Buddhism and Islam, were introduced to Indonesia, and their associated linguistic, scientific, legal and administrative achievements and values came to have significant impacts on regional cultures. These new influences were not spread evenly across the archipelago, and even where they were influential were never adopted in their entirety. But they had a major effect in shaping not just the history of their times, but also the Indonesia of today.

The second driving force was trade, both within the archipelago and, especially for the states in the centre and the west, internationally. The trade networks which developed during this period linked the states of the archipelago together, and connected them to the world beyond, especially to China and the Indian subcontinent. And as we will see, these trade routes were not only channels for the exchange of goods, they were also conduits for the exchange of ideas and of people.

The rise of the state

The first eight centuries of the Current Era provide only fragmentary evidence about the nature of Indonesian societies. What is clear is that this was the time that the first states—as opposed to societies or communities—started to emerge in the archipelago, and that trade was a driving force in this development.

It is impossible to say with any certainty just when Indonesians first became involved in trade with peoples outside their local regions, whether in other parts of the archipelago or beyond. Certainly we have no extant records from Indonesia itself which would help resolve this problem. Evidence from the countries with which Indonesia traded, however, especially China, suggests that perhaps as far back as 500 BCE at least some of the ports on Java's north coast were routinely trading with mainland Southeast Asia, south China and the east coast of the Indian peninsula. This trade involved the export of Javanese products such as rice, but also the spices and sandalwoods of eastern Indonesia, which suggests that there were both intra-regional and international trading linkages in operation in which the Javanese ports participated.

By the first century BCE, clear evidence exists of the extent of the region's participation in international trade. The emperors of Rome began to receive cloves from the Maluku region of eastern Indonesia, sandalwood sent west from Indian ports and timber that might have originated in Nusa Tenggara Timor (Lesser Sunda Islands). In his *Natural History*, the Roman historian Pliny the Elder suggests that Indonesian outrigger-equipped boats might have been trading with the east coast of Africa by the first century CE. This suggestion is strengthened by the fact that the island of Madagascar, off the African east coast, was settled at least as early as 700 CE by peoples speaking a language which originated in southwest Kalimantan. By the first century CE Java was also tied-in to the trade route that linked China to the Roman empire in the Mediterranean, a truly international network.

Starting in about the fourth century CE, the region's international trade began to experience a modest, but in historical terms important, expansion. In part this expansion was directed westward across the Bay of Bengal, as the ports on the east coast of the Indian peninsula sought to make up for the loss of trade from the Roman empire, now in decline, by trading with southeast and east Asia. And in part the expansion was northward, to southern China, where the breakdown of the Western Chin empire in the fourth century meant that the southern Chinese states no longer had access to the Central Asian trade routes, along which they had previously secured access to western commodities and to Buddhist holy sites and teachers in India. The only way to restore access to these goods and locations was via the sea route south around the southeastern extremity of the Asian mainland and then north and west to India.

While this sea passage had been known to traders for centuries, it had a reputation for being very dangerous: ships that ventured this way ran the risk of attack by pirates. So long as the potential for trade along the route was not particularly great, nobody was going to make much of an effort to bring it under control. By the early fifth century, though, a growing volume of trade between China and Japan on the one hand, south and west Asia and Europe on the other, was passing through the Straits of Melaka. The Chinese Buddhist monk Faxian (Fa Hsien) passed along this route in 414 on his return to China after spending some years in India studying Buddhism and collecting Buddhist texts. A number of small states grew up in the region, seeking to participate in the seaborne trade by offering services ranging from supplying ships with food and water to protection from raids by pirates—though often they were the pirates themselves.

Many of the goods that moved along this trade route were those that had earlier travelled overland—with one very important difference. Along the overland route, the Chinese had previously imported a variety of goods from western Asia, goods generically referred to as 'Persian'. These included fumigants, perfumed woods, and gums and resins. Chinese trade records of the time show that these products continued to be received, via southeast Asia. However, careful analysis of these records, and of remnants of the goods themselves, shows clearly that many of the original Persian items had been replaced by goods from the Indonesian archipelago. Just when this substitution began is not known, but it seems to have become well established by about the seventh century.

By this time the Indonesian ports were experiencing their first international trade boom, boosted not only by the expanding trade with China but also by increasing Arab demand for Indonesian products, especially spices from the Maluku islands such as cloves, nutmeg and mace, and increasing Indonesian demand for exports from south Asia, such as cotton cloth.

Until quite recently it was generally believed that Indonesian participation in the commercial shipping now passing through the archipelago was limited: that the main carriers of cargoes were foreign ships, crewed by foreigners, primarily Indians or perhaps Arabs. More recent research has established that this picture was inaccurate, and that Indonesians were active both as builders of substantial ships, and as their crews, in the early years of the Current Era. One Chinese document, for instance, dated to the third century CE, says of boats from the region that 'the large ones are more than fifty meters in length and stand out from the water four to five meters . . . They carry from six to seven hundred persons, with 10,000 bushels of cargo [c. 6000 tons deadweight]'.

Not just trade goods passed along these trade routes: information and ideas came too. Of particular importance were religious ideas and philosophies, and their allied cultural attributes. This was the time that states influenced by the Hindu and Buddhist cultures of India were beginning to appear in Southeast Asia, both on the mainland and in the archipelago. Buddhist texts dated to the fifth century CE and clearly inspired by Indian thinking have been found in west Kalimantan and Brunei, and in west Java. Chinese records of this time, such as the reports of travellers who had visited the region, and of embassies from the region which had visited China, noted that many local rulers seemed to have been influenced by Indian religious cultures. By the seventh century these ideas were well established in the western and central parts of the archipelago.

The question of just how Hindu and Buddhist culture first came to the archipelago has attracted the attention of scholars for well over a century. At first the general feeling was that Indians must have colonised at least some of the Indonesian islands and in this way transplanted their cultural ideas. By the middle of the twentieth century, however, the continued absence of any persuasive evidence to support this theory led to its rejection by most scholars.

The locus of explanatory emphasis then shifted to trade: it came to be argued that as Indonesia was drawn further and further into trading relationships with India, so Indian traders came to the archipelago, settled, and in so doing transmitted Indian cultural ideas to local peoples. Indian traders did indeed settle in the archipelago, often in specific sections of port cities set aside for them—but as traders did not carry much status in Indian society, and were unlikely to have had the education necessary to acquire the sophisticated religious, scientific and literary ideas that were ultimately to be adopted by Indonesians, this view also lost favour with scholars.

The Indians who would have had access to this level of education were the priests or Brahmins, the caste at the top of the status hierarchy. Thus the view was formed that Brahmins might have come to Indonesia, perhaps at the invitation of local rulers, to teach about their culture. The religious and scientific knowledge of these scholar-priests would have been very useful in consolidating these local states and raising both their status and that of their rulers, who might first have heard about Indian culture, in rudimentary form, from the traders.

In the absence of specific evidence, however, the other way of looking at this question is to suggest that it might not have been a case of Indians, of one caste or another, bringing elements of their culture to Indonesia, but of Indonesians, who certainly had the technology and the skills to sail across the Bay of Bengal, going to India and selectively adopting Indian ideas.

Whichever explanation is preferred, it is likely that a key element of the transmission of Indian-derived ideas to Southeast Asia came from the region itself, and not from India.

The first quasi- or proto-states in Indonesia—'state' here meaning a political institution standing above local communities, with a ruler owed allegiance by its members, with a coherent set of laws—probably emerged in Java around the fourth or fifth centuries of the Current Era. We know of a state called Tarumanegara, ruled at one time by a king called Purnavarman, which was located in present-day west Java in that period. Its centre or capital might have been located around Tanjung Priok, today the port of Jakarta, or at a site reasonably close by. Its rulers were Hindus, though apparently people of fairly eclectic beliefs. Contemporaneous Sanskrit language inscriptions found in Kalimantan also refer to a state called Kutei on the Mahakam river.

By the seventh century, according to Chinese sources, there were two states in particular in the archipelago that were dominant: Ho-ling in Java and Srivijaya in Sumatera.

Hindu and Buddhist societies

We first hear of the state of Ho-ling—we still know it only by its Chinese name—when it appears in Chinese records as having sent a trade delegation to China in 640. By this time it held a crucial position in archipelago trade, probably having displaced Tarumanegara as the primary commercial intermediary between Java and the eastern islands. It also occupied a pivotal place in the long-distance trade between China and India. But Ho-ling was not just a trading entity. It also had a strong agricultural base in the fertile and well-watered soils of the coastal plain facing the Java Sea, and the Kedu plain in the south-central region of the island. The rice produced in this hinterland not only fed the population of the state, but was also important as an export commodity.

Ho-ling's religious orientation was Buddhist although, as was the situation in many regional societies newly introduced to the Indian religions, the faith had a strong admixture of pre-existing religious beliefs.

Early in the eighth century, Ho-ling merged—it is not clear precisely under what circumstances—with a state based on the Kedu plain that was called Mataram, the first of two such-named states based in central or eastern Java which were to emerge in the pre-colonial era. Both Hinduism and Buddhism were represented in Mataram, the balance of religious authority tending to swing between them.

Mataram produced the oldest temples still in existence in Indonesia, located on the Dieng plateau northwest of the city of Yogyakarta, and dating back to the fourth century. The height of Mataram's monumental achievements was reached with the construction in the eighth and ninth centuries of the massive edifice of the Borobudur, the largest Buddhist building in the world, located 60 kilometres northwest of Yogyakarta. Construction of the elaborately sculpted Borobudur was a huge engineering undertaking, involving the quarrying of over a million stones and their cartage (or haulage) up a hill. Clearly Mataram must have been a prosperous state to have been able to afford to devote so much of its resources, especially of skilled and unskilled labour, to a project which, although of great religious and artistic merit, would produce no economic return.

Like Ho-ling, the basis of Mataram's economic strength lay in a combination of a strong agricultural base focused on the production of rice, and an extensive and profitable international trading network. Mataram's merger with Ho-ling enabled it to take over that state's trading links with China.

Let us turn now to the island of Sumatera.

As we have noted, by the fifth century CE a growing volume of trade between China and Japan on the one hand, south and west Asia and Europe on the other, was passing through the Straits of Melaka between Sumatera and the Malay Peninsula. A number of harbour principalities had emerged to service this trade. Many of these states were also traders in their own right, gathering produce from around the archipelago for onward shipment to China and India.

By the seventh century, one of these states had outstripped the others, establishing its dominance over the waterways of the region. This was Srivijaya in Sumatera, the first major state in the Indonesian archipelago about which we have clear information. Its capital, at least initially, was located at or near the present-day city of Palembang, though by the end of the eleventh century it had shifted to Jambi. Srivijaya controlled the flow of trade through the Straits of Melaka for about 600 years, until the thirteenth century—twice as long as the Dutch colonialists were in Indonesia, and more than three times as long as the British were in Malaysia.

To think of Srivijaya as a 'state' in conventional twentieth-century terms, as a political entity with defined boundaries, a central government with clear authority over the territory enclosed within those boundaries and to which the citizenry owed allegiance, would be misleading, however. Srivijaya was more like a confederacy, centred on the royal heartland around the capital and with vassal states surrounding it, both inland and, more importantly, at river mouths and small harbours along both sides of the Straits of Melaka. These latter states played an important role in the Srivijayan economic system, acting as collecting points for local produce to be fed into the wider trading system centred on the Srivijayan capital, and also guaranteeing the security of trade through the region.

To some extent these states acknowledged Srivijayan suzerainty because of the latter's military power, especially that of its navy; but Srivijayan rulers were astute enough not to push the issue of suzerainty too far. Vassal states were allowed a considerable degree of local freedom, which increased the further away they were from the Srivijayan capital, though always with the proviso that they did nothing to challenge the position of Srivijaya itself. This applied particularly with respect to Srivijaya's control of international trade passing through the region, which was of course the source of the income the state needed to finance its activities, especially the navy that was its weapon of last resort.

The trading networks of Srivijaya were also important channels for the spread of aspects of Srivijayan culture. Thus, for instance, the rise of Srivijaya did much to promote the spread of early variants of the Malay language—indigenous to southern Sumatera—through the central and western parts of the Indonesian archipelago. And, at least according to legend, exiles from Srivijaya were responsible for establishing ruling dynasties in Cambodia, and Melaka on the Malay Peninsula.

The Srivijayan capital was a cosmopolitan place, with many foreigners living there more or less permanently. Its residents included Chinese, Javanese, people from various parts of the south Asian subcontinent, including Bengalis and Gujeratis, and Persians from west Asia. Srivijayans, too, resided overseas, and especially in Canton where, from late in the seventh century to the middle of the eighth, they were seen as the leaders of the resident foreign trading community.

The Srivijayans were not simply merchants and traders; they were also skilled boatbuilders and navigators. The state became an important trading power in its own right, its vessels sailing as far north as Canton in southern China and as far west as the Arab countries of west Asia. Although the Chinese undoubtedly had considerable shipbuilding skills, they had concentrated these skills primarily on the construction and operation of riverine and coastal shipping up until the tenth century, when Chinese traders began to visit Srivijaya in their own ships. Until this time, trade between Srivijaya and China had been carried on by Srivijayan merchants, in ships built and crewed by Srivijayans.

One measure of the close links between Srivijaya and China was that, at irregular intervals, the rulers of Srivijaya sent missions to China carrying gifts to the Chinese emperor, gifts which are usually called 'tribute'. The first of these missions went to China in 670–73. To the Chinese, such tribute indicated that the state sending it acknowledged the overlordship of China and its own inferior position. The tribute system also served to guarantee a flow of needed imports into China at a time when, for whatever reason, Chinese merchants themselves could not travel overseas to secure those goods. Srivijaya— and other Southeast Asian states that at some time or other also sent tribute to China—viewed the matter rather differently, however. They saw their gifts more as a means of ensuring continued access to an important market.

Srivijaya was also a major centre of Buddhism and Buddhist learning, attracting many foreign pilgrims. The Chinese scholar and pilgrim Yijing (I Tsing), for instance, late in the seventh century visited Srivijaya twice on his way to and from India, learning the Sanskrit language in which many Buddhist texts were written, and studying the Buddhist religion.

Srivijaya went into decline from about the twelfth century, for reasons which are still in dispute. Some argue that the causes were essentially political and military. The Javanese kingdom of Mataram was at war with Srivijaya in the early part of the eleventh century, and at much the same time, in 1025, the capital was invaded by forces from Chola in India, the ruler and many of his officials being captured.

While these political and military developments were possibly quite significant in weakening and then destroying Srivijaya's power, probably more important were developments in the state's trade relationship with China. Srivijaya's near-monopoly on trade with southern China was broken as the Chinese themselves began to take a much more active role. Chinese merchants began to venture south on Chinese-owned ships, rather than waiting in the southern Chinese ports for Srivijayan merchants to come to them. And these Chinese merchants, for sound commercial reasons, wanted to deal with a variety of suppliers, not just one. This destroyed the essential element of the Srivijayan commercial, and state, order: monopoly control of trade through the Straits of Melaka. With this gone, and with smaller, formerly vassal states being able to trade directly with southern China, Srivijaya lost its control over those states, and in any case lost its capacity to pay them, given that its own revenues were substantially reduced.

Srivijaya was one of the strongest, most long lasting and certainly the best known of the trading states of early Southeast Asia. In its essential characteristics—a small state bureaucracy, reliance on international trade, contacts with the outside world—Srivijaya was typical of similar trading states that have been located throughout the archipelago at various times right down to the present day. Singapore, for instance, may be regarded as the modern descendant of Srivijaya.

Late in the ninth century, with Srivijaya still at its zenith, the Javanese state of Mataram was expanding, perhaps in response to a resurgence in the China trade and the prosperity that was bringing to Java's ports. Early in the tenth century, the palace of the king was moved east from inland central Java to the delta of the Brantas river, in the vicinity of the present-day city of Surabaya. The reasons for this shift have been much debated. The issue is of interest here since it focuses our attention on a variety of aspects of the workings of the state of Mataram: the role of religion, the relationships between ruler and the ruled, the relative significance of inland and coastal states, and the economic and demographic bases of Mataram society.

At one level, the reason for the move seems obvious. In late 928 or early 929 Mt Merapi, a volcano located near the then capital, erupted violently, ejecting large quantities of ash over the surrounding countryside. This rendered much of the local rice-farming land temporarily unusable: it was now impossible for the state to support its large population on its substantially reduced agricultural base. This alone would have dictated a move, but the need to do so would have been strengthened by the fact that the eruption would have been seen by the inhabitants as a sign of the gods' displeasure—natural disasters of this kind were typically seen as having this religious meaning. Thus a move of the capital, and therefore of a large proportion of the population, would have been vital to the continued existence of the state of Mataram and its society, in both physical and religious terms.

Another reason advanced by some scholars is that in order to build the Borobudur, and the other great religious monuments of the age, the rulers of Mataram had had to withdraw large numbers of people from agricultural production. The implication here is that the movement of the capital might have been driven by the movement of the people, not by its ruler: people who wanted to flee the exorbitant labour demands of the state.

However, to suggest that the capital might have had to follow the people does not fully resolve the problem, since it does not indicate why it was moved to the Brantas delta, as opposed to anywhere else in Java. In trying to explain this fact, once again we probably cannot go past trade. By this time the region was experiencing the beginnings of the next great boom in seaborne trade, which demanded a shift in the focus of economic and political activity away from inland Java to the coast. And along the north coast of Java, the Brantas delta region was best suited to access this trade.

The last major ruler of Mataram was the legendary hero-figure Airlangga (r. 1016–1049), the son of a marriage between the daughter of the king of Mataram and the ruler of Bali. Until the tenth century CE, Java and Bali seem to have lived separate lives, with little formal contact. The north coast of Bali participated in intra-regional and international trade, there being evidence of contacts with India going back perhaps to the start of the millennium. Presumably Bali adopted elements of Hinduism, and possibly also Buddhism, from those contacts. In the tenth century, however, the Java–Bali relationship changed markedly, a change symbolised by the marriage from which Airlangga was born. From this time onwards, the norms and mores of the Javanese court were increasingly to become the standard reference points for the Balinese, in terms of defining both their religious and social identities.

Airlangga's reign saw the composition of the epic poem *Arjunawiwaha*, or 'The Marriage of Arjuna', by the court poet Mpu Kanwa. Loosely based on the Indian epic of the *Mahabarata*, it also read as an allegory of Airlangga's life. Airlangga is reputed to have united the various legal codes then prevailing in Java into a single code, though unfortunately no copy of this has survived, leaving us simply to guess at what it might have said.

Airlangga's reign also marked the beginning of the end for Mataram, and the start of the period of transition which, two centuries later, was to see the emergence of Majapahit, perhaps the greatest of all the classical Indonesian kingdoms. In 1016, Mataram suffered a major military defeat at the hands of Srivijaya and slipped into a state of political disorder. Alone of the prominent members of the royal family, Airlangga escaped the onslaught, and set about rallying the Mataram forces so as to expel Srivijaya. By about 1019 he was back in control of the region around Pasuruan on the north coast, east of Surabaya. Bali was brought under control by 1025, and by about 1035 most of Mataram had been restored to Airlangga's control.

Around the middle of the century, Airlangga apparently decided that after his death the state should be divided between his two sons. Quite what he intended to achieve by this is not clear, but the division seems to have taken place, the western portion of Mataram becoming Kadiri, the eastern part Janggala. Of the two, Kadiri, with better access to the sea, was the more powerful. A century later, under Jayabaya (r. 1135–1157) and his successors, Kadiri re-absorbed Janggala, and extended its influence into Kalimantan and Bali. Sumatera seems to have remained outside its control, for even though Srivijaya was now in decline, it was still strong enough to hold off the Javanese.

Kadiri eventually collapsed in 1222, defeated by the neighbouring state of Tumapel in the Brantas River valley in the Malang region, under the command of Ken Angrok. A new capital for the state was established at Kutaraja, close to the harbours of east Java. The city was later re-named Singasari, the same name by which the new state, encompassing the whole of eastern Java, came to be known.

The last king of Singasari was Kertanegara (r. 1268–1292). Born into the princely families of both Janggala and Kadiri, he reunited the two halves of the kingdom. He also had imperial ambitions, seeking to establish his authority over much, if not all of the archipelago. Under his rule, Singasari's forces extended the state's influence eastward into Bali and westward to the Straits of Melaka, taking advantage of the decline of Srivijaya. The Straits were largely under Singasari's control by 1286.

Unfortunately this westward expansion brought Singasari into conflict with the Chinese, who were pushing into the Straits at the same time and for much the same reasons: the decay of Srivijaya and the subsequent absence of any hegemonic power which could guarantee the continuation of peaceful trade.

In 1289 the Mongol emperor Kublai Khan, seeing China's influence in the Straits threatened by Singasari, sent emissaries to Java to demand tribute from Kertanegara. Kertanegara refused to pay, and sent the Chinese emissaries home, reputedly after having cut off their noses and ears—though whether this is literally what happened, or whether it simply means that the envoys were ritually humiliated, is unclear. In any event, in 1292 Kublai Khan responded by sending a military expedition comprising as many as 1000 vessels and 20 000 soldiers to Java to enforce collection of the tribute.

However, before the expedition arrived, important political changes had taken place in Singasari. Jayakatwang, ruler of the previously subordinated Kadiri, had killed Kertanegara and taken command of the state. When the Mongol army arrived in east Java, the surviving son-in-law of Kertanegara, Raden Vijaya (also called Kertarajasa), persuaded its commanders to assist him to defeat Jayakatwang; this done, he tricked the Mongol army into laying down their weapons and attacked them, killing many and driving off the rest, leaving him firmly in command. He established his palace at Majapahit, in the Brantas River valley south of Sarabaya, and Majapahit became the name of the state.

Not all the merchants and sailors involved in the punitive Mongol expedition returned to China. Quite a number stayed, either voluntarily or otherwise, subsequently contributing an injection of Chinese technology and manpower to Javanese culture. One of the results seems to have been a change in the technology of shipbuilding, with certain Chinese techniques bolstering existing Javanese practices, including the greater use of iron nails and the introduction of bulk-heads to divide up the cargo space.

Initially, the main task facing Kertajasa and his immediate successors as rulers of Majapahit was to bring a few remaining rebellious parts of Java under their control. This was achieved early in the fourteenth century, thanks in large measure to the leadership provided by another great hero-figure, Gajah Mada, chief minister to the great ruler Hayam Wuruk (r. 1350–1389), the great-grandson of Kertanegara.

Under Hayam Wuruk, Majapahit was to become the most substantial state in the Indonesian archipelago; it might even have been the biggest in Southeast Asia, although considerable care needs to be taken in interpreting the data on this point. The *Negarakrtagama*, an epic poem composed by the court poet Prapanca in 1365, includes an extensive list of regions which, it asserts, were part of the Majapahit empire, ranging from the western tip of Sumatera to the southern Philippines and east to New Guinea. The poem also mentions states on the Asian mainland which, although not described as vassals of Majapahit, are nonetheless said to be under the protection of Hayam Wuruk. It seems likely that these states had a relationship to Majapahit similar to that which the tributary states of Southeast Asia had to China: they were in a commercial relationship with Majapahit, and were under an obligation not to act in ways which would have gone against the interests of Majapahit, but they were not subordinate or inferior in quite the way that terms such as 'tributary' or 'vassal' would normally imply. What does seem clear, though, is that Majapahit's authority extended into Bali, Sumatera and Kalimantan.

Coinciding with the growth of Majapahit, and indeed one of the reasons for that growth, was the rising Chinese and European demand for Indonesian spices, mostly nutmeg, mace and cloves from Maluku but also pepper from Sumatera and western Java. These spices had a wide variety of uses: as food preservatives, as flavour enhancers, as cures for a range of common ailments, even as aphrodisiacs.

By the middle of the fourteenth century, Majapahit's merchants and sailors were predominant in the spice trade with Maluku, buying up the spices at their place of origin and bringing them back to Javanese ports for storage and onward shipment to China and Europe. Many of these merchants and sailors would have been Javanese, from Majapahit's heartland; others would have been drawn from the indigenous trading networks which Majapahit absorbed into its own as its authority extended out around the archipelago.

Trade between Indonesia and China increased substantially during the Majapahit era, as much because of changes in commercial policy in China, especially following the establishment of the Ming Dynasty in 1368, as because of developments in Indonesia. The first of the Ming emperors took the view that trade with Indonesian states, and others in the southern region, should be controlled by the state and not by private traders; thus they forbade individuals to engage in it. One result of this ban seems to have been an increase in the number of Chinese traders resident in the Indonesian ports, unable to return home for fear of punishment but nevertheless continuing to participate in trade from the southern end.

In the place of private traders the Ming emperors wanted to see official trading relationships established, characterised by the sending of tribute missions from the south, and of trading-cum-diplomatic expeditions from China. The biggest of these expeditions were the seven led by Zheng He (Cheng Ho) in the first three decades of the fifteenth century, all of which spent substantial amounts of time in Indonesian waters. The harbours of east Java, especially those of Gresik and Surabaya, played an important role in the repairing and revictualling of Zheng He's ships.

It was not just in the political and commercial fields that Majapahit reached substantial heights, however—like many of the states that preceded it, Majapahit was an important cultural centre. Its greatest literary achievement was the *Negarakrtagama*, while Majapahit artists and architects, developing a distinctively East Javanese style, reached heights which were close to those seen in central Java at the time of the building of the Borobudur.

Majapahit's culture was influential across the archipelago, many other states and societies imitating its manners, its clothing and its forms of cultural expression. Perhaps the most-quoted evidence of this influence is contained in the *Hikayat Banjar*, 'The Story of Banjar', which was written sometime between the fifteenth and seventeenth centuries. This text reported that the ruler of Banjar, on the south coast of Kalimantan, had ordered his elite not to dress like Malays, Dutch people, Chinese, Siamese, Acehnese or Makasarese: 'You should not even follow [our] old customs of dress . . . We have now set up a country of our own, following the ways and manners of Majapahit.' Admittedly, this reference to Majapahit might not have been specifically to the state of that name; it might have been meant as a general reference to Java. Nonetheless, the point that Majapahit was seen as being synonymous with Java, and as representing the height of cultural achievement, seems clear.

In addition, Javanese myths, texts, placenames, words, titles and nobility and even *krisses* have been found through much of southern Sumatera, especially around Palembang, and in Lampung, in Kalimantan, and on several of the islands east of Java, notably Bali, but also Lombok and Sumbawa. Javanese figures, often attributed to Majapahit culture, appear in the foundation myths of many other states and societies from Sumatera and the Malay Peninsula to the Maluku islands.

3
THE AGE OF COMMERCE: 1400–1700

The period from the mid-fifteenth to the late seventeenth centuries of the Common Era has been identified by several historians as the Age of Commerce in Indonesia and much of the rest of insular Southeast Asia. This chapter explores the reasons for this identification of international trade as the dominant characteristic of the era, and examines the impact of this trade on the development of Indonesian states and societies.

During the thirteenth century east–west trade passing through the archipelago had begun to rise; from about the beginning of the fifteenth century it started to boom. In both China and Europe, the two main markets for Indonesian products, economic, social and demographic changes were increasing significantly the demand for Maluku spices and black pepper. And, as noted in the previous chapter, between 1403 and 1433 China sent seven state trading expeditions to Southeast Asia, commanded by the great admiral Zheng Ho, at least in part to search for these spices.

Maluku spices had long been traded internationally north and west from Indonesia, though not in large quantities. Black pepper was a newer element in the trade. At first, Indonesian traders, especially in the Sumateran ports, imported pepper from India and sold it on to China: they were doing this at least by the early part of the twelfth century. Later in the same century, pepper vines were introduced to Java. Pepper cultivation then spread to Sumatera, and by early in the fifteenth century the Sumateran port principalities had become substantial producers of pepper in their own right, and were selling it to China in place of the Indian crop. They were thus doing what Srivijaya had done successfully seven centuries earlier: substituting a local product for an imported one, securing for themselves not just the profits from trade, but also from production.

The effect of the rising international demand for these products was to increase competition between merchants wanting to secure supplies direct from the producers. This in turn encouraged a host of smaller ports in the archipelago, from Aceh in northern Sumatera across to Ternate and Tidore in the Maluku islands, to establish direct trading links with foreign purchasers.

The trade boom brought prosperity for those Indonesians who participated in it, and certainly changed their societies. But it also brought, or at least substantially strengthened, the presence in the archipelago of two forces which were to play leading roles in the events of the succeeding centuries: Islam and Europe.

The spread of Islam

Up until about the fourteenth century, the various Indonesian states were primarily Buddhist. It was through the trade networks that Islam came to Indonesia and supported Buddhism.

We do not know for certain when Islam first appeared in the archipelago. The first hard evidence we have is a gravestone marking the burial of a Muslim in east Java, dated 1082. We do not know, however, whether the person buried there was an Indonesian Muslim or a foreigner.

We are on firmer ground when we look to Sumatera at the end of the thirteenth century. Marco Polo, who visited the island in 1292, noted in his diary that the state of Perlak, on the northeast coast, was by this time Muslim. The neighbouring state of Pasai was probably also Muslim by the same time, to judge by a royal tombstone found here, dated to 1297 and written entirely in Arabic.

The channel through which Islam flowed into the archipelago was trade.

By the thirteenth or fourteenth century, most of the traders taking Indonesian spices west to Europe were Muslims from south Asia and the Middle East. Some Chinese traders were Islamic too, especially those coming from Fujian province with its long history of prominent roles in trade and administration being played by foreign-born and local Muslims.

For many Indonesian traders, conversion to Islam made sense simply because it gave them something in common with their south Asian and Middle Eastern trading partners, who showed a preference for dealing with fellow believers. For Indonesians without any particularly strong religious beliefs of their own, or who were finding their beliefs unable to provide coherent and persuasive answers to the increasingly complex range of questions posed by the changing world within which they lived, conversion to Islam offered spiritual benefits as well as commercial ones.

For local rulers, conversion to the new religion offered more than economic benefits. In particular, the faith gave them direct access to fellow Muslim rulers in south Asia and the Middle East, and especially to the Ottoman empire, then a major world power. Such contacts enhanced their political standing in the eyes of their populations and—perhaps more importantly—in the eyes of potential rivals. They also provided a conduit for the supply of military equipment, especially firearms (including cannon), and military advisors.

The conversion to Islam of the entrepot of Aceh, at the northern tip of Sumatera, in the mid-fourteenth century, and of Melaka, on the other side of the Straits of Melaka, perhaps half a century later, marks the point when the spread of Islam through Indonesia became significant.

From Sumatera, Islam followed the trade routes east. Gresik, an important port just to the west of Surabaya in east Java, was converted a decade after Aceh. Then followed Ternate, 2000 kilometres to the east in the Maluku islands (1460), Demak in central Java (1480), Banten in west Java (1525), Buton in southwest Sulawesi (1580) and Makasar in south Sulawesi (1605).

By the early decades of the seventeenth century, Islam had been introduced to virtually all the major coastal societies of the archipelago, but from this point it made no further substantial territorial advances.

The beginnings of colonialism

If Muslim dominance of the spice trade route back to Europe had had the effect of boosting the spread of Islam in the archipelago, it also contributed, though less directly, to the colonisation of the region by European powers. Political power in Europe was gradually shifting westward from the Italian peninsular states to the Atlantic coast, and in particular to Portugal and Spain. The merchants and political leaders from these rising powers were not content to see their supplies of

Indonesian spices controlled by the well-established Muslim-dominated chain of intermediaries passing through the Red Sea and the Levant. Toward the end of the fourteenth century and early in the fifteenth, in an effort to bypass the Muslim traders of the Middle East, Portuguese navigators and merchants sought a sea passage to Asia. They pushed south down the west coast of Africa, around the Cape of Good Hope and across the western side of the Indian Ocean to India itself. In 1511 they captured Melaka, and finally reached the Maluku islands in 1512, where they established a base on the island of Ambon. They then turned their efforts to collecting spices, trying to secure a monopoly on the trade; they also set about converting the local population to Catholicism.

The Portuguese presence had a significant impact on the dispersion of both trade and traders around the archipelago.

By capturing Melaka the Portuguese had ensured that, for the moment at least, no one power held even a quasi-monopoly of the primary entrepot at the eastern end of the spice route to Europe. But they soon found that what they had captured at Melaka was simply a location, not a trading function. Many of the Asian traders who had previously used Melaka's markets and storage facilities now dispersed to other ports, among them Aceh and Jambi in Sumatera, Banten, Cirebon, Demak and Surabaya in Java, and Makasar in Sulawesi.

Aceh, at the northern tip of Sumatera, became the dominant power at the western end of the archipelago, and the entrance to the Straits of Melaka. By the 1570s it had extended its influence southward, absorbing the neighbouring states of Pasai and Pidië. It was at the height of its power under the rule of Sultan Iskandar Muda (r. 1607–1638).

By the late sixteenth century, Banten in west Java had emerged as the most important pepper-trading port in the region, and a major revictualling and warehousing site for traffic of all kinds passing through the archipelago.

In the east of the archipelago, by the beginning of the seventeenth century Makasar was dominant. It had benefited considerably from the Portuguese capture of Melaka in 1511, attracting many traders from Indonesia and other parts of Asia who did not wish to do business with the Portuguese: Malays and Javanese in particular. Dutch and English traders too used Melaka's trading facilities. Although they were rivals both commercially and politically, the trade passing through Makasar was too important to rule it off limits to either power. Moreover, it was independent of Portugal, their common enemy. Makasar had become the key to regional trade in which the most important items were spices from the Maluku islands and slaves, either from Sulawesi itself or from islands to its immediate north and south. Other important commodities passing through Makasar included pepper from Banjarmasin in Kalimantan and Jambi in Sumatera, cotton and iron from India, gold and silver dollars from Manila and sugar and gold from China. Makasar itself was a significant exporter of rice (at least until well into the seventeenth century) and cloth.

By 1637, when Matoaya, the greatest of the early rulers of Makasar, died, the Makasar empire had reached its greatest extent, stretching from Lombok in the west to the Kei Islands off New Guinea to the east.

One of the key characteristics of the Muslim port states was their cosmopolitan nature. By early in the sixteenth century, all of them had substantial communities of people from the Indian subcontinent, Persia and the Middle East, and important roles were played in virtually all of them by Muslims from other parts of Asia.

Given their later and highly equivocal position in Indonesian society, it is useful to note in particular that by the sixteenth century there were also substantial numbers of people of Chinese descent, or mixed Chinese-Javanese descent, residing in the ports of Java (and in many other islands of the archipelago). Among them was a significant number of Muslims. Of the nine 'saints'—the *wali songo*—said by Javanese legend to have brought Islam to the island, Raden Patah was not the only one apparently of at least partial Chinese descent.[1]

Indeed, during the fifteenth and sixteenth centuries, while China forbade its citizens to travel abroad, those who by whatever means did manage to get to Southeast Asia had little option other than to remain, and to do so meant assimilating into the local communities. Apart from anything else, there was little possibility of renewing either their cultural roots or their numbers through the arrival of new people and ideas from China. It was only after direct contacts between China and Indonesia were renewed after 1567 that the region saw an increase in the numbers of ethnic Chinese who maintained their connections with China.

Majapahit, the dominant inland Javanese state, remained under Hindu influence for much longer than the ports, although the evidence of gravestones suggests that from the middle of the fourteenth century onward, at least some state officials were Muslims though the rulers were not. Majapahit was unusual, though not unique, among the Javanese states in that it had both agricultural and maritime bases. And it was at least in part this combination which gave it its strength. Its ports gave it considerable income from regional and international trade, far beyond what it could have earned simply from its own produce. Its agricultural production gave it a measure of economic security which states relying solely on trade did not have, its surpluses of rice in particular giving it the resources it needed to finance its trade with Maluku, China, India and Europe. Control over trade seems to have been the more important element in the maintenance of its power, however.

By the early years of the sixteenth century, Majapahit—its capital now near Kediri in east Java—was crumbling. The trade that had been so important in its emergence as a regional power was ultimately the cause of its downfall. Majapahit's powerful trading role had depended on its capacity to monopolise the trade routes running through the archipelago. So long as it had this power, it held the whip hand over potential rivals and rebels. The great expansion in demand for the archipelago's products had meant greater incentives for rivals to seek access to the region's exports, and the alliance of trade with Islam gave those rivals an additional impetus to break away from Majapahit's control.

By this time the most powerful of these rivals was the port city of Demak, located on Java's north coast (the *pasisir*). Under its expansionist and proselytising ruler Sultan Trenggana (r. 1504–1546), Demak pushed south and east into the heartland of Majapahit. In 1527 Majapahit succumbed, and thus the last of the Hindu–Buddhist states of Java disappeared, a thousand years after they had first emerged.

Although Majapahit was defeated militarily and politically, its moral and cultural influence persisted. The state of Demak, for instance, claimed to be the legitimate, hereditary successor to Majapahit on the grounds that Raden Patah, founder of Demak's ruling Islamic dynasty, was the son of the last king of Majapahit and a Chinese princess. The story is probably apocryphal, but it illustrates not just the mixed ethnicity of the port elites but also the significance they attached to demonstrating links to Majapahit. Although at one level the religious enemy of the Islamic ports, at another Majapahit was still the Javanese heartland, its values the ultimate legitimator of leadership.

Demak, however, was not long left to enjoy its success. In 1546 Sultan Trenggana was murdered; there followed a war over the succession to the sultanate, which destroyed Demak as a state and brought to a halt its pretensions to island-wide sovereignty. In its wake, the pattern of inter-state conflict intensified, a two-fold division of power on the island ensuing. One power focus lay to the east, among the ports of the pasisir, and was centred on Surabaya; the other lay inland, centred first on Pajang and then on Mataram, an emerging Islamic south-central Javanese state with its capital near the present-day city of Yogyakarta. By the seventeenth century, Mataram had become the most powerful of the Javanese states, bringing the coastal states under its control. The appeal of Islam for Mataram—and for other inland societies—lay not in the democratic, egalitarian qualities which had led to its ready acceptance in the cosmopolitan port states, but more in its mystical qualities.

As we have already noted, inland Javanese societies were organised on a strictly hierarchical basis, to which the egalitarian traditions of Islam were not particularly attractive. Mataram for most of the seventeenth century, under rulers such as Agung and Amangkurat I, was a centralised and absolutist state: there was nothing egalitarian or democratic about the way these rulers went about their tasks. Another important factor promoting Islam here was that its most active missionaries were Sufis, members of a mystical Islamic sect. The ideas they promoted, including the veneration of saints and pilgrimages to sacred places, fitted in quite easily with many pre-existing religious beliefs and practices in Java.

The rulers of Mataram were the central element in both the political and the religious structures of the state. And here we can see that, although now Muslim in form and symbolism, in many respects Mataram continued to follow the practices of its Hindu and Buddhist predecessors. Indeed, like the earlier rulers of Demak the rulers of Mataram did much to stress that they were the legitimate successors to the rulers of Majapahit, even though there had been a considerable hiatus between the fall of Majapahit and the rise of Mataram.

In earlier Javanese states, the ruler was seen as the reincarnation of a god; since the inhabitants of Mataram were now formally Muslim, this interpretation was no longer open to their rulers, but they were certainly regarded as having a special relationship to Allah. And they retained the pre-Islamic idea that they were responsible for ensuring that the state was in a condition of equilibrium, of harmony and tranquillity. Any absence of equilibrium—as shown by deliberate actions, such as rebellions against the ruler by disaffected nobles, or through natural phenomena, such as earthquakes, volcanic eruptions or floods —was evidence that the king was failing in his job, and thus possibly liable to be removed.

There was theoretically no limit to the power of the ruler. In practice, though, a major limitation was presented by the sheer size of the state, and the resultant difficulty of ensuring that the ruler was aware of what was happening in all parts of the realm, and that his wishes would be obeyed throughout the kingdom. In fact, the direct power of the ruler was strong only at the centre of the state, in its capital. The further from the centre, the weaker the power of the ruler.

Outside its core heartland, administration of the state was in the hands of the *priyayi*, a largely hereditary aristocracy. Formally at least, the priyayi had a very strongly developed set of values and norms, which stressed status and etiquette, refinement and self-control. Ordinary people were everything the priyayi were not: coarse, emotional, unrefined.

From the priyayi was drawn the group of men who represented the ruler in the districts and regions outside the capital: the most common term for such officials was *bupati*, a term still in use today for the Indonesian official who heads a shire or a county.

The bupati, while officially the representatives of the ruler, in fact usually exercised very considerable local autonomy. A significant link between the ruler and his various bupati was taxation. It was also through the taxation system that those local officials earned their incomes. Officials were not paid a salary; rather, they had the right to keep the difference between the taxes they could extract from their regions, and the net tax they paid to the ruler. This would clearly have put the bupati in a very powerful position to squeeze the local population in some cases, but not always. Until two or three centuries ago, Java as a whole was underpopulated: people who felt they were being treated too harshly by their local bupati were usually able to retaliate simply by moving on to an uninhabited, and thus untaxed, region. Since with no people the bupati would earn no income—and with no taxes being paid to the ruler would soon be without a job and perhaps without a life as well—there was a strong incentive for bupati to treat their local populations, if not generously, at least with a degree of self-interested compassion.

The wealth brought by the trade boom also contributed to the development of major urban centres in the archipelago. The first Europeans to travel in Indonesia during the age of commerce reported finding cities that were substantial by European standards. It seems likely that cities such as Aceh, Banten, Demak, Surabaya and Makasar all had populations exceeding 50 000 in the sixteenth or seventeenth century, on a par with many European cities of the day.

Indonesian ships, especially those of the Javanese, were by the global standards of the day also substantial: the Portuguese, when they first arrived early in the sixteenth century, routinely remarked on the size of the vessels they encountered. Ships of 500 or more tonnes, sometimes built in the Pegu region of Burma but more often in the north coast ports of Java, including Jepara and Rembang, were particularly useful in the rice trade, characterised as it was by the need to transport large quantities of a commodity whose value was small relative to its volume. Small vessels would almost certainly not have proven economical. Other large ships were used as troop-carriers in major military expeditions. The word 'junk' originally came into the English language, and similar words into other European languages, from the Malay word *jong* for this kind of vessel.

For much of the period covered by this chapter, local rulers regarded the European presence in the archipelago as of little consequence and saw no necessity to abandon longstanding political and other feuds with their neighbours in order to band together to expel them. This was to be a fatal error—albeit one which is most obvious in hindsight.

As we have noted, the Portuguese were the first Europeans into the archipelago. But following not far behind them were the English, the Spanish and, most importantly for us here, the Dutch. Their motives were much the same as the Portuguese, though of course we must add in the emerging rivalries between these powers. Each wanted to secure a monopoly of the Indies trade; each wanted to exclude the others.

The first Dutch voyages to the Indies took place in the 1590s. The first fleet, of four ships and 249 men, set out in April 1595. Two years later three of those ships, with a total of 89 surviving crew, made it back to Amsterdam, proving that it was possible for Dutch ships to reach the

Indies, successfully evading the Portuguese. As a result, a flurry of ships headed towards the spice islands; 22 of them in 1598, for instance.

Initially these voyages were extremely profitable: one expedition, sent by a company based in Amsterdam, returned a profit of 300 per cent. However, the number of ships reaching the islands, and the volume of spices they bought for sale back in Europe, soon had the effect of increasing the prices demanded by the spice producers and lowering the prices that could be commanded in Europe. As a result, the central and provincial governments in the Netherlands urged the major Dutch trading companies to combine their efforts, and to form a single company in which they would all be shareholders. In this way, 'wasteful' competition could be eliminated. Thus on 20 March 1602, the United East India Company (the Vereenigde Oost-Indische Compagnie or VOC) was established.

The VOC was a joint stock company, in which six regional chambers of commerce, Amsterdam being the most prominent, held the shares. It was governed by a board of seventeen directors. In some respects it was similar to other trading companies being established at the same time, such as the English East India Company, but in other respects it was innovative. Most importantly, shareholders invested their money in the Company, not in individual voyages. This gave the Company's directors the opportunity to pursue long-term rather than short-term objectives, to take strategic decisions rather than having to return a profit on each and every voyage.

The first major VOC base in the archipelago was at Ambon, which it seized from the Portuguese in 1605. Quite quickly the Company's officers realised that this was a far from ideal site for their regional headquarters, most importantly because they needed to participate in the intra-Asian trade networks, linking the Indies with China, Japan and India, as well as in the inter-continental trade to Europe. There were two major reasons for this.

One was that the intra-Asian routes were profitable in their own right. This was, after all, the reason why generations of Javanese,

Malay, Chinese, Gujerati and other traders had been engaged in them. The other reason was that exploitation of these networks was necessary in order for the Dutch to participate profitably in the intercontinental spice trade that had drawn them here in the first place. For the Company, the basic problem with the spice trade was finding a way of paying for the goods it purchased. The Netherlands itself produced almost nothing that the spice producers wanted. The Srivijayans, the Melakans, the people of Majapahit and other local traders, when buying spices in Maluku, offered primarily food—particularly rice—and cloth in exchange, goods which were in high demand in the spice islands. The Dutch had to adapt their trading practices to this fact; in other words, they had to acquire food and cloth with which to buy spices. And this food and cloth could come from Java, China, Japan, India, or places in between.

The intra-Asian trade routes passed through the western, not the eastern, part of the archipelago. Thus began the search for a site in the west which could serve as both the major warehousing and transshipping site for goods being traded within the Asian region and as the regional administrative headquarters of the Company.

The site initially chosen was the port of Banten, on the northeast coast of Java. Already a thriving harbour principality at the turn of the seventeenth century, Banten drew its commercial strength from the trade with China: it was a crucial hub in the Chinese trading networks in the region, whose importance had been boosted considerably by the movement there of many of the Chinese who had been excluded from Melaka by the Portuguese. It had replaced Melaka as the most important pepper port supplying the Chinese market by the end of the sixteenth century. It was here the Dutch traders had made their initial Indonesian landfall. But other foreign traders were here as well: notably the strongest European competitors of the Dutch, the English. The ruler of Banten himself was not particularly keen on having the Dutch set up a large-scale and potentially permanent enterprise here, being concerned—with considerable justification—

at the impact that the Anglo-Dutch rivalry would have on his state.

The Dutch thus decided to look for a new site, in roughly the same region, but one over which they would be able to exercise greater control. They eventually settled on a fine natural harbour at the mouth of the Ciliwung River, near a relatively small port principality called Jayakarta. In 1610 they concluded a contract with the Jayakarta prince permitting them to build warehouses and establish their headquarters here. They named their settlement Batavia. Subsequently renamed Jakarta—a variant of Jayakarta—it is today the capital of Indonesia.

The decision to establish this base at Batavia was an important and necessary commercial step: it allowed the Company to build the warehouses, victualling and ship-repair facilities and so forth which were necessary for its trading operations. But the very success of this endeavour gradually changed the kind of role that the Company was to play in the archipelago, in at least two important ways.

First, the establishment of a major base meant that the Company had to devote some of its resources to managing the people and materials being gathered there: in other words, it had to become something of a territorial administrator. To be sure, at first the territory to be administered was not extensive; but the initial aim of the Company's founders had been to avoid becoming territorially involved in the archipelago at all, precisely to avoid the costs which such a move would inevitably bring with them.

Second, the establishment of this base inevitably brought the VOC into conflict not only with the English, already established at Banten, but also with neighbouring Javanese states, which not surprisingly resented this intrusion into their realms. Banten itself claimed that Jayakarta was part of its territory, and thus that Batavia was on its soil. More importantly, the VOC also fell foul of Mataram. Just as Batavia was being established, Mataram under Sultan Agung was reaching the peak of its military power and geographical extent.

Banten and the English each made several attempts to seize control of Batavia in the first decade of its existence, some of which went close to success. But ultimately neither was militarily strong enough—or, for that matter, politically strong enough—to dislodge the Company's forces. Mataram, though, should have been a different matter.

For some time after its establishment, Mataram paid little attention to Batavia. The settlement was regarded as a relatively minor irritation compared with the much more important issue of bringing the trading states of the north coast pasisir under Mataram's control. The VOC itself sought to establish friendly relations with Mataram, sending ambassadors to its court, bringing with them tribute in the traditional manner.

By the 1620s this situation had changed significantly. Mataram captured the major east Javanese ports of Gresik, Tuban, Pasuruan and Surabaya between 1621 and 1625, effectively giving it control over east and central Java. For the first time since the fall of Majapahit, an inland state controlled the trade passing through Java's north coast ports. Sultan Agung now turned his attention to Batavia, which stood between him and effective control of all of Java.

In 1628 and 1629, Mataram laid siege to Batavia, the first time nearly succeeding in capturing the position. The second expedition, though, proved less fortunate, and revealed the state's strategic weakness. Mataram had great land-based strength, being able to bring up an army of perhaps 160 000 men to besiege the VOC position. But to provide all those men with food, supplies had to be brought in along the north coast, by sea: there was simply no way that the quantities of food required could have been taken to Batavia by bullock cart, the most efficient means of land transport then available. Unfortunately, the Mataram navy—a not inconsiderable force by Indonesian standards—was substantially less skilled and less well equipped than the navy of the VOC. The Company was thus able to interdict Mataram shipping, and thereby to cut off, or at least greatly reduce, the supply of food to the army outside Batavia's walls. In the end, Sultan Agung had to acknowledge his incapacity to take the town, and pulled back from it.

This reverse certainly did not mean that Mataram was no longer a major power: the VOC post was still a nuisance rather than a major challenger for power, albeit a nuisance Mataram could well do without. But it did mean that the VOC had established itself as an important local power, able to justify its presence in Java by military strength. For the next century and a half, the VOC and Mataram engaged in a struggle to control Java, a struggle that would eventually exhaust both sides.

At the same time that Mataram was being forced back from Batavia, Aceh, the strongest Indonesian state in the western part of the archipelago, also suffered defeat at the hands of the colonialists, this time the Portuguese. The Portuguese capture of Melaka, as we have seen, resulted in most Asian shipping shifting to other harbours, including the important Islamic pepper port of Aceh—which had never accepted the presence of the Portuguese in Melaka, from either a religious or a commercial viewpoint.

In the 1620s, the greatest of the Acehnese rulers, Sultan Iskandar Muda (r. 1607–1636) invested enormous quantities of material and human resources in an attempt to crush the Portuguese presence in Melaka. Having been rebuffed in a direct attack, he shifted tactics, gradually encircling Melaka by conquering its surrounding Malay states. He finally laid siege to the city in 1629—but was defeated. His navy was ultimately no match for that of the Portuguese, nor could he rely on the support of his Malay subjects in the struggle.

But Portuguese influence in the region more generally was on the wane and that of the Dutch rising. In Maluku, the Dutch eliminated the Portuguese and the Spanish from Ternate by 1606 and Tidore 60 years later. Local rulers were forced into concluding agreements with the Dutch, recognising the latter's sole right to participate in the spice trade.

In 1620–23, in their efforts to ensure control of the nutmeg production from Banda, the Dutch all but wiped out the indigenous population of the island, replacing the local people with Eurasians and others believed to be more loyal to the Company and more accommodating to its demands. Cloves came under its control in the 1650s, when it captured the island of Ambon. Being in a monopoly position, the VOC was also able to reduce substantially the participation in the spice trade of Javanese, Buginese, Malay and other traders operating out of ports on both sides of the Java Sea and the Straits of Melaka.

But the Dutch were still confronted by the power of Makasar, the key spice trading entrepot in eastern Indonesia. In the first half of the seventeenth century, the rulers of Makasar were committed to keeping their port open to traders from all around the region, and from around the world. In particular they saw free trade in spices, the most important of the commodities produced in the region, to be in their best interests. One ruler of Makasar is famously quoted as having written: 'God made the land and the sea; the land he divided among men and the sea he gave in common. It has never been heard that anyone should be forbidden to sail the seas'.

Free trade was not on the Company's agenda, however; its aim was to monopolise the spice trade and thus maximise its own profits.

Other traders, including Muslims from Maluku and from other parts of Indonesia, together with Europeans such as the English and the Portuguese, not surprisingly refused to recognise this self-proclaimed Dutch monopoly, and actively sought to break the Dutch hold on the trade. What was free trade to them became smuggling to the Dutch, in which Makasar came to play a central role. As we have seen, it quickly developed into the major centre of resistance to the Dutch attempt at monopoly, with Malay, Javanese, Gujerati, English and Portuguese merchants all using its facilities. Makasar also maintained a strong military presence in the east, in the spice islands, to protect its commercial interests there. The VOC's pretensions to power in the eastern archipelago could not succeed so long as Makasar remained unchallenged.

The Dutch launched a series of naval expeditions against Makasar in the first half of the seventeenth century, but none was successful. In 1656, though, they managed to seal off the clove pro-duction in Maluku, having finally managed to defeat the local Muslim traders, making it very difficult for the merchants in Makasar to get access to the spices. The VOC, however, wanted to finish Makasar off, once and for all. Following a pattern already established in other conflicts in the region, they sought allies among Makasar's regional enemies. There are two great ethnic communities residing in the Makasar region: the Makasarese and the Buginese. The conflicts between these two groups were legendary, and in some senses continue to the present day. The Dutch found allies in their struggle against the Makasarese among the Buginese, and especially in one of the greatest Buginese leaders, Arung Palakka.

In 1660 the Dutch struck a deal with Arung Palakka in which the latter agreed to provide troops to support the Dutch in their attacks on Makasar, in return for which he expected to be able to free the Buginese from Makasarese overlordship. The Makasarese tried to negotiate an alliance with Mataram in Java, and thus force the Dutch to fight on two fronts, but the Mataram ruler dismissed the proposition. In 1667 a combined force of Dutch and Buginese troops, together with Ambonese soldiers in Dutch employ, attacked Makasar and forced it to the negotiating table. Two years later, again supported by Arung Palakka, the Dutch attacked and destroyed the last major fort held by the Makasarese.

As a result of these combined military actions, the Indonesian and foreign traders were driven out of Makasar, and the city's independence destroyed. Many non-Dutch traders, both local and foreign, transferred their activities westward to Banjarmasin in southeast Kalimantan, which tried to replace Makasar as the regional centre of trade, but with little success. Many Makasarese traders and soldiers moved to Java (where ultimately they came to be regarded by the Dutch as posing a threat to their control of trade through the pasisir ports). No longer would Makasar pose a threat to Dutch ambitions in the eastern part of the archipelago. The port continued to play an important role in regional trade, but as part of the larger Dutch trading machine, not in its own right.

The Buginese soon found that they had effectively swapped their Makasarese masters for the Dutch, and many left the region to settle in other ports, re-establishing their trading networks. By the eighteenth century they had secured control of the Riau region and thus the entrance to the Straits of Melaka.

By the mid-seventeenth century, such was their degree of control over the Maluku spice trade, the Dutch were able to sell spices in Europe at about seventeen times the price for which they had bought them in Maluku, with none of the profit passing into Asian hands. Thus not only did the spice producers suffer; so did the trading inter-mediaries—Javanese, Malay and others—who had been the mainstays of the spice trade, the rice merchants who had supplied rice to those intermediaries and the multitude of others who had become dependent on participation in or support for the spice trade for their living.

The VOC had clearly begun to make the transition from being simply a trader to being a regional power.

Controlling the supply of pepper to the European market was more difficult to achieve than controlling the supply of spices, but even here the Dutch had a considerable measure of success. Sumatera was the key region, with significant amounts of pepper being produced in Aceh in the north, the Minangkabau highlands in the mid-west and the Lampung region in the south. In the north, Aceh was by now consider-ably smaller than it had been in its heyday, but it was still a regionally significant port for the export of pepper, as well as tin, camphor, gold and silk. Politically—and economically—it had not recovered from its defeat by the Portuguese in 1629, and the exercise of Dutch naval strength was sufficient to persuade it to surrender its pepper (and tin) producing regions to the Company. Under the terms of the Painan Contract, negotiated in 1663, the Dutch secured a complete monopoly on various products passing through Acehnese ports, including pepper.

Further south, the Dutch had established a strong presence in Padang, the only important port on the western side of Sumatera facing the Indian Ocean, and one of the two major export outlets for the products of the Minangkabau highlands, chiefly rice, pepper and gold. The Dutch established a warehouse here as early as 1666, though their influence remained confined to a tightly circumscribed area around the port itself, and did not penetrate inland to any significant extent. (They were strong in the port itself but, like the Portuguese in Melaka, could not extend that influence further afield.)

The other major outlet for Minangkabau products was eastward, down the long and meandering rivers that flowed eventually into the Straits of Melaka. This region was still nominally independent, but in fact was commercially under the influence of Melaka, by this time a Dutch territory. Thus the Dutch managed to lock up the exports from the Minangkabau region quite effectively, although the Minangkabau heartland remained untouched by Dutch influence, the Minangkabau state remaining politically and administratively independent of foreign control.

The Dutch were not the only colonial power with a physical presence in Sumatera. In the south of the island, at Bengkulu, the English East India Company had a base called Fort Marlborough whose origins dated back to the early seventeenth century and the intrusion of the Dutch into west Java. We have already noted that when the Dutch arrived at Banten they found the British there ahead of them and moved further to the east to establish their base at what became Batavia. Over time Dutch influence spread back into Banten, and in 1682 the Dutch were able to get the ruler of Banten to give them a monopoly of trade through the port, and to expel the British. This was a major blow to the British, since it meant that the only way they could now get access to the valuable pepper exports of west Java and southern Sumatera was by going through the Dutch. An alternative base had to be found. After some searching around, in mid-1685 an agreement was reached with a local ruler in south Sumatera for the establishment of a British base at Bengkulu, under the administration of the Presidency of Madras in India.

4
ECONOMIC DEMISE, POLITICAL DECLINE: 1600–1800

By the middle of the seventeenth century, the power of many of the Indonesian states, built up through the profits earned in trade and given spiritual strength by Islam, was beginning to wane. Political and economic strength was being dissipated in intra-state struggles, especially in the inland centres which, on the face of it, ought to have been able to supplant the much smaller coastal ones, but which by and large failed to do so. By the end of the eighteenth century, the stage was set for the rise of the age of European imperialism.

The age of commerce ended for Indonesia as it began: with changes in demand for the products that Indonesia supplied to international markets. The second and third quarters of the seventeenth century saw economic crisis replace boom in most of the economically advanced world, including Europe and China. Prices were falling, population numbers stagnating or even declining, and political crises challenging established rulers and state systems.

Indonesian traders were also hit by regulations issued by the Japanese government in 1639, closing that country off to all international trade except with China and the Netherlands. Up until this time, direct trade between China and Japan had been banned, in theory if not in fact, as one of the ways the ban was overcome was through the exchange of goods in overseas ports. One of the most important of these ports was Banten in west Java, whose role in the Chinese trade networks across the region has already been noted. When the Japanese government decided to close the country off from the rest of the world, this trade network collapsed virtually overnight.

The external world had changed in other ways too. In 1567 the Ming Dynasty in China had repealed the regulation prohibiting its citizens from engaging in private overseas trade, thus freeing Chinese traders to once again sail direct to Indonesia to collect the goods they wished to import. This they had begun to do, and in large numbers, squeezing out many of the Indonesian intermediaries who had been carrying goods north to China.

The reactions of the Indonesians and the Dutch to all these external forces were rather different, reflecting in large measure the different kinds of options they faced.

The general Dutch response was to try to preserve as much of their volume of trade as possible, which meant driving down the purchase prices they paid for Indonesian commodities as far as they would go, and eliminating their competitors. In this respect, the crisis really did little more than confirm the Dutch in the policies they had been pursuing to that moment.

The effects on Indonesian producers were more substantial. In many areas they retreated from the marketplace, which was increasingly left to the Europeans and ethnic Chinese—although, as will be seen, at least some of the European traders were no better placed to cope with the economic downturn than their Indonesian competitors had been. Right across the archipelago, we see peoples who had formerly been producers of cash crops—notably spices and pepper—destroying those crops, and planting instead subsistence crops, especially rice.

Not all Indonesian producers reacted in this way to the pressure of the market. Some of the pepper producers of Sumatera, for instance, who had also developed a strong market for cotton cloth from India while demand for their pepper was strong, responded to the decline in the demand for pepper by switching to the production of substitutes for formerly imported goods. As the economic decline began, not only had their incomes from pepper production declined; due to political upheavals in India the quality of the cloth they imported had fallen as its price had risen. This presented the pepper producers with a dilemma: they had become accustomed to consuming cloth to the point where giving it up was extremely difficult, but they no longer had the income to purchase it as before.

What they did was to stop planting pepper—after all, the market no longer wanted their crop—and plant cotton instead. Not only did this cotton enable the producers to meet the Sumateran demand for cloth; they were also able to supply cotton to weaving centres in other parts of the region, filling the void left by the disappearance of Indian cloth. Among the emerging cloth centres was Java, whose batik industry was also given a boost by the availability of local, and affordable, cloth. So the picture was not one of totally unmitigated gloom.

For the more powerful, absolutist rulers such as Sultan Agung of Mataram, these developments were particularly worrying, for they had come to rely on the income generated from trade as an essential backup to their political power. Finding themselves bereft of that backing, they, or their immediate successors, generally reacted by seeking to safeguard what political power they had at the expense of commerce. Thus Agung launched a series of attacks on the once-again rebellious ports of the Javanese pasisir, which found themselves caught between Dutch commercial pressure to the north, and Mataram's military pressure from the south.

Many Indonesian cities, once major cosmopolitan centres of considerable size attracting peoples from right around the region, faded back toward their provincial origins. In the case of those overrun by the Dutch, large numbers of their inhabitants, both locals and foreigners, fled. While often a search for personal safety and survival, this was also a search for new commercial opportunities: the traders among these people knew that the Dutch would not permit them the freedom they needed to carry on their businesses as before. This was the fate that befell Makasar when it came under Dutch control in 1669, Banten in 1682, and other trading centres such as Palembang, Banjarmasin, Ternate and Kupang at much the same time.

The retreat from the cash economy had a variety of knock-on effects. Given that they had less income, Indonesians also had less to spend on the commodities they had previously bought freely. For example, imports of Indian cloth by private traders in Batavia, for sale in the north Java ports, fell dramatically in the late seventeenth century, from a peak of 60 000 pieces in 1685 to only about 5000 pieces in 1705. Over the same period, the value of cloth exports from Batavia to the north coast ports fell by more than 90 per cent. Although the significance of this decline might be clouded somewhat by the fact that Indian cloth was used chiefly not for clothing but as a store of wealth, a form of money, the message that there was a major decline in the welfare of the inhabitants of the ports seems inescapable.

Indonesian traders were hit hard, as evidenced by the substantial decline in the size and number of Indonesian ships engaged in archipelagic and regional trade at the end of the seventeenth century, compared with the figures for a century or so earlier. The situation was made worse by the fact that in 1651 Sultan Agung prohibited his subjects from travelling abroad and in 1655 closed all Javanese ports and ordered the seizure or destruction of all Javanese vessels. What commerce remained no longer needed the large cargo ships for which the Indonesians had been known at the start of the age of commerce. Being relegated in effect to the much smaller coastal routes, traders switched to smaller, shallower-draught vessels. The days of Indonesian dominance of seaborne trade were over.

The questions remain, however: Why were Indonesian states and their producers and traders, by and large, unsuccessful in meeting the challenge of changed trading circumstances? Why did the region's participation in global trade in the sixteenth century not lead to the development of local forms of capitalism, which might in turn have led to the emergence of local states comparable with those that emerged in Europe and Japan at much the same time, and would have enabled Indonesia to weather the trade bust?

Early European observers argued that the fundamental commercial weakness of the local states lay in the fact that their rulers had no respect for private property, and were inclined to confiscate it arbitrarily. Thus no private citizens could feel secure in their wealth, nor could they rely on being able to pass on accumulated wealth to their descendants. Under such circumstances, investment in infrastructure which would preserve or create wealth such as ships and strong, defensible warehouses for the storage of trade goods was unattractive. Rather, wealth was going to be held in forms that could be easily hidden and readily transported in case of danger. Under such circumstances, wealth clearly was not being put to commercially productive work. Thus, once the supply of profits dried up, the local economies collapsed.

Other historians have pointed to the fact that, unlike the case in the countries of western Europe, state rule and commercial activities were tightly linked in the Indonesian states; their rulers either held trade as their own monopoly, or else permitted only those merchants with whom they were in alliance to trade, thus preventing the emergence of a class of capitalist entrepreneurs independent of the state. When trade declined, the power of the state was threatened, and under such circumstances most state rulers reacted in defensive ways, seeking to shore up their political power by other means. They were not commercial risk-takers; they were conservative politicians.

The other explanation often given relates to the arrival in the region of the Europeans; that the Europeans were sufficiently powerful—militarily and commercially—to defeat the local states and traders. It is clear that from about the mid-1500s to the mid-1600s the major Indonesian trading states fell to hostile forces, most of which were either European in origin, or in which Europeans played important roles even though the Europeans were by no means demonstrably superior in matters of either commerce or technology.

In the case of spice production in the Maluku islands, the VOC was certainly the crucial factor in destroying local producers and traders after it established its monopoly from the middle of the seventeenth century. It used this monopoly power ruthlessly.

In all probability, none of these factors on its own was decisive. But taken together, their force was virtually unstoppable, especially in those states that had come to depend on trade for their incomes—and this meant virtually all the major Indonesian states at this time. From this point on, the states tended to turn inwards, to be concerned chiefly with intra-regional affairs. What had been a region with vibrant, exciting links with the outside world—links which might have been based on trade, but which also brought great ideas both spiritual and secular—became, if not isolationist, then certainly far less open to the world than it had been.

This development had an important impact on local societies. Up to this point, there was certainly no sense in which we could talk of an Indonesian society or nation extending right across the archipelago. There was, nonetheless, a web of trading contacts linking coastal peoples together. Virtually all the ports of the region had substantial non-local communities of traders and sailors: Javanese, Malays, Buginese, Acehnese, Bantenese, and also locally based (and often locally born) Chinese. By gradually monopolising inter-island and international trade, the Dutch were weakening, albeit not completely breaking, these ties and eventually the social links they represented as well. Further, the Dutch were cutting off the Indonesians from routine contacts with the wider world beyond the archipelago, and thus denying them the stimulus that such contacts had previously provided. Indonesia was becoming isolated not just from the international marketplace for goods, but also from the international marketplace for ideas.

The only winners in this situation seemed to be the VOC and the Chinese traders.

Extension of VOC control

Over the rest of the sixteenth century and into the seventeenth, the VOC gradually extended the regions under its control. The establishment of Batavia had marked the beginnings of a change in the status of the Company, from an entity solely concerned with trade to a regional administrator. Following Mataram's failed attempts to seize Batavia, the Company began pushing out into the Javanese hinterland and along the north coast. By the end of the seventeenth century it was the dominant power in the Priangan highlands of west Java, and eastward from Batavia along the north coast through to the eastern end of the island. Mataram in central Java for the moment remained independent, but was becoming increasingly concerned at Dutch encroachments into its territory.

In the area immediately surrounding Batavia, land was brought under direct Company rule, often by military conquest. It was then sold off to private citizens, some from the Netherlands, some from other parts of Europe and others from China: the Chinese population of Batavia in particular grew rapidly after the establishment of the VOC settlement. Out of a population of just over 27 000 in 1673, nearly 3000 were Chinese, while there were just over 2000 Europeans and 700 Eurasians. Indeed, the Chinese had played a crucial role in the development of Batavia since its very foundation, so much so that Batavia was in many respects as much a Chinese colonial town as a western one. The inflow of Chinese picked up even further pace after the Company's annexation of Banten in 1683, which brought with it control of much more land. The Company set about producing sugar from these lands for the Middle East market but, lacking a local labour force to work the land, used Chinese immigrants instead.

The Chinese, for the most part, remained in communities distinct from those of the indigenous population, contrary to the cosmopolitan experience of the fourteenth and fifteenth centuries when ethnic Chinese in Indonesia (and other parts of Southeast Asia) were forbidden to return to China and thus cut off from cultural or genetic renewal. Now both these things were possible. As a result, we see both a resurgence of Chinese ethnic identity and an increased Chinese dominance of regional trade with China itself and, almost as a by-product, of domestic trade as well.

Nevertheless, we should be wary of lumping the ethnic Chinese into the one basket as if they constituted a single community with a single role to play in Indonesian society. To say that most merchants were ethnic Chinese is not to say that all ethnic Chinese were merchants. At the margins at least, the boundaries between the ethnic Chinese and indigenous societies remained in many respects as blurred as they had always been. At one end of the social and economic scale, Chinese craftspeople and labourers blended in with local societies; at the other end, some ethnic Chinese had been almost completely absorbed into the Javanese aristocracy. In the middle of the eighteenth century, for instance, the local rulers of Pekalongan, Batang, Sidayu and Semarang were all of ethnic Chinese descent.

Decline of Mataram

During the second half of the seventeenth century, the power of the kingdom of Mataram was clearly on the decline from the time of the death of Sultan Agung in 1646 and the succession to the throne of his son Amangkurat I. The ports of the pasisir were once again in conflict with the authority of the Sultan.

The VOC became increasingly concerned about this situation, since its major interest in Java was in ensuring access to the island's resources. Its policy was to work through the established ruler of Mataram, who did the actual collecting of revenues through his subordinates, revenues which were then split with the Company. In return, the Company gave the ruler political and military support. Not only was this an efficient system of administration from the point of view of the Company, the Company also believed that it reflected the way that things had always been done in Java.

In Batavia's view, Javanese kingdoms were centralised and absolutist, and its approach to Javanese politics was based on the need to maintain this principle. But the Dutch were misreading the situation: the Javanese state was not always as centralised and absolutist as they imagined. The ruler of Mataram might, in a formal sense, have been sovereign along the north coast, but in practice his authority depended on his relationship with the bupatis of those regions. In some cases the Sultan was sufficiently strong to be able to appoint his own men to positions of bupati—though there was no guarantee that the local populations would willingly follow the instructions of those so appointed. In other cases the Sultan had to negotiate with local leaders, sometimes bribing them for their support, sometimes cajoling them, sometimes holding members of their families hostage as a guarantee of their loyalty, sometimes arranging marriages between them and his female relatives.

Even when the Sultan could be confident that the pasisir rulers were loyal, and able to impose their wills on their populations, these relationships were still of a personal rather than an institutional kind.

57

The result was that the Mataram state was held together not so much by the absolute power of the ruler as by the network of ties with regional overlords that the ruler was able to enforce.

Despite its misunderstanding of both the complexity of these relationships and the nature of the authority of Mataram, the VOC's policy committed the Company to supporting the ruler of Mataram in conflicts with his nominal vassals, including the rulers of the north coast states.

Perhaps the single most significant episode in such conflicts was the revolt led by Trunajaya in 1676 in Madura. A relative of the ruler of Madura, Trunajaya had seized power in the island in 1671, and rejected the overriding authority of Amangkurat I of Mataram. The Sultan could hardly allow this act of defiance to go unheeded. He sent his son to Surabaya, the port city across the narrow straits from Madura, to try to bring an end to the revolt, but he failed. In September 1676, Trunajaya and his army crossed the straits to Java and started a campaign along the north coast. Within about two months, Trunajaya's authority was acknowledged by most bupatis along the coast as far west as Cirebon. The fact that Trunajaya was able to gather to his army many Javanese, to supplement the Madurese he had brought with him, testifies to the extent of discontent with the rule of Amangkurat in Java itself. Further, Trunajaya played very effectively on Islamic sentiment, exploiting what many Javanese saw as the anti-Islamic attitudes of Amangkurat, and on messianic beliefs among the Javanese, portraying himself as the Just Prince, the *Ratu Adil*, come to free the Javanese from the chaotic rule of Amangkurat and return Mataram to the lost glories of an earlier golden age. The myth of the Just Prince was deep-seated in Javanese society and was typically invoked by rebels against contemporary authority to justify their rebellion.

This challenge clearly placed Amangkurat in a very difficult position: the continued existence of Mataram hung in the balance. Trunajaya was in control of much of the pasisir and of east Java, and indeed in 1677 captured the Mataram capital, Plered. Unaided,

Amangkurat seemed to have no chance of bringing the pasisir regions back under control. The Company was the only force capable of helping him regain the kingdom—but the Company was controlled by the infidel Christians, a fact which would only weaken his Islamic credentials further and give strength to his opponents.

The Company did not really wish to become embroiled in a war from which the commercial returns were doubtful. The situation was made even more difficult for Batavia by the presence among Trunajaya's supporters of soldiers from Makasar. Having fled their home on its capture by the Dutch in 1674, these Makasarese had originally gone to Banten, but after some conflict with the Sultan of Banten had moved to east Java, where they were warmly welcomed into the armies of Trunajaya. Batavia feared that not only would they strengthen the fighting capacity of Trunajaya on land, but also that their well-known seafaring skills would enable Trunajaya to control the sea lanes along the north coast.

The Governor-General in Batavia, Johan Maetsuyker, tried to use diplomacy rather than force to resolve the problem, but ultimately this proved impossible. The Company finally decided to send a military force to assist the ruler of Mataram—now Amangkurat II, who had succeeded his late father—to defeat the rebellion, and at the same time to expel the Makasarese. The Dutch succeeded in both these endeavours.

Amangkurat established his new court of Kartasura, close to the present-day city of Solo. The cost of Dutch support for his rule, though, was high. Directly or indirectly, Mataram granted the Company all the revenues derived from the pasisir ports; a monopoly over the trade in textiles, opium and sugar; and the right to build shipyards and fortresses wherever it wished in Java.

Over the following eight decades, the VOC helped succeeding rulers of Mataram to secure their authority by intervening in the three Javanese Wars of Succession (1704–1708, 1719–1723 and 1746–1757). In so doing, the VOC went some distance to helping to create the kind of Javanese state that it imagined had always been present. By assisting

Mataram in its disputes with local rulers of the pasisir, the Company was intervening in a centuries-old state of conflict—or at least tension—between the conservative courts of the inland and the more outward-looking, and certainly more Islamic, coastal states. The rulers of Mataram were grateful for this military assistance—but every time the Company intervened on the side of the Sultan, there was a price to pay. And that price was usually the surrender of more rice or more timber or more gold to the Company, and sometimes the surrender of more territory to the Company's control. To balance these losses in revenue, the Sultans had to impose more and more taxes on their peoples, an imposition which ultimately proved counterproductive.

But there was also a sense in which the Company's very success in strengthening the position of the Sultans weakened its own position. The dominant political issues in the court of Mataram in the first part of the eighteenth century were not to do with the VOC, but rather with the relations between the court in Kartasura and the lords of the pasisir regions to which it laid claim. The VOC came into these considerations to the extent that it could help or hinder the process of exerting control over those states. The Sultan was willing to accede to the Company's wishes—with or without good grace—so long as he was in need of the Company's support in conflicts with recalcitrant vassal states. But once most of those vassal states had been subdued, then Kartasura started to question why Mataram still needed the support of the Company. This situation—and indeed the sheer complexity of the political situation in Java in the eighteenth century—is well illustrated by the so-called Chinese War of 1740–1741 and the subsequent Third Javanese War of Succession, 1746–1757.

The Chinese War, 1740–1741

During the reign of Pakubuwana II, who came to the throne as a teenager in 1726, Mataram had felt sufficiently confident of its strength to pressure the pasisir rulers to stop sending tribute to the Company; by 1732, only Cakraningrat IV, the ruler of West Madura, was still sending tribute, primarily, it would seem, because he saw the VOC as a useful ally in his own conflicts with the Mataram court. Within Mataram itself, re-negotiation of the 1705 treaty with the VOC in 1733, which resulted in increased payments being made to the Company, fanned growing resentment of the state's relations with the Dutch. It has been argued by some that the increased payments did not add to the burden of Java's rural economy, and might well have provided additional economic opportunities for some entrepreneurial Javanese. But for those of Pakubuwana's opponents who were critical of his relationship with the VOC, the revised treaty provided further ammunition. There was an ethnic element here too, in that the agents charged with collecting much of the rice which was the Company's due were ethnic Chinese, which caused resentment in some quarters. In fact, both Mataram and the VOC made extensive use of ethnic Chinese as tax collectors in the territories they controlled.

In late September 1740, VOC officials in Batavia believed they had uncovered evidence of a planned Chinese rebellion. The basis of the plot was that Chinese residents in Batavia believed that the Company was planning to expel, and possibly kill, those of them who were surplus to Company requirements, and therefore were planning a pre-emptive strike. Open hostilities between the two sides erupted in early October. The Company's forces were dominant, and a search of the Chinese quarter of the city turned into arson and mass murder. The slaughter lasted three days and it left approximately 10 000 Chinese dead. These killings sparked the so-called Chinese War, which quickly spread right along the north coast as far as Surabaya.

Initially, the fighting seemed to be going strongly against the Company. Semarang was surrounded in June. By July 1741, the Company's positions at Juwana and Rembang had been overrun and the garrison in Demak, including Buginese and Balinese soldiers as well as Dutch, forced to withdraw.

In Mataram, Pakubuwana II was indecisive in confronting what was clearly one of the most politically complex crises he had ever encountered. Among his advisors at court there were those who counselled him to side with the Chinese in the hope of expelling the Company from Java, and those who were all for supporting the Company—ideally, holding back until the Company was on the ropes, and then stepping in to rescue it, at the price of rescinding the oppressive Java–VOC treaties. Eventually Pakubuwana decided to side with the Chinese, presumably having concluded that the VOC was heading for defeat. In late July, Mataram forces beseiged the Company position in Kartasura. The VOC held out for three weeks but then fell, its commander being among the dead.

This disaster convinced the Dutch that they had to accept the only real offer of assistance they had received, from Cakraningrat IV, assistance which proved decisive. The combination of the westward sweep of Cakraningrat's Madurese forces and the steady reinforcement of the Company's coastal fortresses from its headquarters in Batavia meant that by about November, the military initiative had passed to the Company. The seige of Semarang was broken in November 1741, and Mataram's armies in the east were retreating before the Madurese.

Pakubuwana was facing defeat. In a desperate bid to preserve his position, he now tried to rebuild his bridges with the Dutch. The Company was wary of his approaches, but nevertheless sent a negotiating team to Kartasura. News of this development angered many of Pakubuwana's internal critics, men who had supported the war against the VOC. They turned their armies against Pakubuwana, and at the end of June 1742 captured and looted Kartasura. Within a year, Pakubuwana's position had changed from contemplating whether to intervene militarily and rescue the VOC in its war with the Chinese, to having to seek the VOC's support to restore him to his throne, now that Kartasura was occupied not by the Dutch but by a combined Chinese–Javanese force.

The VOC provided this support—but, adding to Pakubuwana's humiliation, it was not VOC troops which ousted the Chinese and their allies from the court, but the largely Madurese armies of Cakraningrat. Pakubuwana was eventually escorted back into Kartasura by VOC forces in December 1742, but the court was a shambles, most of its buildings destroyed and its treasures—sacred swords, jewellery, gamelan sets, manuscripts and so forth—looted.

VOC support had come at enormous cost. The whole of the north coast was ceded to the Company, along with the income from toll-gates, markets and various duties and taxes levied by Mataram. Partly because of the level of destruction of Kartasura, in 1746 the capital was moved to the village of Solo (also called Surakarta).

Not all of Mataram's princes accepted the compromise that Pakubuwana had negotiated: in 1746, the Third (and final) Javanese War of Succession broke out. This time, in order to get Company support, Pakubuwana II—already a dying man—made the ultimate sacrifice: on 11 December 1749 he formally ceded sovereignty over Mataram to the VOC. The Company now decided that the old principle of seeking to maintain the unity of Mataram was neither feasible nor necessary, and sought the division of the state between the rival claimants.

On 13 February 1755, the Treaty of Giyanti was signed, dividing what was left of the kingdom of Mataram into two parts. One part, with its capital in the city of Solo, was headed by Pakubuwana II's son, Pakubuwana III. The other part, with its capital 60 kilometres to the west in Yogyakarta, was ruled by Pakubuwana II's half-brother Mangkubumi, who took the title Sultan Hamengkubuwono I. The treaty was not immediately accepted by all parties to the dispute: fighting went on for another two years. In 1757, though, an uneasy peace settled on Java when Pakubuwana III's territory was divided, with a portion going to his cousin Mas Said, who took the title Mangkunegara I. The final act in the saga of the destruction and division of Mataram took place in 1813, when Hamengkubuwono's territory was also split, part being hived off under the rulership of Pakualam I. In this way the four royal houses of contemporary Java were established, all with at least some claim to be the inheritor of Mataram tradition.

Dutch and Javanese reactions to the Treaty of Giyanti varied somewhat. On the one hand, for the Javanese states the end of the wars of succession brought a period of peace and material prosperity unprecedented for at least 150 years, a period which was to last until the outbreak of the Java War in 1825. In the absence of constant struggles for power within the state, and rebellions against it from the provinces, the states' resources could be devoted to more productive uses. There was never any real chance that there would be reunification of the states, but neither was there any real likelihood of hostilities breaking out between them.

Nevertheless, rivalry between the royal houses became the central feature of Javanese politics for the remainder of the eighteenth century and well into the nineteenth; in some respects it remains to the present day. Certainly, during this period royal rivalry was a much more important fact of political life in the respective courts than was the presence of the Dutch. The Dutch remained, in an important sense, peripheral to the 'real politics' of Java, the struggle between the royal houses for supremacy. The Dutch had a role to play only in the sense that they could be called upon to support one house against another.

For the Dutch also the treaty had both positive and negative aspects. It was bad, in the sense that they now had to deal with two (and then four) Javanese rulers instead of just one. This certainly added to the political costs of the Company's Java policy, and probably its financial costs as well. And there were problems inherent in trying to exercise the sovereignty in Java that the treaty had promised them. Having formal sovereignty was no guarantee of the capacity to exercise it. The Dutch had won the war by political as much as by military means, and even in victory their military strength was debatable. In some respects, the Javanese states came out of the conflict more powerful than the Dutch.

On the other hand, peace was inherently more profitable than war. The Company had previously strengthened the garrison it maintained in Mataram in case it had to fight to impose a solution to the conflict on the rivals. Now that a peaceful resolution of the dispute had been achieved, these forces could be withdrawn and many units demobilised, resulting in a considerable saving of money. And the half century or so of peace which followed the signing of the Treaty brought considerable prosperity to Java.

The Company outside Java

I want to turn now to other parts of the Indonesian archipelago, to see how the Company was faring outside Java.

The Dutch started to push seriously into the Minahasa region of north Sulawesi towards the end of the seventeenth century, particularly after the defeat of Makasar in 1669. A contract of agreement with leaders of nineteen *walak*, or local communities, in Minahasa was concluded in 1679 by the Governor of Ternate on behalf of the Company. The aim of this agreement, revised in 1699, was to secure for the VOC the northern approaches to the spice islands, especially from the Spanish who had been active here and further north in the Philippines. In addition, the people of Minahasa were to supply the Company with rice and timber, though here the returns were rather less than the Company had expected. Despite being nicknamed 'the bread basket of the Moluccas' by early Company visitors, the region's deliveries of rice were generally lower than expected, and unreliable. Apart from any agricultural reasons for this, it seems that the Dutch often lost out in the rice market to Buginese traders who bought rice here for sale further north and west, in Sulu. The Buginese were also more attuned to the demands of the Minahasa market, supplying it with goods, such as their own distinctive cloth, which were in much greater demand than anything the Dutch had to sell. By the end of the eighteenth century, rice supplies to the Company had virtually ceased.

The Dutch had even less success in their attempts to order the political and social lives of the Minahasans. The Company was concerned, as in Java, with the maintenance or creation of a stable society that would facilitate achievement of its economic goals. Thus at the end of the sixteenth century the VOC recognised three walak leaders as the leaders of the whole Minahasa region, authorised to arbitrate and determine matters of law, subject only to the requirement that they inform the Company's representatives in advance of issuing judgements. These leaders were expected to create conditions of stability and order across the region. However, they enjoyed their new privileges to the full, to the point where their actions were seen by many Minahasans as simply unacceptable. In places, people moved away to lands beyond their control and that of the Company, disrupting agriculture and trade and thus further endangering the already fragile rice deliveries to the Company. In other regions open warfare broke out. The Company let the system die out in the early eighteenth century, although there was a temporary revival in the 1730s. The attempted imposition of this new form of local leadership had brought more unrest than stability.

Much the same could be said of the Company's attempts to eliminate local warfare, in the expectation that this, too, would stabilise society. Indeed, it may well be argued that the introduction of new commodities into Minahasa—agricultural crops such as maize, as well as firearms—might actually have made conflict between the walak more likely rather than less, as neighbours sought dominance over each other. Right through to the end of Company administration at the end of the eighteenth century, relations between walak were characterised by hostility rather than by unity.

At the northern end of Sumatera, by the end of the eighteenth century the territory owing allegiance to the Sultan of Aceh had contracted substantially from its heyday two centuries earlier. Aceh now effectively controlled only the northern tip of the island. It was, though, still an important trading state, selling pepper, camphor, tin, gold and silk, among other items. Despite the Painan Contract, supposedly limiting trading relations to the Dutch, other traders—both local and foreign—continued to visit Aceh. The Americans, for instance, were trading regularly with Aceh by the end of the eighteenth century. Indeed, there was a strong American presence in Sumatera, both trading and consular, long before there was any such presence in other parts of the archipelago. In 1802, for instance, 21 American ships visited the so-called 'pepper ports' of Aceh, Americans going on to effectively dominate the trade in pepper here until the middle of the nineteenth century. Acehnese traders also continued their commerce with the east coast of the Indian subcontinent. One of the more interesting items exported to India from Aceh was war-elephants, though this trade declined as the Indian rulers adopted more European styles of warfare.

Further south, there was a VOC garrison in Palembang, but it was limited to fewer than one hundred men under the terms of the treaty with the Sultan of Palembang; the treaty noted that greater numbers would draw into question the continued sovereignty of the Sultan over the region.

To the west, the Dutch retained their foothold at Padang, and with it their access to the Minangkabau highlands. In the south, though, the British were still present in Bengkulu, enabling them to retain a strong position in the south Sumateran pepper trade.

Overall, neither the Dutch nor the British had much of a physical presence on the ground in Sumatera in the eighteenth century. Both were concerned primarily with trade, and saw formal treaties with local rulers as being the best way to go about ensuring the success of their trading ventures. In many respects, the Dutch saw their major rival on Sumatera as the British rather than any local Sumateran ruler; and the British returned the compliment.

The VOC moved into Kalimantan rather later than into the other major islands. It established its first post at Pontianak on the west coast, for instance, only in 1778, in response to a request from the Sultan of Pontianak, whose own state only just predated the Dutch arrival. In seeking Dutch support and protection in his competition with local rivals, the Sultan was doing something that other small regional states had been doing for centuries.

By the last decade of the eighteenth century, on paper at least, the VOC seemed to be at the peak of its power. It controlled, either directly or via political alliances, many of the important ports in the archipelago, and about two-thirds of the island of Java. It was militarily the single most powerful state in the region. It looked prosperous, paying dividends during the eighteenth century of between 20 and 40 per cent.

And yet in 1799 the Company was bankrupt; its charter was allowed to lapse and it collapsed, its overseas activities—including those in Indonesia –taken over by the Dutch Crown. How could this have happened?

The collapse of the VOC

The first point to make here is to recognise, once again, that answers to historical questions in Indonesia can rarely be sought in Indonesia alone. The region's openness to the rest of the world, through trade, religion and politics, was such that it was routinely vulnerable to changes in the international environment. Thus it was for the VOC. Although the Asian headquarters of the Company were in Batavia, the VOC's Asian operations actually extended over a very wide area, ranging from Japan and China across to India. Any search for an explanation for the collapse of the Company cannot look simply at Indonesia; conditions prevailing in other parts of the east and south Asian worlds also need to be taken into account.

One important consideration was that the Dutch were losing control of the lucrative trade with China, particularly to the British. The latter had realised, much more quickly than the Dutch, that private traders were the way of the future, just as state-chartered companies had been two centuries earlier. Although the English East India Company was to survive until the middle of the nineteenth century, as early as the late seventeenth century private traders from Britain were playing increasingly important roles in intra-Asian trade.

The impact of events in Europe cannot be disregarded either. The Fourth Anglo-Dutch War (1780–1784) was a disaster for the VOC. The Company lost 70 per cent of its total assets, including extensive shipping and facilities, to the British, on top of the costs incurred as a result of the War.

In terms of Indonesia-based reasons for the Company's collapse, the one usually given is that as an institution the Company faced what turned out to be an impossible conflict between its activities as business venturer and as territorial administrator—that is, a conflict between trade and politics. When it was established two centuries earlier, the VOC represented an imaginative and innovative response to the commercial challenges the Dutch faced in the archipelago, and its efforts to monopolise trade in and with the archipelago brought it substantial profits. Initially the Company had focused its activities on trade, avoiding as far as was possible acquiring direct control over territory or peoples.

However—so this line of argument goes—by the later years of the eighteenth century the VOC had outlived its role as innovative trading company and was failing to adapt to the new role it faced; in particular it had acquired an extensive territorial empire but failed to evolve an efficient means of administering that empire.

Under an external appearance of prosperity, the Company was now in deep financial difficulty. One sign of the difficulties it faced was that its debts rose during much of the eighteenth century while its profits fell; much of the 'profits' it used to support the dividends it paid to its shareholders actually came from short-term borrowings. A great deal of potential profit was being siphoned off by its representatives in the archipelago: despite quite horrific punishments meted out to those of its employees who were discovered violating the Company's ban on private participation in trade, many did engage in such trade. Corruption in business is no new phenomenon in Indonesia.

This argument has come under some criticism in recent times, some authors arguing that the roles of merchant and quasi-state were actually complementary rather than competitive: that had it not been for the Company's latter role, it could not have played the former one. Yet it is clear that the way the Company combined these activities did not always work.

The legacy of the VOC

How might we assess the impact of the VOC and its employees on Indonesian states and societies? From the preceding it can be seen that in the political, military and economic arenas VOC influence was substantial, but not overwhelming. The strength of the Company was primarily a reflection of the weaknesses of its opponents, and especially of the fact that there was no unity of action among the Indonesian states that were its competitors. The Company's military successes—in Makasar, for instance, and on the north coast of Java—were made possible by the participation of Indonesian forces on the Company side. It was only at sea that the Company's technology and organisational skills gave it a clear edge over its Indonesian competitors.

Within the Indonesian states, even those in Java which had come under greatest Company pressure, the focus of attention of court elites was still on local rivals, the Company being seen as a force which was either a useful ally or a dangerous enemy in conflicts with those rivals. The Company, while clearly recognised as foreign, was nonetheless also seen in some sense as a state operating within the established norms of inter-state relations.

For the merchants and traders, the impact of the Dutch presence was more substantial, in that it had pushed them out of profitable markets and the carrying trade. However, the Company was by no means the only force responsible for the gradual squeezing out of Indonesians from regional and international trade, and in any event suffered a similar fate itself. To the extent that Indonesians were participating in international trade during the age of commerce they were subject to the vagaries of the international market: to the whims of consumers half a globe away, and to the changing political and strategic conditions in north Asia and in Europe. With or without the presence of the Company, it is likely that Indonesian merchants and traders in the eighteenth century would have seen their share of international trade much decreased from that in the sixteenth century.

For the bulk of the population, the peasants, the Company's presence for the most part had remained invisible. Even at the end of the eighteenth century, most Indonesian territory and peoples were not under Dutch control. Some Indonesians, it is true, by 1800 had adopted the religion of the Dutch—and that of earlier European powers, the Portuguese and the Spanish. But over most of the archipelago, Christianity had made little impact. The only places where there was any possibility of the Dutch exerting a degree of social and cultural influence had been the urban areas, for the Dutch in the Indies were overwhelmingly urban dwellers. Yet even if we look at the culture of the urban areas at the end of the eighteenth century, what is striking is the paucity of Dutch influence.

Indeed, it could well be argued that in terms of urban culture, the Dutch had come under the influence of the Indonesians rather than the other way around. This can be seen, for instance, in the development of Batavia, the only place in the archipelago where the Company established a civil settlement of any size. Early efforts to establish a Dutch city, complete with canals and Dutch-style cool-temperate climate housing, were soon abandoned as being quite unsuited to the region. What emerged was a new type of city, drawing on Europe for some of its features, but increasingly reliant on local borrowings, the germination of a unique culture combining Dutch and Indonesian elements, commonly referred to as *Indische* (or 'Indian') culture.

5
ESTABLISHMENT OF
EMPIRE: 1800–1900

The preceding centuries saw the arrival in Indonesia of a variety of European powers, competing with Indonesian states and with each other for control of the trade flowing through the region, but by the late eighteenth century, despite the collapse of the VOC, the Dutch were the strongest of these foreign powers. Indeed, the Dutch were probably as strong a force as any individual Indonesian state, especially since the division of Mataram in the middle of the century. Despite this, the Dutch did not enjoy a predominant position in the archipelago; for they still faced considerable local and European competition.

By the end of the nineteenth century the situation had changed dramatically. No other foreign power now had a presence in the region, with the minor exception of the Portuguese in East Timor, and no Indonesian state of any substance stood out. The Dutch colonial state dominated all but a few peripheral parts of the archipelago— colonialism seemed triumphant, and was certainly triumphal.

The triumph of colonialism was fragile. We have already seen that the Dutch capacity to enforce a monopoly on trade in the major exports of the archipelago had been severely damaged by the activities of the English East India Company and private British traders in the first half of the eighteenth century, and by the Dutch defeat in Europe in the fourth Anglo-Dutch War of 1780–1784. It would hardly be an exaggeration to say that the Dutch came to control the Indonesian archipelago in the nineteenth century in part because it suited their main international trading rival, the British, to allow them to do so, and in part because—as in previous centuries—their Indonesian opponents were never willing to forgo traditional rivalries to form a united front against them. The Dutch empire in the Indies came about largely by default.

The initial consolidation of empire came in Java, where the Dutch presence was historically the strongest, at the turn of the nineteenth century. At this point both the remaining Javanese states and the Dutch administration were in transition.

One of the arenas of greatest turmoil was the Yogyakarta-based state ruled by Hamengkubuwono II, successor to his father Hamengkubuwono I, who had died in 1792. Hamengkubuwono II was a much less astute ruler than his father, and the state quickly became divided on numerous issues, ranging from nominations to the bureaucracy to the Sultan's personal behaviour (especially with respect to religious matters) to the level of taxation imposed on both peasants and aristocrats.

The Dutch administration was facing even greater challenges. Following the collapse of the VOC in 1799, administration of the Indies had fallen to the Dutch government. But the Netherlands fell to Napoleon Bonaparte in 1806, and Napoleon's brother Louis was placed on the Dutch throne. Committed to the liberal ideals of the French Revolution, Louis appointed Herman Daendels as Governor-General of the Indies to put these ideals into practice.

Daendels was a radical thinker who wanted to modernise the colonial administration on Java and eliminate elements of feudalism such as forced labour and delivery of crops. He also wanted to extend the territory under direct Dutch rule, and the courts in Solo and Yogyakarta to treat the representatives of Batavia not as ambassadors of a foreign state, but as representatives of the sovereign power.

Overshadowing Daendels' efforts were the effects of the Napoleonic Wars. The British had established a naval blockade of the Indies, and were threatening an invasion, thus administrative reform had to take second place to fortifying Java against the threat of British attack. Under Daendels' direction, a highway was constructed along the north coast of the island to facilitate the movement of troops and materiel, major armaments factories were established and the locally recruited army expanded from 4000 men to 18 000 men.

These developments all had to be paid for—and the only way Daendels could do this was by going against some of the very principles he had previously championed. In order to raise money he permitted the renting and selling of land to European and Chinese entrepreneurs. In order to raise a workforce to undertake war-related construction work, forced labour was expanded. These and other measures increased substantially the burden placed on the Javanese, and the peasantry in particular.

The royal courts, however, did little to resist these further encroachments on Javanese hegemony. In 1810 one of Yogyakarta's regional officials launched a rebellion against the Dutch, but it was easily put down. Daendels then demanded that Hamengkubuwono II take personal responsibility for the rebellion, and pay Batavia compensation. When he refused, Daendels marched on Yogyakarta in late 1810, captured the city and forced the Sultan to abdicate in favour of his son, Hamengkubuwono III.

All this effort, however, was finally in vain. Daendels completed his term of office in May 1811, but in September the same year, after a short military campaign, the colony of Batavia was captured by the British. Hamengkubuwono II took advantage of the confusion this inevitably aroused, and proceeded to depose his son.

74

The British appointed Thomas Stamford Raffles, later to become famous as the founder of modern Singapore, as Lieutenant Governor-General of the Indies. Raffles quickly came to the view that Hamengkubuwono II was unacceptable as a ruler. Uncovering an exchange of letters between him and the ruler of Solo, which implied a plot to attack the British, in 1812 Raffles sent a military expedition against Yogyakarta to depose Hamengkubuwono. The city was bombarded and then stormed. The Sultan was captured and his son reinstalled as ruler.

Raffles proposed following the same general principles Daendels had espoused in administering the lands now under his control: the abolition of forced labour and forced deliveries. But to compensate for the loss of government revenue from these changes, he proposed the imposition on Javanese farmers of a land rent tax. This would be collected by the bupati, acting now as agents of the British government: as British tax collectors, in other words.

Like Daendels, though, circumstances prevented Raffles achieving all that he wanted. In 1816, as a result of the ending of the Napoleonic Wars in Europe and the re-assertion of Dutch independence, the British handed back to the Netherlands the territory they controlled in the Indies.

By this time, Hamengkubuwono IV had ascended the Yogyakarta throne, but the state was moving rapidly towards economic and political collapse. A major problem was that the annexation of Yogyakarta lands by Daendels and then Raffles had deprived many officials of their living, since they no longer had people or land under their financial control. But the Dutch themselves were not in a much better state, for the cost of their involvement in the Napoleonic Wars had been extremely high; economic recovery seemed a long way off. Thus both the rulers of Yogyakarta and the Dutch were concerned to find alternative ways of making a living out of the island.

For their part the Dutch raised tolls and customs duties substantially; Raffles had taken over these forms of taxation from the

Sultan in 1812, in a move ostensibly aimed at curbing corruption and lessening their burden on the peasants. The Dutch Resident in Yogyakarta also encouraged court officials to rent out the land still under their control to European and Chinese plantation entrepreneurs. It became standard practice for the officials to receive advance payment of rentals from those entrepreneurs.

These actions bore heavily on the peasants. They had to supply labour to work the land rented to foreigners, and the fact that an increasingly large amount of land was being put under plantation crops meant that they had less and less land on which to plant food crops for themselves, rice in particular. The population of Java had increased rapidly in the half-century or so of peace which had followed the Treaty of Giyanti; it was now facing an increasingly critical problem of food supply, and in 1821 there was a particularly poor rice harvest. While it was certainly not due entirely to the appropriation of rice fields for the cultivation of plantation crops, this was one of the factors involved, and overall the peasants felt they had good cause to be aggrieved at the practice of renting land.

The system was abolished in 1823, not because of its impact on the peasants but because of a change in colonial policy. The new Dutch Governor-General, van der Capellen, believed that the state, not private entrepreneurs, should play the leading role in the exploitation of Java's abundant land and labour. Land rented by private entrepreneurs therefore had to be returned to its owners, any pre-paid rentals refunded and compensation made for any improvements the renters had made to the land, such as irrigation systems supporting sugar cultivation. The problem with this was that in many cases the bupati had already spent the money they had received for rentals, and were thus placed in severe financial difficulties. For this they blamed both the Dutch, for obvious reasons, and also the rulers of Yogyakarta, arguing that the latter had aided and abetted the Dutch.

We thus have a situation in the early 1820s where a solid wedge had been driven between the bulk of the Javanese peasantry and many of the regional and religious officials on the one hand, and the court rulers and the Dutch on the other. This divide was to result in the so-called Java War of 1825–1830, the last significant war to be fought in Java between local forces and the Dutch until the late 1940s. It cost over 200 000 lives, the overwhelming majority of them Javanese, although 8000 Dutch soldiers were killed as well. While the monetary cost of fighting the war almost bankrupted the victorious Dutch, it was a war that they, and their local allies, clearly won.

The central figure in the forces opposing the Dutch was Prince Diponegoro, a son of Hamengkubuwono III and thus a direct descendent of Sultan Agung. He had been brought up away from the court, in the care of his great-grandmother, and his education had followed both Javanese aristocratic and Islamic traditions, a combination unusual in court nobility at this time.

Being of royal blood, Diponegoro wielded considerable influence among peasants and aristocrats alike, an influence consolidated by the fact that he was clearly not a participant in the government of Yogyakarta, despite being from the royal family. Diponegoro was also seen as a focus for Islamic dissatisfaction with the conduct of the court and the extent to which it was coming increasingly under the influence of the Christian Dutch.

But there was one other element in this equation, a factor that substantially strengthened Diponegoro's position as the focus of opposition to the court elite, particularly in the eyes of the peasants: Yogyakarta in the early 1820s was experiencing a string of natural disasters. The rice harvests had been poor. In 1821 a cholera epidemic had struck; in 1822 the volcano Mt Merapi, situated immediately to the north of Yogyakarta, had erupted. These disasters combined to convince many that the Sultan was losing his right to rule, and that there would soon emerge a new sultan. Just as Trunajaya had done nearly two centuries earlier, Diponegoro encouraged the view that he was the Just Prince, come to take over the throne and thus free his people from oppression and return the kingdom to a state of harmony and tranquillity.

If Diponegoro was increasingly seen as an ally by those Javanese opposed to the rulers of Yogyakarta, conversely he was increasingly seen as an enemy by both those rulers and the Dutch. By the mid-1820s the latter were actively seeking ways of bringing him to heel. A decision to drive a road through his ricefields in Tegalrejo finally provoked him into outright opposition to the court and its Dutch allies. A combined Dutch–Javanese force was despatched to Tegalrejo in 1825 to capture him, sparking off the war.

Initially Diponegoro's forces were quite successful, scoring victories against the Dutch and the Sultan's forces as far east as Madiun, and along the north coast. Surabaya was threatened. The city of Yogyakarta was itself besieged and supplies of food cut off. By about 1828, though, a stalemate had been reached. The Dutch were finding the cost of the war so high that they started seriously to consider cutting their losses and abandoning Yogyakarta altogether. But one last effort was to be made to capture Diponegoro—by whatever means.

Diponegoro was invited to meet with the Dutch commanders in the town of Magelang, to the north of Yogyakarta, ostensibly to discuss a truce. Instead, he was captured and on 28 March 1830 sent into exile in Sulawesi.[1] Such was the reliance of the anti-Dutch forces on Diponegoro's leadership that with his capture the resistance to the Dutch largely dissipated. Some skirmishing continued for a few years, but the war was effectively over.

The Diponegoro (Java) War marks a watershed in Javanese and Indonesian history more important than the collapse of the VOC in 1799. The capture of Diponegoro marks the end not just of an era in Javanese history, but also of an age, an age in which the Javanese states were independent political entities, able to determine both their internal and their external political structures and relationships. It was the last of the priyayi-led wars or rebellions; after Diponegoro's defeat, the priyayi were increasingly absorbed into the colonial state.

The Java War was not the only Indonesian war in which the Dutch were engaged in the 1820s, however—they were also fighting a protracted war in the Minangkabau highlands of west Sumatera.

For centuries Minangkabau had been an important agricultural and commercial centre, and a stronghold of Islam. Secular political authority in Minangkabau lay in the hands of an aristocratic elite, comparable in many ways to the Javanese priyayi. Like their Javanese counterparts, the Minangkabau elites were hereditary, and ruled their regions largely as independent fiefdoms, acknowledging only the loose hegemony of the ruler of the state. Late in the eighteenth century, though, and into the nineteenth, Minangkabau society was undergoing a major shake-up that was to upset the balance between its various political elements.

The aristocratic rulers had traditionally based their economic well-being on their control of the trade in gold. By the middle of the eighteenth century the gold mines were beginning to peter out, and thus the economic strength—and the political strength—of the rulers began to decline.

At the same time as the gold trade was drying up a new commodity was beginning to impact on Minangkabau society: coffee. High-quality coffee had for some time been a major product of the highlands—but it was a crop grown by ordinary peasant farmers, not controlled by the aristocratic elite. The international demand for Minangkabau coffee rose at the end of the eighteenth century, especially following the appearance at Padang of the first American traders. The result was to pour extra resources into the hands of the coffee farmers, people who had not previously enjoyed much wealth, and certainly very little political power.

This inflow of money into rural Minangkabau was one of the major factors behind the strengthening of Islam at this time. Many rural boarding schools or *pesantren*—in Minangkabau, as in many other parts of the archipelago, a key factor in spreading the Islamic faith—took to growing coffee to boost their incomes. The prosperity the coffee boom brought to rural Minangkabau society also meant that more people were able to afford to make the pilgrimage to Mecca than ever before. This was significant in itself, but was made doubly so because of the influence of the puritanical Wahhabi Islamic reformist movement, at that time sweeping through Arabia.

Some of the Minangkabau scholars who were studying in Arabia came under the influence of the Wahhabis. In 1803, according to Minangkabau folklore, three of these scholars—known as *Paderi*— returned to Minangkabau and set about organising a reformist movement. They were opposed to gambling, cockfighting, much of the matrilineal customary law, the consumption of alcohol, opium and tobacco: in general, those parts of everyday Minangkabau life which they regarded as being in conflict with the true principles of Islam.

This reformism sat rather uncomfortably with many elements of Minangkabau society. For one thing, through their attacks on matri- lineality, the Paderi were directly attacking the legitimacy of the aristocratic elite—which had a vested interest in seeing the established order of things continued. Many ordinary Minangkabau were also dis- turbed by what they saw as the excesses of the Paderi. They found it difficult to understand, for instance, why they had to imitate the lifestyle and forms of clothing used by Arabs in the desert in order to be good Muslims in Minangkabau. They could not see what the con- nection was between purifying the faith and the way in which women walked, the direction their eyes pointed, the wearing of a beard by the men and so forth.

In the first decade of the nineteenth century, this tension erupted into a civil war between forces supporting and opposing the Paderi. Initially the fighting went the way of the Paderi. In 1815, most of the Minangkabau royal family was murdered, giving the Paderi a major victory. Their forces then pushed north into the Batak highlands, trying to convert their inhabitants to Islam.

We need now to move back in time a bit, and look at how the British and then the Dutch reacted to these developments.

Colonial reactions

The British, who had taken Padang from the Dutch in 1795, initially took little interest in the conflict in the Minangkabau highlands. But when Raffles took up his appointment as Governor of the British-controlled territories in Sumatera in 1816, he tried to extend the region under Padang's control, sending an expedition into the highlands to establish a series of British outposts. Raffles was prepared to deal with the aristocratic elite and to give them some kind of support in their conflict with the Paderi in return for trade concessions, but he was defeated by the passage of time; in 1819 the British returned Padang to the Dutch, and thus ended his Minangkabau exploits.

After the return of Padang to the Netherlands, there remained (for the Dutch anyway) the irritant of the British presence in Bengkulu. For the British there were a few Dutch irritants around too: the Dutch settlements at Melaka, and in India. In 1824 Britain and the Netherlands negotiated the Treaty of London, in which a clear dividing line was drawn between the interests of the British and the Dutch in Southeast Asia, running through the Straits of Melaka. Thus Bengkulu was handed over to the Dutch, and Melaka to the British. The Dutch also undertook to recognise British sovereignty over Singapore. The treaty was strongly opposed by Raffles, who saw it as ending for all time his chances of building a British empire in the archipelago. So it was; but he was unable to persuade London to his point of view.

The treaty as a whole was of major historical significance. For the first time in recorded history, the great trade route of the Straits of Melaka was clearly divided between rival powers, one on each side of the Straits, rather than being under the hegemony of one state. This treaty is the reason why the present-day border between Malaysia and Indonesia runs where it does, down the middle of the Straits; and why that boundary is thus defined geographically rather than by following any clear ethnic or economic line of division.

Meanwhile, the restored Dutch Resident at Padang, following Raffles' line of thinking, urged Batavia to support a move into the Minangkabau. Batavia was largely unmoved by these representations, but they were seized upon by leaders of the Minangkabau aristocracy, and especially by those who had sought refuge from the Paderi in Padang. They tried to make a deal with the Dutch Resident, offering territorial and other concessions in return for support against the Paderi. Batavia consistently told the Padang Resident not to encourage such advances; but he seems just as consistently to have ignored his instructions. In February 1821 the Padang administration made an agreement with fourteen local leaders, under the terms of which Minangkabau was to be ceded to the Dutch in return for protection from the Paderi. In this way the Dutch found themselves committed to war in Minangkabau.

This war was fought in two stages. The first ran from 1821 to 1825, during which neither side made much impact on the other. In late 1825 the Paderi leader Tuanku Imam Bonjol and the Dutch military commander de Steurs signed an agreement to halt the hostilities. The Dutch were able to withdraw the bulk of their troops and redeploy them to Java to fight Diponegoro. The Paderi used the cease-fire to send emissaries north, seeking military support from the Acehnese.

Following the conclusion of the Java War, the Dutch were able once again to focus their attention on the Paderi. They reinforced their garrisons in Minangkabau using not only the troops with which they had fought Diponegoro but also, ironically, some of the troops who had fought *against* them, on the side of Diponegoro.

The Dutch were on the offensive again by 1832. And this time, despite receiving support from Aceh, the Paderi were soon in retreat. In 1837 the main centre of resistance, the town of Bonjol, was captured; Tuanku Imam Bonjol himself escaped, but shortly thereafter surrendered and was sent into exile. The Paderi War was effectively over by the end of 1838, although unrest continued in some regions until late in the 1840s.

Although Batavia may not have approved of the action that had initiated this war, and even at its conclusion may have resented its cost, it nonetheless saw that control of the Minangkabau highlands could be profitable.

Control of the Minangkabau heartland gave the Dutch considerable influence over the trading states stretching to the east and the south of Minangkabau to the Straits of Melaka, which effectively depended on their access to Minangkabau products to earn their living. With the Dutch securing a hold over those products, it was relatively easy to step in and gain control of the states as well. Having already acquired Bengkulu from the British, by the middle of the nineteenth century the Dutch had control over virtually the whole of southern Sumatera.

Both the Java and Paderi Wars cost the Dutch dearly, in personnel and in resources. And at much the same time, in Europe, the Dutch had fought a costly and ultimately unsuccessful war in 1831–1832 to prevent the establishment of the Kingdom of Belgium in the former southern provinces of the Netherlands. The financial losses resulting from all these wars had somehow to be recovered—and once again, Dutch eyes turned to the Indies as a source of the revenue needed.

The Cultivation System

For much of the nineteenth century, Dutch politicians and colonial officials were divided between those who saw state capitalism as the best means of exploiting the resources of the Indies, and those who saw private enterprise as a better and more efficient vehicle for that exploitation. The high point of state capitalism came with the introduction in 1830 of the Cultivation System—sometimes known in English, rather misleadingly, as the Culture System, following the Dutch term *Cultuurstelsel*.

The creator of the System was Johannes van den Bosch, appointed Governor-General in 1828. Van den Bosch's view of colonial administration was that since the only reason to have a colony was to make a profit out of it, every colony had to be run along the lines which produced the greatest net return. He did not believe that this could be achieved by freeing the Javanese of the obligation to surrender produce or labour to their rulers. In fact, the reverse was the case: only by requiring the Javanese to make payment of such produce and labour could the maximum profit be derived.

His Cultivation System required villages to set aside one-fifth of their rice fields for the production of a crop nominated by the government, and suitable for the European market. The main crops required were coffee, sugar and indigo; others included tea, cinnamon, tobacco, silk and cochineal. In return, the peasants would be exempt from payment of land rent. Villagers also had to provide labour to work on the government's crops. The processing of the crops was to be undertaken by European and Chinese entrepreneurs.

The Cultivation System was confined almost entirely to Java, although it was also used for coffee production in the Minangkabau highlands after the Paderi War, and in Minahasa, chiefly in the uplands of Tondano. In neither of these regions, however, was output anything like that of Java. Minahasa produced perhaps 35 000 *pikuls* (approximately 2 187 500 kg) of coffee per year for instance, compared with 191 000 pikuls (approximately 11 937 500 kg) in Minangkabau and nearly 1 million pikuls in Java.

The System was a great financial success. The Dutch national debt, incurred between 1815 and 1830, amounted to 37.5 million florins. In the first decade of operation of the Cultivation System, Java produced a net profit averaging f.9.3 million *per year*; in its second decade, the average annual surplus remitted to the Netherlands rose to f.14.1 million. These revenues not only enabled the Netherlands to pay the costs of its wars, both successful and unsuccessful; they also allowed the country to embark on a period of unprecedented prosperity and economic progress. It was the profits from agricultural production in Java that built the Netherlands' railways, canals and military fortifications.

The System was also a great success for the Dutch Crown, which in 1824 had established the Netherlands Trading Company (Nederlandsche Handel Maatschappij or NHM), which was granted monopoly rights to purchase the products of the Cultivation System, transport them to Europe, and to sell them there.

But how did the System impact on the Javanese peasants upon whom it was imposed? Different sections of the Javanese peasantry, and peasants in different parts of the island, were affected in different ways, but one common factor was that the System meant additional labour demands on virtually every male inhabitant of rural Java. In some regions—especially in the less sparsely populated parts of east and west Java—it was not uncommon for villagers to flee their homes in order to avoid this labour burden. They were able to do this well into the nineteenth century because of the substantial amount of unoccupied land still available in these parts of the island.

In other areas the peasants rebelled against the new demands being made on them. In several of the regions where sugar cane was cultivated, for instance, there was a significant increase in reports of cane mysteriously catching fire just before it was due for harvesting. There were also marches, parades and sit-down demonstrations in protest at the new impositions. For many others, however, there was little that they could do to mitigate the demands the System made on their land and their labour.

The impact on the peasants was exacerbated by the way in which the System was commonly administered. Both the Dutch colonial officials and the local officials who had responsibility for running the System were paid, in part, by way of a commission on the cash crops produced. Thus both had an incentive to push up production of such crops at the expense of food crops. Many village heads also became particularly adept at manipulating the System for their own benefit, to the disadvantage of their fellow villagers. Village heads were further estranged from their village populations by the demands of the System; increasingly, they had to rely on the coercive power of the state, and not their own political abilities, to maintain their positions.

As early as the mid-1830s, some colonial officials were reporting on the adverse effects of the System on the peasants in some areas, especially in north-central Java and the eastern part of west Java. One colonial administrator wrote, in a report dated 19 January 1835, about a visit he made to an indigo-producing region of west Java:

> On the roads as well as the plantations one does not meet people but only walking skeletons, which drag themselves with great difficulty from one place to another, often dying in the process. The Regent [bupati] of Sukapura told me that some of the labourers who work in the plantations are in such a state of exhaustion that they die almost immediately after they have eaten from the food which is delivered to them as an advance payment for the produce to be delivered later.[2]

The crisis deepened in the 1840s and 1850s. Major famines struck parts of central Java in 1843 and at the beginning of the 1850s. Many people fled their homes in search of food elsewhere, often ending up in the cities, especially in Semarang, the biggest city in central Java. The death toll caused a scandal in the Netherlands, where there were many expressions of public outrage at what was going on in the Indies. This concern was given additional vigour by the publication in 1860 of the book *Max Havelaar*, written by a former colonial official named Eduard Douwes Dekker under the pseudonym Multatuli ('I have suffered much'). The book was an indictment of both the Javanese officials—bupatis and village heads in particular—and the Dutch officials who, at best, could be said to have done nothing about the abuses of the System with which they were in daily contact, and at worst could be seen as having actively connived in those abuses.

Recent research has shown that the effects of the Cultivation System were not as unremittingly negative as these reports and assessments would suggest. Javanese peasants were not simply passive subjects of Dutch colonial policy, unable to do anything substantial to direct their own fates. Rather, many were initiative-takers, able to respond imaginatively to the challenges the System threw at them. The extra cash which the System injected into the countryside, together with the improvements in local infrastructure, at least in some areas stimulated the peasants into new commercial entrepreneurial activities. According to this line of argument—and it is a powerful one—the System might have been applied harshly, and was morally indefensible, but it did materially benefit at least some Javanese.

What were the traditional rulers of Java doing at this time to look after the interests of their subjects? Basically, nothing: their minds were on other things. While the Cultivation System was at its peak, the courts of Java, deprived of any real political power, were undergoing a cultural renaissance of sorts. The middle and later decades of the century saw a flourishing of cultural activities centred on these courts. The Dutch were happy to support these activities: they seemed to strengthen the 'traditional' aspects of Javanese society and to show that colonialism was not interfering in those aspects. And—more pragmatically—while the leaders of the courts were concerned with the increasingly intricate details of dance and theatre, they were not engaged in political activities that could have been directed against the Dutch.

We know considerably less about the impact of compulsory coffee cultivation on the peoples of Minangkabau and Minahasa, but there is no reason to believe it was substantially different from the Javanese experience.

Just as the initiative for the imposition of the System came from the Netherlands, not Indonesia, so it was with its abolition. The most vocal Dutch opposition to the System came from the growing industrial and capitalist class, emerging as a result of the economic development financed by the revenues from the Cultivation System. These industrialists, the founders of the Liberal Party, came to oppose continuation of the Cultivation System for two rather different sets of reasons.

One was that it was causing very considerable suffering for the Javanese people. Of itself, it is doubtful whether this concern would have been strong enough to enable the liberals to bring about a change in colonial policy. Of greater significance was the on-going debate about the nature of colonial administration, and specifically the question of whether it should be the state or private enterprise that ran the colony. Being representatives of the emerging capitalist class, the Liberals wanted to see the elimination of state capitalism and its replacement with private enterprise.

The first evidence that the Liberals had sufficient strength in the Dutch parliament to direct colonial policy came in 1854 with the passage of a law on colonial government (*Regeerings Reglement*).

The dismantling of the System itself began in 1862 with the freeing-up of the cultivation of pepper. This was followed by cloves and nutmeg in 1864 and tea and indigo in 1865. The last crop to be freed-up was coffee: it remained subject to compulsory cultivation right through to 1917. By 1867 the peasants had been substantially freed of their obligation to provide labour services and land to their bupatis and village heads. This, too, was consistent with Liberal opposition to forced labour; and it meant that there was now more free labour available in Java for hiring to work on estates managed by Europeans. The ending of the Cultivation System is usually dated to 1870, the year in which a law was passed reforming the colonial sugar industry. With the passing of the Sugar Law, it was just a matter of time before the remainder of the System was brought down.

Let's turn now to look at the last 30 or so years of the nineteenth century, and at the form of colonial administration in place in Indonesia during that time.

Liberal Era

The period 1870–1900, generally referred to as the Liberal Era, saw a substantial flow of Dutch private capital into Indonesia, primarily for investment in agriculture. The key legal provision shaping the pattern of this investment was the Agrarian Law of 1870. The Law had two essential features. First, it provided that the only people who could own land in Indonesia were Indonesians: that is to say, people belonging to one of the ethnic groups indigenous to the archipelago. Europeans and Chinese were thus prevented from becoming or remaining landowners. Second, the Law made provision for the leasing or renting of land by foreigners; it was on the basis of these leases that the major late nineteenth-century privately managed plantations were established.

Until the middle of the 1880s the bulk of this investment was made by private planters funded by the major financial institutions in the Netherlands, but in 1883–85 the colonial economy of Java went into severe depression, hitting the sugar industry in particular. The depression showed up the essential weakness of individual private capitalists: they did not have the financial strength to weather this kind of crisis. What happened then was perhaps thoroughly predictable— the banks and finance companies took over the businesses of the ailing private entrepreneurs. Thus what we see emerging in the last fifteen or so years of the century as the major players in the colonial economy are large agribusiness conglomerates, usually clustered around Dutch-based banks or finance houses.

The expansion of western economic influence into Java during the Liberal period was not limited to the cultivation of commercial crops in large privately owned plantations; it also involved the export to Java of manufactured goods produced by Dutch industry. For the first time in its history as a subject of Dutch colonialism, Java was emerging as an important market for Dutch products, not just a source of raw materials.

Europeans were not the only ones in a position to take advantage of the improved climate for private entrepreneurs in the Indies: the Chinese community resident in Java also benefited. The vast bulk of the Chinese were urban dwellers, concentrated in the cities and towns of the north coast of the island: the ports on the inter-island trading route. This was in part at least because there were strict controls on their movement to other places in Java. They were, for instance, banned from entering the rural parts of west Java until 1872. A few did penetrate into the inland areas of central Java and take up residence there, as tax agents, commercial agriculturalists or traders, but in absolute terms their numbers were small.

By late in the century, ethnic Chinese capital—much of it released by the ending of government tax agencies in which much of it had been invested—was pushing hard into areas of manufacturing which had thus far remained locally owned, driving out indigenous entrepreneurs. It is no coincidence that when the nationalist movement began early in the twentieth century, one of its first major bases was among Javanese businesspeople forced out of the batik industry by competition from ethnic Chinese.

Ethnic Chinese also continued their involvement in less savoury elements of the economy, many reaping huge profits from the government-controlled opium dens, pawnshops and gambling houses, thus contributing to the further impoverishment of the Javanese. An indication of this is that although purchases of rice and cotton goods continued to fall during the closing years of the century, revenue from opium, gambling and pawnshops soared.

The Liberal Era was to see a decline in living standards among the Javanese peasantry, especially after the depression of the mid-1880s and the emergence of the major agribusiness enterprises controlled by banks and finance companies. This decline in living standards can be measured in a number of ways. We can, for instance, look at what people were eating. For the vast bulk of the Javanese, rice was the preferred staple food, and in the latter part of the nineteenth century rice consumption was falling. In 1885, for instance, the average Javanese consumed about 119 kg of rice; by 1900 this had fallen to 103 kg. In counterpoint to this decline, the consumption of less-favoured foods such as maize and cassava increased.

Wages and working conditions also declined. A government enquiry into Javanese welfare, held at the beginning of the twentieth century, noted that after 1885 there had been what it rather coyly referred to as 'a more or less strong reduction of wages'. But it was not just that wages for the Javanese working on European-managed estates fell. The displacement of local products such as animal manure and hand-woven baskets by imported fertilisers and imported hessian bags meant that local producers lost important markets for their goods as well.

But we cannot blame Liberal policy alone for this decline in living standards. There was clearly at least one other force at work, which was to become of increasing importance during the twentieth century. This was the rate at which the Javanese population was growing. Again, hard data are not easy to come by, but it seems clear that the population was growing at a much faster rate than was food production, although there was some falling off of the rate of population growth in the last years of the century.

The extent to which the welfare of the Javanese was declining in the late nineteenth century was such as to cause concern in the Netherlands and, eventually, some significant changes in colonial policy. We take up this matter in the following chapter, looking at the adoption of the so-called Ethical Policy in 1901.

East coast of Sumatera

Outside Java, the pattern of Dutch interaction with local states and societies in the late nineteenth century was rather different. I want to look first at the Dutch forward movement in the east coast region of

Sumatera, roughly the middle third of the eastern coastline. This movement differed substantially from Dutch contact virtually anywhere else in Indonesia in that it did not involve any significant conflict with local peoples, and was led primarily by private individuals rather than government officials.

The key to developments here was tobacco.

Tobacco was introduced into the archipelago by the Portuguese in the sixteenth and seventeenth centuries; it was grown mostly in Java, especially in the central and eastern parts of the island, but during the VOC period it was never a major export commodity. In the early nineteenth century, Raffles had tried to promote its cultivation; van den Bosch included it within the Cultivation System, but as it was not particularly successful, it was one of the first crops withdrawn from the System, in 1866. Freed up from government control, tobacco cultivation became rather more profitable, particularly in the Besuki region of east Java.

By the 1860s in Sumatera, tobacco was being produced in small quantities by local farmers in the east coast region controlled by the Sultan of Deli. Jacobus Nienhuis, the son of an Amsterdam tobacco broker visiting the Deli region, found the quality of the tobacco being produced here first rate. He secured a lease on land along the Deli River, put in a small crop of his own and, after harvesting and processing, sent it to Amsterdam. Here it found a ready market, especially as the outer wrapper for cigars.

To take tobacco cultivation further, though, Nienhuis needed three elements, the classical inputs to any industrial enterprise: land, labour and capital.

The capital was not too difficult to organise. A number of Dutch finance houses expressed an interest, but eventually Nienhuis formed a joint venture with the NHM, the Crown company, setting up the company Deli Maatschappij in 1869.

Land presented a slightly greater problem. The pioneer planters soon discovered that to produce high-quality tobacco required soil conditions which could only be sustained if the land was used to plant tobacco for only one year in a cycle of eight years, or even longer if the soils were not very good. Thus a plantation required at least eight times as much land as could be planted to tobacco in any particular year.

Luckily for the planters, Sumatera's east coast was largely unpopulated at this time. The Malay Sultans here found it very profitable to lease out this land, hitherto unused—or at least not used by them or by any people paying them tribute—to the planters.

This left the planters with the problem of acquiring labour. The fact that the land was largely uninhabited, while it was advantageous in terms of securing large leaseholds, made for difficulties in recruiting a labour force large enough for successful cultivation of tobacco and the other crops which followed, such as rubber, tea and sisal.

At first the Deli planters recruited Chinese workers from Pinang and Singapore, and then directly from south China itself, and by 1870, of about 4000 labourers employed in the tobacco estates, all but 150 were Chinese. This method was soon found to be problematic, however. The British colonial authorities in Singapore and Pinang insisted that any recruiting which had to be undertaken via their Protectorate for the Chinese, which had to assure itself that working conditions, wages and so forth were adequate. The planters naturally did not welcome this 'interference'. Recruitment direct from China avoided this problem, although it meant dealing with the representatives of the Chinese Emperor—not necessarily a much more desirable relationship. Costs were also high.

As a result, by the 1890s Chinese labourers were being replaced with men brought in from Java. By 1915, most of the estate labourers were Javanese.

To regulate the employment of the labourers, in 1880 the colonial government enacted the Coolie Ordinance. Although framed in a way that seemed to protect the interests of both parties, in fact the Ordinance worked very much in the favour of the employers. The most infamous part of the Ordinance was the so-called Penal Sanction, which provided that if a labourer left his place of work without permission he committed a criminal offence. The employer could report the missing labourer to the local colonial authorities, who would then use their police force to find the absconder. Once caught, he could be subject to imprisonment or flogging as punishment, before being returned to his employer.

Conditions prevailing in the labourers' compounds on the estates also left much to be desired. Employers provided—or perhaps more precisely 'permitted'—gambling, opium and prostitution, the results of which often meant that at the end of his initial period of engagement a labourer was in debt either to a money-lender or, indirectly, his employer, and thus could not avoid signing on for a further term of employment.

By late in the century, the conditions under which the coolies worked on the plantations were coming under increasingly critical review in the Netherlands. The Minister for the Colonies (who, as many critics pointed out, had made his fortune as a planter in Sumatera), initially dismissed the criticism, but in 1902 the publication of a book called *Millioenen uit Deli* ('Millions from Deli') had much the same effect on Dutch public opinion that *Max Havelaar* had had half a century earlier. The pressure to withdraw the Penal Sanction was becoming stronger, but although moves to eliminate it began in 1911, it was not withdrawn until 1936.

The tobacco industry prospered during the 1880s, with the opening up of more and more plantations in the Deli, Langkat and Serdang regions. Early in the 1890s, however, the industry faced a major crisis. World tobacco prices in 1891 were half what they had been a year earlier. In part this was because of massive overproduction on the part of the industry, in part because the United States had imposed high import duties on foreign-grown tobacco, with the result that by 1891 there were no American buyers in the world market.

Between 1890 and 1894 no fewer than 25 tobacco estate-owning companies in Sumatera collapsed; tobacco production, which had reached a record of 236 323 bales in 1890, fell to 144 689 bales in 1892. The crisis shook out of the industry many of the speculators who had sought to cash in on the initial boom. They were replaced by more pragmatic businesspeople, concerned to put the industry on a more financially and scientifically stable footing.

The danger of an economy dependent on a single crop had become obvious, thus efforts were made to find new commercial crops to supplement tobacco. Coffee was tried in the Serdang region south of Deli, but competition from Brazilian coffee meant that it was not very profitable, so cultivation ceased altogether within a few years.

Rubber, however, proved much more profitable. Serdang became the centre for rubber cultivation, in the same way that Deli was the centre for tobacco. In the early years of the twentieth century rubber cultivation grew rapidly; it became the engine of growth of east Sumatera, just as Deli tobacco had been a few decades earlier.

About 35 years after Nienhuis established the first tobacco plantation in Deli, the landscape of east Sumatera had been changed dramatically, transformed into one of large estates stretching for 200 kilometres along the coast. This was commercial agriculture on an industrial scale.

The other economic development in this region, which was to have enormous significance for Indonesia, was the production of oil.

The first commercial oil wells in Sumatera, located on the east coast in the region of Langkat, were owned by individual Dutch entrepreneurs. In 1890 a group of Dutch bankers backed by the Crown floated the Royal Dutch Company, which took over most of the individual concessions. By the late 1890s, however, Royal Dutch was in financial difficulties, stemming chiefly from the competition it was experiencing from its American rival Standard Oil (Esso). But a series of shrewd refinancing deals with European-based financiers and the expansion of the company's area of operations to Kalimantan brought Royal Dutch back to profitability by about 1905. Its major Indonesian rival, more powerful in Kalimantan than in Sumatera, was the

London-based Shell Transport and Trading Company. In 1907 the two companies merged to form Royal Dutch Shell, which thus became the predominant oil production company in the Indies, and one of the largest in the world—which it still is.

Let's turn now to Aceh, the northernmost region of Sumatera.

Aceh

At the end of the eighteenth century Aceh was a wealthy and independent state, and the region's most important pepper exporter. In the first decade of the nineteenth century, annual pepper exports from Aceh probably amounted to around 2500 tons out of a total Southeast Asian figure of 9000 tons. The later collapse of the VOC created an opening in the international pepper trade which was filled by foreign traders, notably the Americans and the Chinese.

Aceh's most important trading connections were across the Straits of Melaka, and particularly to the British trading station of Pinang, whose merchants and traders thus had a vested interest in Acehnese affairs; in particular, they had an interest in seeing that there was no unnecessary interference with the pepper trade there from either the Dutch or local rulers.

Aceh's wealth brought with it domestic political problems. By the early 1800s the political power of the Sultanate of Aceh had declined considerably from its heyday a century earlier. It still claimed sovereignty over the north Sumateran ports, whose trade was mainly in pepper, manifested in the persistent demand by the Sultan that all trade in pepper pass through his capital. But the Sultan was rarely able to enforce this demand and most of the time, regional chiefs, or *ulee-balang*, based in the north coast ports conducted their own trade in pepper independently of the Sultan. The more pepper they were able to export, the greater their revenues, and thus the greater their independence from the capital. Control of the trade in pepper was very much a political matter, shaping the relations between the centre of the state and its regions.

By the second decade of the century, the conflict between the Sultan and the uleebalang had heightened to the point where the Sultan was considering asking the Dutch to intervene on his side. In an attempt to forestall such a move, Raffles travelled to Aceh and concluded an agreement with the Sultan committing the British to recognising the Sultan as the legitimate ruler of Aceh; in return for this the British were to be permitted to station a consular agent in Aceh and to have free access to all Acehnese ports. Other European and American powers were to be denied the right to establish permanent bases in Aceh, and Aceh agreed not to negotiate any treaties with these powers without British agreement.

However, England did not confirm the agreement. More importantly, in the 1824 Treaty of London the British government effectively gave away the political concessions Raffles had secured. We have already noted that this treaty involved the swapping of Bengkulu in south Sumatera for Melaka, and Dutch recognition of the British position in Singapore. It also provided that the British renounce all previous political connections with Aceh; that the Dutch would respect the independence of Aceh; and that the British would have the freedom to trade anywhere they wished in Sumatera, free from any Dutch interference or discrimination.

From the point of view of the British traders, this was a far better deal than the one Raffles had negotiated: there was no burden of financial or military support for the Sultan, and at the same time they retained their right to trade freely with Aceh.

For Aceh, the treaty was also attractive, as it ensured that neither the British nor the Dutch challenged its independence. And indeed, for the next two decades, there were no direct external threats to Aceh's independence. This, of course, did not mean that the internal threats to its existence were any the less pressing. Certainly the conflict between the Sultan and the regional rulers did not abate.

By about the middle of the century the external situation was beginning to change, however, and Aceh's independence was coming under much more serious challenge.

Following the Dutch victory in the Paderi War, Dutch influence by the 1860s extended right up to the southern edges of Aceh, and threatened to envelop a number of states which the Sultan of Aceh claimed as his vassals. Not surprisingly perhaps, the Sultan began to cast around for allies. After advances to France and Turkey were rebuffed, he approached Britain. The British ought to have been a better bet: the Treaty of London, after all, had committed Britain to supporting Aceh's independence and preserving the right of British merchants to trade freely with it—but at the very time the Acehnese wanted some support, Britain was on the point of changing its policy.

The reasons for this change can be found in the establishment of what became British Liberal policy in the Indies in the 1850s and 1860s. One reason behind the British signing of the Treaty of London had been preservation of access to Acehnese ports. But as trade in the Indies was being freed-up following the general liberalisation of colonial policy, Acehnese independence became less crucial to the British: they could get access to Acehnese trade even if Aceh was under Dutch control.

Moreover, it was evident that the Dutch were not the only ones with their eyes on Aceh: the French and the Americans both had designs on the place. London's view was that it was better that the Dutch control Aceh than either of these more formidable colonial powers.

Thus in 1871 the British and the Dutch concluded the Sumatera Treaty, which in effect revoked the provision in the Treaty of London by which the British and Dutch guaranteed the independence of Aceh. The way was now open for the Dutch to intervene in Aceh without fear of any formal British reaction. Since the Sumatera Treaty also provided that British traders would be treated equally with Dutch traders in any territory in Sumatera brought under Dutch control, there would be no protest from British commercial interests either.

The Aceh War

The Sultan of Aceh now began an even more frantic search for allies. He first approached the Italian Consul in Singapore, then the American Consul. The Italians gave the Sultan short shrift, but the Americans clearly had some sympathy for his position. However, the Dutch, on learning of this development, and using the argument that the Americans were about to intervene in Aceh, launched what a century later would be called a pre-emptive strike. In April 1873 they landed a force of 3000 men at the Acehnese capital and proceeded to assault the Sultan's palace.

This force easily captured the palace, and forced the Sultan to flee. But the Acehnese just as easily regrouped and counterattacked ten days later, compelling the Dutch to withdraw. This did not mean that the Acehnese had won; merely that they had secured an extra couple of months in which to prepare for a second assault, but their subsequent pleas for support from Turkey, Britain, France and the United States fell on deaf ears. At the end of 1873, the Dutch sent in a much stronger expeditionary force, at the same time blockading the Acehnese coast to prevent the movement of goods in and out.

The Aceh War thus started in earnest; it was to last 30 years, and be by far the most costly in Dutch colonial history. At its peak the Dutch force in Aceh numbered over 10 500 men—about one-third of the total strength of the Royal Netherlands Indies Army, the Koninklijk Nederlands Indische Leger (KNIL). The Dutch lost around 15 000 men dead and 10 000 wounded. Acehnese casualties are much harder to estimate, but there were probably about 25 000 killed.

The 1873 Dutch expeditionary force found it relatively easy going at first, capturing the capital, announcing that the Sultanate was abolished and that Aceh had been annexed—but this initial success was misleading. Many of the coastal uleebalang were quite willing to submit to the Dutch, since in return the Dutch agreed to lift the naval blockade of their ports and allow the resumption of trade, but when the Dutch tried to move into the interior, where the bulk of the population lived, and establish an apparatus of civil government, they struck trouble. They found that it was virtually impossible to conquer and hold the countryside, and that civil government officials—almost entirely Dutch—were easy targets for guerilla attack.

The Acehnese resistance was led now not by the Sultan or the uleebalang, but by the religious elite, the *ulama*. The war took on a decidedly religious aspect, Islam being represented as the defender of the Acehnese against the attacks of the infidel Dutch.

Dutch casualties began to mount. By the mid-1880s, the cost of the war was reaching the level where it was close to politically unbearable in the Netherlands. In 1885, the Dutch commander in Aceh introduced a new tactic, the so-called Concentration System, which involved the building of blockhouses and watchtowers around the capital, linked by a railway and telegraph lines.

This policy did little to save Dutch lives, for although fewer men might have been lost to enemy action, disease within the defended area was rife, leading to many deaths. Dutch morale was low, their troops being cooped up behind wire and fortifications and prevented from retaliating against the Acehnese, who kept making pin-prick attacks on the forts and sabotaging the railway.

It was not until the 1890s that the Dutch finally hit on a successful strategy against their opponents. This strategy had two elements, one military and the other civil. The military element was the formation in 1890 of lightly armed flying columns of Indonesian troops commanded by Dutch officers, armed and trained for jungle warfare. The flying columns were soon recording important victories against the Acehnese forces.

The civil element in the counter-guerilla operations was suggested by Snouck Hurgronje, the very influential colonial government adviser on Islam. Snouck took the view that the religious leaders, the ulama, could never be persuaded voluntarily to cease fighting the Dutch, and thus that they would have to be crushed completely by the army. Then a new locus of regional power would have to be found to take their place. He suggested that the uleebalang be used in this capacity. The uleebalang, he suggested bluntly, could be bought off with promises of important positions in the Dutch administration. He was right, and in this way the Dutch were able to drive a deep wedge into Acehnese society between the religious and secular elites.

There followed a bloody military campaign that, by about 1903, brought most of Aceh under the control of the Dutch and their uleebalang clients. The Aceh War is generally reckoned to have ended in that year, though fighting was to continue in some areas for another decade.

The other islands

In most other parts of the archipelago, by the end of the nineteenth century Dutch force of arms had also prevailed. In Bali, although the north part of the island had been seized by the Dutch in the middle of the century, the southern part was still free at the turn of the twentieth. As part of the drive to 'tidy up' the colonial map and incorporate into the colonial state all the remaining corners of the archipelago, the Dutch then launched a drive, first political and then military, against the independent rulers of south Bali.

There was no doubt which side would emerge the winner in this conflict, at least in the political sense. But the events which brought the conflict to an end were deeply shocking to the Dutch. In early September 1906, Dutch troops landed at Sanur in the Kingdom of Badung, today a major beach resort popular with international tourists. The troops marched overland to Den Pasar, the capital of Badung, and besieged it. On 20 September the King of Badung, members of his family, court and followers marched out of the city and into the guns of the Dutch. When they refused calls to halt, the Dutch troops opened fire on them at point blank range; about 1000 Balinese died. They had quite deliberately committed mass suicide, an action known in Balinese as *puputan*. Two years later, the same scene was played out in the last remaining independent Balinese kingdom, Klungkung: here 300 people died.

In other parts of the archipelago, Dutch colonial forces fought a series of wars—albeit considerably smaller than the Java, Paderi and Aceh Wars—to bring the rest of the region under their control: against Palembang (1825), Banjarmasin (1860), Lombok (1894 and 1907) and Bone (1905). They even fought the Chinese for control of goldmines in west Kalimantan in 1884. Boundaries of colonial possessions were agreed with the British in Malaya (1824), New Guinea (1828), Serawak (1859) and Sabah (1891), and with the Portuguese in Timor (1904).

Thus at the end of the century the outline of the colony of the Netherlands Indies, and thus subsequently Indonesia, was virtually complete.

The colonial infrastructure

But the colony of the Netherlands Indies was a patchwork of territories, rather than an integrated unit. There were a number of territories under direct control, but more extensive were the so-called 'native states', which had agreed to accept Dutch suzerainty in return for greater or lesser degrees of local autonomy.

The end of the nineteenth century saw the gradual establishment of the organs of colonial government, in fields such as education and public administration. Especially following the collapse of the Cultivation System, the colonial government fell back into activities that were more traditionally those of government: public administration and the provision of public works or infrastructure. In this latter area we see substantial activity in the last part of the century, particularly in Java. Thus the government was involved in building railways, expanding ports, improving communications links, supplying gas and electricity and so forth.

Educational opportunities were also improved. The colonial government made the first budgetary allocation for state-run schools in 1848. The main function of these schools was to prepare their pupils, drawn mostly from the aristocracy, for positions in the public service. A Department of Education, Religion and Industry was established in 1867 with responsibility for overseeing the Indonesian educational system.

The last two decades of the century saw a considerable expansion of primary education. In 1882 there were 300 primary schools for Indonesians in Java and 400 in the Outer Islands, with a total enrolment of around 40 000 students, of whom just 44 were girls. By 1897 the number of schools had nearly doubled, and the number of pupils more than doubled. At the turn of the century, there were about 150 000 Indonesian children in primary schools of one kind or another—but the biggest expansion of schooling had been brought about not by government effort but private, especially by the Christian missions that increased their teaching presence in the Indies dramatically after about 1890.

6
TIMES OF CHANGE
1900–1945

Few Indonesians looking at the situation in the Indies at the beginning of the twentieth century—and even fewer Dutch people—could have imagined the extent of political and social change that would take place in the ensuing four and a half decades. In 1900 the colony of the Netherlands Indies extended from the western tip of Sumatera into the western half of the island of New Guinea. The political will of local states and leaders seemed exhausted. By 1945 the scene had changed beyond recognition. On 17 August in that year, the nationalist leaders Sukarno and Mohammad Hatta proclaimed Indonesian independence. A provisional Constitution had been drawn up, a government and parliament established and an army formed. Young people were playing prominent roles in national-level politics. A sense of being Indonesian was gaining strength around the country. The position of Indonesian as the national language, the language of politics, government administration, education and the news media was firmly established. Dutch colonialism, while not yet defeated, was clearly on the retreat. The question was not whether the Dutch colonial presence in the Indies would be eliminated, but rather when and how.

It would be easy to conclude that the Indonesian nationalist movement, emerging in the first decade of the century and a prominent part of the political and social landscape by the 1920s, had been remarkably successful. In the space of less than half a century, it had apparently not only defeated Dutch colonialism, but also succeeded in overcoming historical ethnic and religious differences between Indonesians. And these are the terms in which many Indonesians today view that movement.

The nationalist movement did accomplish much. But changes to the international political, economic and security environments also had a major impact on the direction of Indonesian history. Moreover, Indonesian society in 1945 still had many deep divisions within it, along religious and ideological lines, and to some extent ethnic ones as well.

Indonesian history in the first half of the twentieth century is a complex mix of the local and the imported, of assertive youth and more conservative parents, of religious unity and division, of a society united in pragmatism but divided on principle. Above all else, this history is one of a society in the process of great upheaval.

I want to look now at a number of ways in which these changes were taking place.

The start of the twentieth century was marked by a significant shift in Dutch colonial policy. As noted in the previous chapter, by the last years of the nineteenth century, the conditions under which many Indonesians were living were beginning to attract critical attention in the Netherlands. Some of those expressing such criticisms undoubtedly had genuine humanitarian concerns. But others had more selfish motives: Dutch manufacturers, for instance, wanting to sell their goods in the Indies, were obviously concerned at a fall in the welfare of the population since this would reduce their profit.

In 1901 the Liberal Party was swept from office in the Netherlands, replaced by a coalition of rightist and religious parties that proclaimed themselves determined to return to Christian principles of government. The Queen's speech from the throne that year spoke of the Netherlands' 'ethical obligation and moral responsibility' to the peoples of the Indies, and heralded the introduction of the so-called Ethical Policy. The ostensible aim of the policy was to raise the welfare of the Indonesian population; in addition Indonesians were to be brought into closer contact with the ethically and morally superior Dutch civilisation, in the expectation that this would ensure their loyalty to the colonial regime. One firm supporter of this policy proclaimed: 'How glorious is the aim that we pursue! It is: the formation out there in the Far East of a social entity which is indebted to the Netherlands for its prosperity and higher Culture, and thankfully recognizes this fact'.

Under the auspices of the Policy, a variety of new programs was introduced. Services to agriculture were extended through the improvement of irrigation systems, and the setting up of agricultural advisory services, scientific research programs and so forth. Education was made more widely available, especially at the primary level, though several tertiary institutions were also opened. In an effort to reduce population pressure in Java—already perceived to be a problem—a program of moving Javanese (and later Balinese) peasants to Sumatera was begun. Reforms were introduced in the public administration system, including the introduction of advisory councils at the regency, residency and national levels.

The Policy petered out in the depression of the early 1930s without necessarily having achieved much in terms of its ostensible objectives. However, as will be noted shortly, the policy changes it brought in had a substantial impact on Indonesian society.

A second important set of changes was taking place in what might at first seem a very straightforward issue not readily amenable to change: the language people spoke.

On 28 October 1928, the Second All Indonesia Youth Congress, meeting in Jakarta, adopted what has become known as the Youth Pledge. This Pledge had three elements, one of which read: 'We, the sons and daughters of Indonesia, declare that we recognise, as the language of unity, the Indonesian language'.[1]

The language that the Congress called 'Indonesian' was a modernised form of a much older language, Malay, originating from the Riau area of Sumatera and the southern part of the Malay Peninsula. It was the first language of only a small proportion of the inhabitants of the Indies. However, Malay was widely spoken throughout the archipelago, being the language of inter-ethnic trade and of Islam. It was also largely a non-hierarchical language, and thus one that appealed to the spirit of modernity and democracy which inspired many of those who attended the Youth Congress.

By the beginning of the century there were 33 Indonesia/Malay language newspapers being published in the Indies, mostly in Java. By the 1920s a modern Indonesian literature was beginning to appear. The first modern Indonesian novel, published by the Dutch government publishing house Balai Pustaka, appeared in 1922: called *Sitti Nurbaya*, it was written by Minangkabau author Marah Rusli. Another of the early novels, *Salah Asuhan*, was written by Abdul Muis, a leading member of the Sarekat Islam political party.

A consistent theme of these early books is that of the predicaments faced by young people caught between the old world of their parents and the new world just emerging around them, which they are helping to shape. At home, these young people are expected to live according to the traditional patterns of life; in particular, a hierarchy based on traditional status, on birth, on age. But outside the home, and particularly at school, they face a very different world. It is a world where they are brought into contact with a much wider range of people: not just Indonesians from other ethnic groups, but also Dutch, Eurasians and Chinese. It is a world where emphasis is placed on the individual rather than on the family or the community, where an individual can aspire to being economically independent, personally responsible for his or her actions, and unhampered by the claims of the extended family. Needless to say, these tensions often led to disappointment and rejection, and occasionally to death. The Ethical Policy also saw a substantial expansion in educational facilities.

At the end of the nineteenth century there were about 150 000 Indonesian children in primary schools of one kind or another. By 1907 this figure had risen to about 265 000 and by 1930 to over 1.5 million. Relative to the population, however, these numbers remained extremely low. In 1930–31, of the Indonesian primary school-age population, only 8 per cent were enrolled in school. By and large these schools did little more than prepare their students to be clerks, minor government officials and the like. The fact that the vast majority of schools used Malay or a local language, not Dutch, as the medium of instruction further limited the educational and career prospects of their graduates.

A very small number of Indonesian children—mostly Christians or members of the aristocracy—was permitted to attend Dutch-language primary schools. One person to receive this opportunity was Kartini, the daughter of the bupati of Jepara, on the north-central coast of Java. In early adulthood she entered into a wide-ranging correspondence with friends, both Indonesian and Dutch, in Indonesia and in the Netherlands. Kartini saw much that was to be admired in Dutch culture, but by the same token was resolutely Javanese in her orientation. A firm believer in education for women, and in women's emancipation, she was the first major female figure in modern Indonesian history. In 1905 she died in childbirth, aged just 25.

Completion of Dutch-language primary schooling opened up the possibility of entering Dutch-language secondary schools and, eventually, universities, either in the Netherlands or, from the 1920s, in Indonesia.

Needless to say, Islamic schools never taught in Dutch, or taught Dutch as a subject. Thus in terms of educational opportunity, religion was of major significance: being a Christian substantially increased your chances of getting a secondary school education and, in time, of getting access to tertiary education. The other factor which had a strong influence on education opportunities was financial status. Even if you were a Muslim, if you came from a family that was well-off you still had a chance for a reasonable education; and this meant, almost exclusively, families of the aristocracy.

The first university-level institution in the Indies, a Technical College at Bandung producing engineers and architects, was established in 1920. There followed a Law College in Jakarta in 1924, and a Medical College, also in Jakarta, in 1927. In 1930 there was a grand total of 178 Indonesians enrolled in university-level courses in the Indies: 3 millionths of 1 per cent of the population.

The 1930s also saw a significant expansion in private schools run by Indonesians and in particular schools which maintained a total independence from the Dutch, to the point of refusing any government funding or other support. These schools are generally referred to in English as 'wild' schools—wild in the sense of not being under the control of the government. In the late 1930s there were about 130 000 students in wild schools of the secular (that is, not Islamic) type— about twice the number enrolled in government-supported schools.

Of particular importance was the school system run by an organisation called Taman Siswa (literally, the 'Garden of Pupils'). The organisation, founded by Ki Hajar Dewantoro[2] in Yogyakarta in 1922, aimed in its schools to develop a sense of Indonesian nationalism while not rejecting all aspects of western culture. In 1936 Taman Siswa had over 11 200 students enrolled in 136 schools.

The other major educational organisation which had a significant impact during the 1930s was the Muhammadiyah, an Islamic reformist organisation established by Kiai Haji Ahmad Dahlan in Yogyakarta in 1912. Education was not the only thing Muhammadiyah was interested in—it also ran hospitals, orphanages and other institutions of a social welfare kind—but it was through its school system that it had its greatest impact on the Islamic community. Its educational philosophies were progressive, and certainly far removed from the rote learning which typified the approach to education to be found in many of the more conservative Islamic schools. By 1938 it had 852 branches scattered throughout Indonesia with 250 000 members, and supported 31 public libraries and 1774 schools.

A fourth major social change in the Indies can be seen in the relations between the racial groups. The barriers between these groups were hardening late in the nineteenth century; by the turn of the twentieth, Indies society was divided along racial lines to a much greater extent than it had ever been.

Formally, the population was divided into three groups: European, Indonesian and what was called 'Foreign Oriental', comprising chiefly Chinese but also smaller communities of Arabs and Indians.

The smallest of these groups was the Dutch, numbering about 94 000 in 1900, around 70 000 of whom lived on Java. The bulk of these people were short-term residents, attracted by the rapid expansion of private agribusinesses in Java and Sumatera from the 1870s onwards. This influx of 'new' Dutch residents had several important effects on European society in the Indies.

Most importantly, it led to a significant 're-Dutchifying' of that community: that is, the newcomers reinforced the sense of Dutch identity among Europeans in the colony. Unlike their predecessors, for the newer arrivals the Indies was essentially a place to make money, and then to leave. There was little sense of attachment to the place, little incentive to learn anything of local cultures, and little opportunity to know any Indonesians except as subordinates at the office, the factory, the plantation or the home. Their culture was not an Indies culture; it was a Dutch culture moved, temporarily, to the Indies.

Women played an important role in this cultural change. In the older, established Dutch resident community, Dutch women were scarce. It was common for Dutch men to take Indonesians as mistresses, and occasionally wives, which facilitated the process of cultural osmosis between the two communities. But the arrival of Dutch families including wives changed this situation. Social life for most of these people revolved around ethnically exclusive social and sporting clubs. There were few opportunities for interaction with Indonesians that were not related to employment or domestic affairs.

This Dutch culture was also increasingly an urban culture. There had been large towns in the Indies before, but it was not really until the influx of new Dutch residents in the late nineteenth century that cities as we know them today, with an urban culture and lifestyle, emerged: with hotels, restaurants, picture theatres, daily newspapers and the like. By 1905, as well as Batavia, there were eight cities with European populations in excess of 1000, six of them on Java.

The 'European' legal classification also included people of non-Dutch background whom Dutch colonial law recognised as having the same status as ethnic Dutch. Thus, for instance, by the early twentieth century all Japanese were classified in this way. There were also a few Chinese, and a very few Indonesians, who had qualified for 'European' status through their professional achievements, their education and, most importantly of all, their demonstrated commitment to the maintenance of Dutch colonial rule.

But the majority of the people in this classification were Eurasian—people of mixed Dutch and Indonesian descent. They far outnumbered the ethnic Dutch: indeed, Eurasians accounted for about 75 per cent of the entire 'European' community in Java in 1900. As in most colonial societies, these people generally found themselves fully accepted by neither of their antecedent communities: the Dutch or the Indonesian. They were, for the most part, permanently resident in the Indies, and while some held quite high positions in public administration, the majority were employed in middle-ranking clerical positions in both the public service and private enterprise, interposed between the Dutch at the top of the system and the Indonesians at the bottom, and with wages to match.

At the turn of the century, their generally higher levels of formal western education, and their better command of the Dutch language, gave Eurasians the edge over Indonesians in competition for such work, even though their wages were rather higher than those paid to Indonesians. Moving into the twentieth century, though, as more Indonesians began to acquire western education and a good command of Dutch, Eurasians found their positions coming under threat. One result was the driving of a deeper wedge between those two communities than there had been previously, something that was to rebound against the Eurasians after Indonesia became independent.

The next largest population group in the Indies was the so-called 'Foreign Oriental'. In 1905 there were approximately 317 000 people classified in this way in Java, with a further 298 000 outside Java. The majority were Chinese, about 44 000 were Arab.

The Chinese community shared many of the characteristics of the European community. Like the Europeans, the numbers of Chinese in the colony had increased significantly in the latter part of the nineteenth century. And, like the European community too, the gender composition of the Chinese community had also altered, with a great increase in the number of women coming in.

The impact of this influx of women on the Chinese community, however, seems to have been a little different from the impact of increased numbers of women on the Dutch community, where the old community was largely absorbed by the new. Among the Chinese the division between the old and new communities, while it was watered down somewhat, remained important.

The long-established community, the *peranakan*, was strongly acculturated to Indonesia. Given that the early Chinese migrants to Indonesia were overwhelmingly male, understandably most of the peranakan had at least some Indonesian antecedents. The more recently-arrived community was called *totok*, meaning 'pure' or 'genuine' (in the racial sense). This community had a more even gender balance, and its members tended to marry almost exclusively within it.

The social and cultural differences between these two communities was significant. Like the Dutch, many members of the peranakan community, and especially those in Java, had developed a distinctive local culture characterised, for instance, by the use of Malay or another local language in everyday speech, rather than a Chinese dialect. The totok community was the opposite. It was a community that was essentially Chinese-speaking, and oriented towards China rather than towards Indonesia.

But even in the peranakan community there was a degree of re-Sinification in the early years of the century, resulting both from a degree of interaction with the totoks and from developments in China. The overthrow of the Manchu Dynasty and the establishment of the Chinese Republic under Sun Yat-sen in 1911 produced an upsurge in Chinese patriotism not just in China itself, but also among many of the ethnic Chinese communities outside China, including Indonesia. Supporters of the Republican movement from China regularly visited Indonesia, seeking support and funds from the Chinese there, and propagandising for their cause. Their activities greatly heightened the sense of Chineseness in many Indonesian Chinese communities, whose members were consequently much more assertive about their Chinese identity than had previously been the case.

The Tiong Hoa Hwe Koan, established to promote Confucianism and probably the most important of the pre-war ethnic Chinese associations, was founded in 1900. Other clan associations, schools, chambers of commerce and the like, all focused on the Chinese community and reflecting a strong sense of Chinese identity, sprang up or were reinvigorated. It was chiefly in response to pressure from associations such as these that the colonial authorities established the first Dutch-language secondary schools for Chinese in 1908—before there were any such schools available for Indonesians—and lifted the restrictions on travel and residence for Chinese in 1910.

Until late in the nineteenth century, the 'average' or 'typical' Chinese resident of the Indies was a peranakan living in Java. This situation was already in a state of flux by 1900, owing to significant levels of in-migration of labourers from China to work on plantations and in the mines; by 1920, the majority of the Chinese population was living outside Java, and was totok.

Chinese immigration into the Indies effectively ceased at the end of the 1920s, which swung the pendulum back, culturally, towards the peranakan community. Indeed, the colony-wide Census conducted in 1930 showed that two out of every three ethnic Chinese in Indonesia spoke no Chinese language at all, and used Malay as their means of everyday communication.

As we have seen, relations between Chinese and Indonesians have ebbed and flowed over the centuries. But the new cultural assertiveness on the part of the Chinese made them worse. The economic divide between most Indonesians and most Chinese was also growing, largely because of the way that many ethnic Chinese were able to benefit from the operations of the colonial economic system, especially after the collapse of the Cultivation System, and by the early years of the twentieth century there was growing tension between the two communities.

Ethnic Chinese and indigenous Indonesians were deeply divided on one crucial question: independence for Indonesia. With very few exceptions, ethnic Chinese did not support the nationalist movement. At best, they remained aloof from the nationalist issue, preferring to direct their attention to Chinese politics. At worst, many actively supported the Dutch position. Leaders of the nationalist movement reinforced this division by discouraging, and in some cases forbidding, ethnic Chinese from joining the emerging nationalist parties. One party, made up of ethnic Chinese and supporting Indonesian independence did emerge—the Partai Tionghoa Indonesia, established in 1932—but it was significant really only because it was the exception.

Ethnic Arabs took a very different position, diametrically opposed to that of the ethnic Chinese. Long integrated with the indigenous communities, and for the most part sharing a religion with them, the Arab community gave broad support to Indonesian nationalism. Individual ethnic Arabs joined nationalist political parties, and at least one major Arab-based party was formed to support independence. There were some Arabs who supported the Dutch, but they were few in number.

The positions these two non-indigenous communities took on the question of independence were powerful factors influencing their relations with indigenous Indonesians; the remnants of that influence remain to the present day.

Finally, let us now turn to what was by far the largest community in the Indies, the Indonesian community—or communities, because it would be misleading to suggest there was as yet a single, Indonesia-oriented community among the indigenous inhabitants of the archipelago, although there were many local leaders who were at this time on the brink of making the transition from a regional to a national orientation; away from concerns primarily about Javanese issues, or Minangkabau issues, or Balinese issues, toward a concern for national, archipelago-wide ones.

There were perhaps three main factors promoting this transition from regional to national orientation. One was the simple—yet for many, unavoidable—fact of colonialism. The extension of colonial authority through the archipelago meant that for the first time leaders of local communities right across the archipelago were confronted with the same colonial rules and regulations, the same colonial officialdom, the same colonial exploitation. Inevitably, willingly or otherwise these local leaders were being drawn into the workings of a state that extended far beyond local and regional boundaries.

The second factor was the changes taking place in Islam, the religion followed by the overwhelming majority of Indonesians. The first of two important forces at work around the turn of the century was Islamic reformism. As we have seen, this reformism had been one of the major factors in the outbreak of the Paderi War in Minangkabau in the nineteenth century; by the early twentieth century its influence was being felt in other parts of the archipelago too. Islamic reformism took a variety of institutional forms, of which the most important was

Muhammadiyah, noted earlier. And—importantly—reformism drew support from Islamic communities right across Indonesia.

The reformist movement did not sweep all before it. The traditionalist community remained strong, and in many areas dominant. Traditionalists were typically to be found in rural areas: their presence was particularly strong, for instance, in east Java. Although some did acquire a western-style education, the bulk did not. For most, the rural boarding school or pesantren was the educational institution of choice.

The success the reformers were having in attracting followers was a matter of increasing concern to traditionalist scholars. In 1926, in an effort to retain support for their understanding of Islam, a group of traditionalist scholars established the Nahdatul Ulama (NU). The leader of this group was Kiai Haji Hasjim Ashari; his grandson, Kiai Haji Abdurrahman Wahid, also a leader of the NU, became the fourth President of Indonesia. The organisation grew rapidly, counting 100 000 members in 99 branches by 1938, and having both youth and women's wings.

Relations between the modernist and traditional communities ebbed and flowed, hostility between them probably peaking in the late 1920s and early 1930s. Relations began to improve by the late 1930s with the growing realisation in both camps that internecine conflict was hampering the development of Islam more generally, and certainly weakening the struggle against the Christian colonialist Dutch. But the differences between them ran deep. They remain significant to the present day, and are epitomised by the contemporary conflict between former President Abdurrahman Wahid from the traditionalist NU and Amien Rais, Parliamentary speaker and power-broker, from the modernist Muhammadiyah.

There were, of course, some institutions in which Indonesians, Chinese, Dutch and other inhabitants of the Indies participated. The Theosophical Society, for instance, drew members from across the demographic spectrum, with the possible exception of the Arab community. But for the most part the various communities lived separate social and political lives. Most sporting, social and youth clubs, for instance, were ethnically based, and often politically based too.

These social and cultural changes were important. But perhaps the greatest changes of all in the Indies—certainly the greatest changes in the Indonesian community—were taking place in the political arena, with the development of parties and organisations aimed at achieving independence for Indonesia. Regionally based, traditionally focused anti-Dutch movements did not cease to exist overnight, but by the 1920s they had all but disappeared from political view, to be replaced by modern, Indonesia-focused organisations. In these organisations membership was individual, rather than collective; parties had networks of local branches, in Java, Sumatera and the other islands, to which individual members belonged; the platforms of the parties were determined at congresses or similar meetings, attended either by the membership as a whole, or by delegates from branches.

The first of these modern movements, ones that might perhaps best be termed proto-nationalist rather than nationalist, emerged in the first decade of the twentieth century. The most important of these organisations were Budi Utomo and the Indische Partij.

Budi Utomo was formed by students at STOVIA (School Tot Opleiding Van Inlandsche Artsen), the medical school in Jakarta, on 20 May 1908, a date commemorated in Indonesian political folklore as marking the beginning of the nationalist movement and the struggle to free the country from the Dutch.

The inspiration for the formation of the organisation came from a low-level Javanese aristocrat, Dr Wahidin Sudirohusodo. He had become particularly concerned at what he saw as the moral and political decline of the Javanese people, resulting from the impact on traditional ideas of both Islam and Dutch colonialism. The only way to restore the dignity of the Javanese, he believed, was through western-style education: through such education the Javanese could rediscover their cultural and historical roots and thus reverse the decline. But it was not the Javanese side of Wahidin's thinking that attracted the STOVIA students—drawn as they were from around the archipelago, not just Java, their orientation was increasingly national rather than regional—it was his commitment to education. These students represented the new emerging Indonesian professional elite, people making their way in the world not through reliance on birth or family connections but through their own efforts, and particularly through education.

The differences between the STOVIA students and Wahidin, and many of the other Javanese aristocrats who supported him, mirrored the changing times: old established elite versus the young emerging one, regional interests versus national ones. These differences came to a head at the Budi Utomo Congress held in October 1908. Here, Wahidin and the ideas he represented asserted their control over the organisation, thus ensuring that it would maintain its essentially Javanese cultural bias, and ultimately avoid offering any serious political challenges to the colonial order. This prompted the establishment of a number of other similar organisations representing regional interests, organisations that were modern in their structure, but largely conservative and backward-looking in outlook. Thus Pasundan was formed in 1914 to promote the interests of the Sundanese, followed by similar groups focusing on Sumatera, Minahasa, Ambon and Timor.

The Budi Utomo was important, though, in starting the political careers of several people who were to become major national leaders in the future. Among them were Tjipto Mangunkusomo and Taman Siswa founder Ki Hajar Dewantoro, both of whom left the organisation after the 1908 Congress.

In 1912, Tjipto and Dewantoro joined with the radical Eurasian journalist Edward Douwes Dekker, grand-nephew of the author of *Max Havelaar*, to found the Indische Partij (the Indies Party). The Party was considerably more nationalist and more politically radical than Budi Utomo. It argued, for instance, that the Indies belonged to all those who were born there, or made their permanent home there, no matter whether they were Indonesian, Eurasian, Chinese, Dutch or anything else. This was the first occasion on which a major political organisation was established which was explicitly intended to cross ethnic boundaries.

The Party was also committed to independence, to be achieved through radical means. Douwes Dekker said:

> As we plan to put an end once and for all to the colonial situation, the *Indische Partij* is definitely revolutionary . . . Revolutionary action enables people to achieve their aims quickly . . . The *Indische Partij* can safely be called revolutionary. Such a word does not frighten us.[3]

It might not have frightened Douwes Dekker, but it certainly frightened the Dutch; in March 1913 the government declared the Indische Partij illegal. Douwes Dekker, Tjipto and Dewantoro all campaigned against the government's decision, but to no avail. Given the option of leaving the colony altogether as an alternative to internal exile, all three left for the Netherlands.

Budi Utomo and the Indische Partij were important beginnings for the nationalist movement, but neither managed to attract a mass base. The first mass nationalist movements were those based on Islam.

As the religion of the overwhelming majority of Indonesians and offering a moral code very different from that of the Dutch, Islam ought to have been a natural pioneer of a united national movement against the Dutch—but such a movement never eventuated. Instead, a variety of Islamic nationalist parties emerged, the primary division between them being not regional but theological: between the reformists and the traditionalists.

The reformists were the first to adopt modern forms of political organisation. Building on an earlier Islamic traders' association, the Sarekat Islam (SI) was formed in Solo on 10 September 1912 under the leadership of Umar Said Tjokroaminoto. Membership of the organisation grew rapidly. By December 1912 it claimed 93 000 members; by April 1913 it had 150 000 members; and in April 1914 there were 367 000 members. In the latter year it had 56 local branches, in Java, Sumatera, Kalimantan and Sulawesi.

The SI membership came from a variety of sources. Its original base had been the Javanese Islamic merchant class, people who were feeling the pinch of increasingly intense commercial competition from ethnic Chinese businesspeople, especially in the batik industry. Other members were rural peasants, especially from Java, where SI recruiters skilfully used the Ratu Adil legend to attract members. And others were drawn from among workers in the industrial centres developing as a result of Dutch economic policy, particularly in cities such as Semarang and Surabaya.

Clearly given such a disparate membership, the SI was not an organisation with a very fixed or even clear set of political principles. Its political objectives, at least initially, were modest: self-government, rather than full independence, to be achieved through peaceful means. Stressing these points, in his address to the organisation's 1913 Congress Tjokroaminoto said: 'We are loyal to the Government', and further: 'we are satisfied under Dutch rule'.

However, within a few years of its formation the SI was to see a determined struggle between two membership factions, each seeking to take the organisation in its own political direction.

One faction was led by Semaun. In 1914, aged just sixteen and a worker on the railways, he had been elected Secretary of the Surabaya branch of the SI. Semaun neatly encapsulates much of the complexity and the fluidity of the early years of the nationalist movement, being also an active member of the VSTP, a railway workers' union, and of the Indies Social Democratic Association (ISDV). The latter was the most radical, leftist political organisation in the Indies, although until 1918 dominated by its Dutch members and led by Hendrik Sneevliet.

Semaun moved to the central Javanese city of Semarang in late 1916, and was soon elected chair of the local branches of both the

SI and the ISDV. Under his leadership the SI grew rapidly in membership—it had 20 000 members by 1917—and became a stronghold of anti-capitalist sentiment. Semaun clearly wanted to draw the SI to the political left. At the organisation's 1919 Congress, he urged delegates to 'join in the class struggle' and declared that the SI 'should become the organization of the worker and small peasant class'.

The other main faction within the SI was led by Abdul Muis and Agus Salim, and centred on the city of Yogyakarta. This faction, while it could not fairly be termed rightist or conservative, was nonetheless clearly non-Marxist, and much more reflective of the commercial background of the original SI membership. This faction was more prepared than Semaun's to negotiate with the Dutch, and to work within the colonial political system. Thus for instance in 1918 Muis and Salim successfully argued that the SI should accept the government's offer of seats in the newly established Volksraad or People's Council.

For the last few years of the decade, the two factions struggled for control of the SI and its affiliated organisations, especially trade unions, a struggle which came to a head in October 1921 at the Sixth National Congress of the party. The previous year, the Indonesian Communist Party (PKI) had been formed, with Semaun as its first Chair. At the SI Congress Salim and Muis introduced a resolution forbidding SI members from belonging simultaneously to any other political organisation. This resolution was quite obviously directed against members of the PKI: no fuss was made about SI members who also belonged to one or other of the smaller Islamic organisations around at this time. It was vigorously opposed by Semaun, and by another rising PKI member of the SI, Tan Malaka, but was passed by a large majority. The Communists thereupon resigned from the party, and the SI's communist-controlled branches, in Semarang and its vicinity, broke away.

The battle between the two sides was now on in earnest, a battle that was fought out in both the countryside and in the cities, in the union movement.

At one level, it was a battle the SI lost. Within four years it had conceded control of a majority of its branches to the PKI, and in the industrial arena was no longer effective. In 1923, it changed its name to Partai Sarekat Islam Indonesia, as if to confirm its national political ambitions, but its heyday was over.

But on another level the PKI also lost out. Gaining control of the SI branches was a hollow victory since the bulk of their peasant membership had, in the process, melted away. In the industrial arena, the party's unions found themselves actively opposed by the government. The latter was quite prepared to use its resources to break strikes, as the party found out when its railway workers' union struck in 1923. In the aftermath of this strike, Semaun was exiled from the Indies; he was not to return until 1957. The union itself saw its membership base shrink from about 13 000 before the strikes to just 535 soon afterwards.

These developments meant that by about 1924 the PKI was floundering organisationally. Underlying its difficulties was an ideological debate about the best arena for party activities: among peasants in the countryside, or among industrial workers in the cities. Eventually, in line with a mid-1924 decision of the Comintern, the Communist International, the party opted for industrial action. In December 1924 it began to wind down its rural activities, transferring its energies to the industrial movement. It also formulated a proposal for the establishment of a Soviet Republic of Indonesia. Then, against the advice of many of its exiled leaders, including Tan Malaka, in October 1925 party and trade union leaders decided to embark on a course of revolution, to be sparked off by strikes in key industries in Java and Sumatera.

The strikes were disastrous. A mixture of organisational incompetence and infiltration of the organisation by government intelligence agents doomed the revolution to failure. Some 13 000 people were arrested, a massive number given that the total membership of the party at this time was probably no more than 3000. Just under half of those arrested were eventually imprisoned or exiled, nearly 1000 being sent to a purpose-built prison camp at Tanah Merah, in what is now the province of Irian Jaya.[4] Other important political prisoners were later sent here, including Mohammad Hatta, the man who proclaimed Indonesian independence with Sukarno in 1945 and was the Republic's first Vice-President, and Sutan Sjahrir, its first Prime Minister. Tanah Merah in time became one of the most potent symbols of the struggle for Indonesian independence; this symbolism goes some way to explaining why all postwar Indonesian governments have insisted that Irian Jaya is a part of the Republic of Indonesia.

The failure of the attempted revolution marked the end of overt PKI activities in Indonesia for two decades. It also drove a deep wedge between many of the leaders who had remained in Indonesia and supported the rebellion, and those outside Indonesia like Tan Malaka who had tried to stop it. The leaders inside Indonesia considered they had been betrayed by the likes of Tan Malaka; betrayed at an organisational level, in that Tan Malaka had actively tried to stop the rebellion, but also betrayed ideologically. Tan Malaka was seen as representing the particular line of communism that sought an alliance with bourgeois nationalists, and was not, in that sense, 'pure'. After the war, Tan Malaka was to establish a political party called Murba, which styled itself 'national communist'. The enmity between this party and the resurrected PKI in the 1950s was intense.

For the rest of the 1920s and the 1930s the nationalist movement was dominated by politicians and parties generally described as being non-Marxist and secular or religiously neutral. These politicians, from whom the first generation of independent Indonesia's leaders were to come, were overwhelmingly young people, born in the twentieth century. They were also male—there were very few women among them—with high levels of education. In this sense, they were beneficiaries of the Ethical Policy, and the ultimate proof of the failure of that policy's aim of using education as a means of tying Indonesians to the Netherlands.

Some of these leaders received their university education in the Netherlands. However, one of the advances brought about by the Ethical Policy had been the establishment of institutions of higher education in the Indies itself. As a result, by the mid-1920s an increasing—albeit still small—number of Indonesians was studying at tertiary level in Indonesia itself.

The person who best personifies the Indonesian-educated secular nationalists is Sukarno, later to be first President of Indonesia, born in 1901. Sukarno's father was Muslim Javanese, a minor aristocrat and a schoolteacher by profession. His mother was Balinese, and a Hindu. Their marriage itself, in a small and incidental way, was symbolic of what Sukarno came to represent: the idea of Indonesian-ness, superseding identification with specific ethnic or religious groups.

Religiously, Sukarno was a Muslim, but more influential was his Javanese cultural background which, while it certainly was not anti-Islamic, at least did not pay very much attention to Islam.

From 1915 to 1920, Sukarno attended a Dutch-language secondary school in Surabaya. Here he was introduced to the world of ideas, chiefly through the library of the Surabaya branch of the Theosophical Society, a library stocked with western as well as Indonesian literature. He became a voracious reader, he later said, introducing himself to thinkers as diverse as Jefferson, Sidney and Beatrice Webb, Marx, Hegel, Kant, Rousseau and Voltaire.

And it was here that his exposure to nationalist politics began. He was sent to board with the family of an old friend of his father, Tjokroaminoto, the SI leader then at the height of his influence within the organisation. Through Tjokroaminoto, Sukarno met virtually all the important nationalist political leaders of his day: H. Agus Salim from Sarekat Islam, Ki Hajar Dewantoro from Budi Utomo, Sneevliet and Semaun from the ISDV and later the PKI. This was a veritable *Who's Who* of Indonesian nationalism.

Sukarno's early life stands in contrast to that of Mohammed Hatta, the man who was to come to epitomise those Indonesian nationalists who were educated in the Netherlands. Hatta was a Minangkabau, born a year after Sukarno in 1902. His initial education in west Sumatera had been in Islamic schools, though he attended a Dutch-language primary school as well. He moved to Jakarta in 1920 to undertake the last two years of secondary school.

Whereas Sukarno's intellectual background up to this point had been a rather eclectic one, without an overarching set of guiding principles or philosophy, Hatta's early history shows him to be much more disciplined and focused. Islam provided Hatta with a ready reference point against which to measure anything that he read or came into contact with. Yet Hatta ultimately declined to join any of the avowedly Islamic political parties. He saw Islam as transcending political boundaries. You could be a Muslim and belong to just about any political party—though in later life he would have drawn the line at the PKI. Islam, he believed, should underlie everything that a Muslim did; it did not have to be put out on show and waved around like a flag.

Like Sukarno, Hatta became interested in politics at an early age. While still in Minangkabau he had been a member of the Young Sumatera League, and in Jakarta had become its Secretary. Unlike Sukarno, though, he had showed little interest in public speaking—and even less talent for it. He was a thinker, a planner, but no great stirrer of public emotions.

In 1920-21, Sukarno and Hatta were faced with the same problem: where to continue their education. And here they split, Sukarno staying on in the Indies, and Hatta proceeding to the Netherlands.

Sukarno studied architecture at the newly established Technical Institute in Bandung. Here he also continued his political education, coming into contact in particular with members of the PKI and with radical Muslims. He also began to write articles for nationalist newspapers. And it was here in 1926, the year after his graduation, that he helped to form his first quasi-political association, the General Study

Club (Algemeene Studieclub). At this time Study Clubs were springing up right across Java. They presented themselves, in good Ethical Policy terms, as being concerned not with politics but with education. And many of them were. But not the Bandung Study Club: it was uncompromisingly political in its outlook, setting Indonesian independence as its goal, to be achieved through active struggle against the Dutch.

By this time a clearer picture of Sukarno's political orientation was beginning to emerge, shaped by both his Javanese cultural background and the particular circumstances of the day. This was the time of the great struggle between the PKI and SI, a struggle that was tearing both organisations apart. Sukarno argued that all elements of the nationalist movement—Islamic, communist and secular—could and should work together towards the achievement of Indonesian independence. Differences between these elements had been exaggerated, or misunderstood; what they had in common, standing above any and all differences, was their commitment to nationalism, their sense of belonging to one nation: Indonesia.

This emphasis on the need for unity in the nationalist movement might have been reflective of Sukarno's Javanese cultural background, with its stress on harmony and the avoidance of conflict. But it also had a pragmatic or tactical edge to it. Given the split in the nationalist movement, and the consequent vulnerability of all nationalist organisations to repression by the colonial authorities, it made good hard political sense to try to unite the parties in the struggle against the Dutch.

While all this was going on, Hatta was studying economics at Rotterdam. In choosing to study in the Netherlands Hatta seems to have been particularly influenced by the views of his mother, and to have gone against the advice of his father. Women had a major influence on many areas of Hatta's life: first his mother and her sisters, and then his wife. The matrilineal culture of the Minangkabau was particularly influential on him.

Once in the Netherlands, Hatta directed his political interests into the Indische Vereniging (Indies Association). Established in 1908 as an association for Indonesians in the Netherlands and for Dutch students who were going to be posted to the Indies in the colonial administration, the Association had gradually been undergoing a change in both membership and direction, away from being simply a social organisation towards one concerned with the political issues of the day in Indonesia. This radicalisation was brought about partly by the arrival in the Netherlands of people such as Ki Hajar Dewantoro, Douwes Dekker and Tjipto Mangunkusumo, all exiled from the Indies for their political activities, but Hatta also played a significant role.

Indicative of the shift in the organisation's direction was its change of name in 1922 to Perhimpunan Indonesia, or Indonesian Association. This change was significant in that the name was now expressed in the Indonesian language rather than in Dutch, and that for the first time ever the term 'Indonesia' was being used in a political context. The basic principle underlying the Perhimpunan Indonesia (PI) was non-cooperation with the Dutch authorities. This meant not working for the colonial government, and not taking part in the instruments of the colonial political system such as the Volksraad (People's Council).

Thus by the mid-1920s there were nationalist movements emerging both in Indonesia and among Indonesians in the Netherlands.

On 4 July 1927, shortly after his graduation, Sukarno took the initiative to transform the Bandung Study Club into the Indonesian Nationalist Association (later Party), or the PNI (Perserikatan Nasional Indonesia). Its goal was unequivocal: independence for Indonesia. Its early members were primarily Indonesian-educated university graduates like Sukarno, but it also included many returnees from the Netherlands.

In defining the ideological base of the PNI, Sukarno started out by saying what it was not: it was not classical Marxism. A central feature of Marxism is the idea of there being a proletariat: workers who own no means of production, who have no capital and who survive by selling all that they possess, in other words, their labour power. Sukarno argued that the concept of the proletariat was not relevant to Indonesia since so many poor Indonesians were not proletarian. They did not survive solely by selling their labour power to others and they did in fact own something with which to produce an income: farming tools, fishing net, a buffalo. The term Sukarno used to describe these ordinary poor Indonesians was *marhaen*. A marhaen was thus rather different from a proletarian, for he (and presumably also she) did own some productive possessions, although still living in abject poverty.

The ideology of the PNI was Marhaenism. Sukarno himself never gave a very explicit description of what Marhaenism was, but we can say that it was vaguely socialist—though not Marxist; anti-capitalist; anti-liberal; concerned for the rights of the community rather than the individual.

The PNI was the first of the major religiously neutral nationalist parties, and was important for that reason alone. But it was also important because it was the political vehicle that brought Sukarno to national prominence. A measure of his standing, and of his commitment to the idea of unity in the nationalist movement, was his formation in December 1927 of an association representing all the major Indonesian-based political parties, including PNI, SI and Budi Utomo: the Union of Political Organisations of the Indonesian People or PPPKI (Permufakatan Perhimpunan Politik Kebangsaan Indonesia).

For a political party to join the PPPKI required simply a commitment to the achievement of Indonesian independence, and to the unity of the Indonesian people in pursuit of that goal. Within the Indies it now seemed as if the nationalist movement was beginning to recover from the disasters of earlier in the decade, to find some degree of unity at last and—probably even more importantly—to have found a leader who had wide popular appeal.

In order to protect the organisation's unity, Sukarno argued from the outset that decisions should not be taken by the divisive western method of voting. Instead, he insisted that the PPPKI reach decisions by what he argued were traditional Indonesian means, of *musyawarah* (deliberation) and *mufakat* (consensus). Under such a system, he argued, all parties were winners; there were no publicly humiliated losers.

At the time the PPPKI was being established, nationalists in the Netherlands and Indonesia were facing a new round of colonial repression. In the Netherlands the leadership of the PI was starting to run into serious trouble with authorities. The single most important factor in this development was what the Dutch saw—with a degree of justification, it must be said—as the increasingly close connections between the PI and communism, both Indonesian and international, particularly following a December 1926 agreement on institutional cooperation concluded between Hatta and Semaun. The upshot was that in September 1927 Hatta and three other leading members of the PI were arrested and charged with encouraging armed resistance to Dutch rule in the Indies.

Feeling, one suspects, that a guilty verdict was inevitable, Hatta decided that he would use his March 1928 trial as a platform from which to expound his views on the political struggle in which the PI was engaged. But the Court found him and his co-defendants not guilty on all counts. In the Netherlands at least, standards of proof applied by the courts in such cases were still high, and largely unaffected by political considerations.

In Indonesia the political mood within the Dutch community was now swinging around to the right and putting pressure on the Governor-General to take action against Sukarno's PNI, which by this time had become the most powerful of the nationalist parties. In May 1929 it claimed 3860 members; by the end of that year, membership stood at 10 000.

Governor-General de Graeff was a fairly tolerant man by the standards of contemporary colonial officialdom, but even he could not ignore the pressures being exerted on him. On 29 December 1929, Sukarno was arrested, along with many other leading members of the PNI.

In August 1930 Sukarno and three other PNI leaders faced court charged on a number of counts, the most important being the catch-all 'disturbing public order'. Sukarno's reaction to his trial was much the same as Hatta's had been two years earlier: forget about what the verdict might be, and simply use the court as a platform to air your political views. But whereas Hatta's plea had won him an acquittal, Sukarno's got him a guilty verdict, and a sentence of four years' jail: his fellow accused, all likewise found guilty, were sentenced to prison terms ranging from fifteen months to two years.

Sukarno's removal from the political scene seemed a masterstroke for the Dutch. The PNI, which had been showing some signs of becoming a mass popular organisation under his leadership, floundered in his absence. Its remaining leaders seemed to have little idea in which direction to turn, and were easily intimidated by the colonial authorities. In April 1931, just months after Sukarno was sentenced, the party voluntarily dissolved itself.

The remnant leaders of the old PNI established a new organisation called Partindo (an abbreviation of Partai Indonesia, or Indonesia Party), but it suffered a distinct lack of success in attracting members, whose numbers, a year after its foundation, stood at only about 3000. Undoubtedly the major reason for this was that none of the people who came forward to lead Partindo in 1930–31 had anything like Sukarno's political skills and personal charm.

By this time, the second stage of the nationalist movement, characterised by parties which sought a mass base, and which were confrontative towards the Dutch, was coming to an end. Both these characteristics had proved problematic, and contributed to the movement's failure to make any real progress against the Dutch.

The third stage of the movement, running through much of the 1930s, saw rather different tactics being adopted, albeit, it must be acknowledged, with not much more success. The nationalist parties of the 1930s were generally cadre-based rather than mass organisations, and a significant proportion of them were prepared to cooperate polit-ically with the Dutch, to varying degrees.

The first of the new parties was the Pendidikan Nasional Indo-nesia, or Indonesian National Education, called the New PNI to distinguish it from Sukarno's old party. It was established in December 1931 by Sutan Sjahrir, recently returned to Indonesia from university studies in the Netherlands. In 1932, shortly after he returned to the Indies, Hatta joined the New PNI.

The party espoused a generally socialist ideology, identifying the indigenous bourgeoisie as one of its enemies. More importantly, the New PNI was a cadre-based party with a hierarchy of leaders. Cadre education was central to the New PNI's philosophy: this was the reason for the organisation's name. Sjahrir and Hatta believed that a major reason for the failure of the old PNI had been the quality of its membership, the bulk of its members having joined not because of a deep-seated understanding of and informed commitment to the principles of the organisation, but rather because of the attraction of Sukarno's personality. With Sukarno gone, that membership had faded away. The New PNI was determined to avoid a similar fate, by ensuring that only trained and committed people were accepted as members.

Sukarno was released from prison in December 1931, having served less than two years of his original four-year term. Invited to join Partindo and to become its head, initially he declined this invitation and instead devoted his energies to trying to bring Partindo and the New PNI together—presumably under his leadership. Failing to persuade Hatta to support the merger, in September 1932 Sukarno threw in his lot with Partindo, and was unanimously elected its Chairman.

At first things seemed to go rather well. By mid-1933, Partindo had no fewer than 50 branches and 20 000 members, but this apparent success was to prove illusory. The year 1932 had brought a number of developments that were to have deleterious consequences for Indo-nesia and for the nationalist movement, developments over which the movement had no control whatsoever.

One was the appointment, in late 1931, of a new and very conservative Governor-General of the Indies, de Jonge, formerly Minister for War in the Netherlands and a Director of the Royal Dutch Shell company. His appointment seemed to herald a new era of even tighter controls on the nationalist movement than had been the case previously.

The second major development that impacted upon the Indies at this time—and most of the rest of the world, for that matter—was the Great Depression. Triggered off by the Wall Street Crash of 1929, it reached Indonesia in 1931–32, and had a profound and long-lasting influence on both the social and economic structure of the country.

This economic crisis should have given the nationalist parties a field day. There is nothing like economic deprivation to make people start to look for radical solutions to their problems. While this may have been obvious to the nationalist leaders, it was also obvious to the leaders of the colonial government—and they had no intention of letting things get out of hand.

In February 1933, a mutiny broke out on the Dutch naval ship *Zeven Provincien*, off the Sumatera coast, in protest at a 17 per cent reduction in pay decreed by the government as a cost-cutting measure. The government quickly put the mutiny down, and then, on the very thinnest of evidence, de Jonge announced the discovery of a plot linking the New PNI and the Partindo to the mutineers. Thereafter police harassment of the organisations' leaders was stepped up, and their meetings were either disrupted or banned. In late June 1933, civil servants were forbidden to belong to either organisation.

On 1 August 1933, Sukarno was arrested for the second time. He had been free for exactly nineteen months. The colonial government was determined not to repeat its mistake of three years earlier, when Sukarno had been able to use his trial as a platform to address the Indonesian people about his political philosophies and objectives—this time, he was not to be given the luxury of a trial at all.

In mid-February 1934, Sukarno was sent into internal exile, first on the island of Flores, and subsequently at Bengkulu and then Padang in Sumatera. Just as had happened with the old PNI after Sukarno's first arrest, Partindo began to collapse. It was not formally dissolved until November 1936, but to all intents and purposes it ceased to function as a political party following Sukarno's arrest.

The colonial government, meanwhile, had not forgotten the New PNI either. Just one week after Sukarno was sent to Flores, Hatta and Sjahrir were arrested and sent to the Dutch prison camp at Tanah Merah. De Jonge as good as admitted that these arrests were preventative and exemplary rather than a punishment for deeds actually committed.

Heavy though this blow was, the New PNI ought to have been able to bear it. After all, it was against this eventuality that the party had committed itself to the production of educated and trained cadres, ready to step into the shoes of any of its leaders who might be imprisoned. However, this was not to happen. A shadow executive did emerge following the arrests, but it was never able to do very much, and was the subject of almost constant government harassment.

Hatta, Sjahrir and Sukarno were not the only nationalist leaders arrested; many of the leaders of Islamic organisations such as the Partai Sarekat Islam Indonesia were also imprisoned or exiled. The effect on the nationalist movement as a whole was disastrous. Added to the fact that Tjokroaminoto, still the most respected Islamic nationalist leader, had died in 1934, by the middle of the decade the non-cooperative nationalist movement was all but dead.

This left those nationalist parties and individuals who were prepared to cooperate, to some degree at least, with the Dutch as the only ones able to operate openly. And the main arena in which they worked was the Volksraad.

Since its foundation in 1918, the standing and composition of the Volksraad had altered somewhat. Originally simply providing advice to the Governor-General, in 1927 it had been given 'joint legislative functions' with the colonial authorities. This gave it the power to discuss the Indies budget, present petitions, draft legislative proposals, suggest amendments to legislation proposed by the government and request information from the Governor-General on specific matters— but in none of these areas did it have the power to compel the colonial government to take any particular action. The colonial government could still, and did, act independently of the Volksraad.

A second change to the Volksraad—potentially of greater significance—was in terms of its membership. In 1931 Indonesians were given the right to fill 30 of its 60 seats; Europeans filled 25, and the remaining five went to 'Foreign Orientals'. Indonesians thus constituted half of the membership of the Volksraad.

Not all Indonesian members of the Volksraad supported independence, however. In the 1931–34 Volksraad, at least four Indonesian members opposed independence; in 1935–38, seven members opposed it.

Among the pro-independence members of the Volksraad, for much of the 1930s the most radical was Mohammad Husni Thamrin, leader of the Kaum Betawi, the Batavia (Jakarta) Association, and head of the political section of the major cooperating nationalist political party of this time, the Parindra or Greater Indonesia Party, formed in December 1935. Parindra was a party of religiously neutral politicians, somewhat conservative in their outlook, whose aim was eventual independence for Indonesia. It had its greatest strength in Java, having been created by the union of a number of Javanese-based organisations and parties, including Budi Utomo. By May 1941 it had about 19 500 members.

Of the members of the so-called moderate left in the Volksraad, the most prominent was Soetardjo, a member of the Javanese aristocracy and the spokesman in the Volksraad for the Association of Indigenous Civil Servants. This group ought to have been supporters of the colonial government, whose interests they served in the course of their employment. However, the 1930s had seen the public service hard hit by a variety of government policies—salary reductions, forced redundancies and the like—intended to help overcome the effects of the Depression. Colonial government policies were having the effect of not only alienating the enemies of the colonial state but also the very Indonesians who in the past had been the backbone of that state.

In July 1936 Soetardjo presented a petition to the Volksraad calling for the convening of a conference to arrange Indonesian autonomy within a Dutch-Indonesian union within ten years. In September, the Volksraad adopted the petition by 26 votes to 20. It was now up to the government in The Hague to respond.

Over two years later, in November 1938, the Petition was rejected. While this was not unexpected, by the same token it left the nationalists in something of a dilemma. Non-cooperation was obviously not a viable political option; but it was looking as if cooperation was not likely to lead to any gains in the struggle for independence either.

By this time as well, the external political situation was beginning to impinge substantially on Indonesian nationalist politics, particularly the growing threat to international peace posed by the fascism of both Germany and Japan. Many prominent nationalist leaders, socialists or Marxists of one kind or another for whom fascism was an enemy rivalling colonialism, now felt it was necessary to consider the extent to which they should make common cause with the Dutch against the fascists.

In April 1937 a group of socialist and Marxist nationalists formed Gerindo, the Indonesia People's Movement. The party argued that the Dutch and the Indonesians both had a vested interest in the fight against the rising tide of fascism in Europe and Asia. Gerindo wanted to participate in this fight—but it could do so only in a context in which the Dutch recognised the legitimate political interests of the Indonesians. Converting the Volksraad into a proper parliament could do this.

This was the first time that an Indonesian political party had proposed joint action with the Dutch against fascism. It was not to be the last; indeed, from now until the outbreak of the Second World War, such calls for joint action increased in intensity. But these calls fell on deaf ears; the Dutch simply refused to contemplate political cooperation with the Indonesians as the price for their support in the fight against fascism.

The other impact of the threat of fascism on the nationalist movement was internal to the movement itself: a renewed interest in trying to bring some sort of unity to it, to make it better able to meet the increasingly complex political challenges of the future. The Gabungan Politik Indonesia (GAPI), the Indonesian Political Federation, was established in April 1939, as a result of initiatives taken primarily by Thamrin. The New PNI declined to join the Federation, but eight other important nationalist parties did join, including Gerindo and the Partai Sarekat Islam Indonesia.

GAPI's membership was primarily drawn from the religiously neutral political parties. The Islamic parties were also attempting to form a united front, and to dissipate years of disunity. In fact, two years before GAPI was established the major Islamic parties had formed the Majlis Islam A'laa Indonesia (MIAI), the All-Indonesian Muslim Congress. Initially this organisation was concerned solely with religious issues, leaving its member parties to pursue their political objectives in other forums, including GAPI. When war broke out in Europe, however, it took on specifically political objectives, and joined forces with GAPI in demanding Indonesian autonomy.

For the Dutch, the European War began in earnest on 10 May 1940, the day German forces invaded the Netherlands. Although Indonesia itself was not threatened directly by these developments, nonetheless martial law was proclaimed in the colony, and all public political meetings banned.

The Volksraad was now quite literally the only place in which the nationalist political parties could voice their opinions—for all the good that it did them. If Batavia had been politically stubborn earlier, when war had first broken out between Britain and Germany, it was absolutely immovable now that the Dutch homeland itself had been occupied. With an optimism which borders at times on the unbelievable, however, members of the Volksraad continued to press motions on the colonial government: motions to have the government replace the word 'inlander' with 'Indonesian' when referring to the people of the archipelago; to define an Indies nationality; and the old favourite, to reform the Volksraad to turn it into a real parliament. All these proposals were rejected out of hand.

In summary, by 1941 the Indonesian nationalist movement was in a politically weak position with virtually all its major leaders— Sukarno, Hatta and Sjahrir among them—either in jail or in exile. Only those parties and leaders prepared to cooperate with the Dutch were permitted to operate legally, and they had been singularly ineffective in securing concessions.

By this time, though, it was not the situation in Europe that was particularly troubling to the authorities in Batavia, but rather the situation in Asia. It had for some time been obvious to many observers that if Japan went to war in this region, the Indies would be a prime target. Only the Indies could supply Japan with sufficient quantities of raw materials such as oil, rubber and tin to sustain offensive operations for any substantial period. The only real question was how these supplies could be secured.

For as long as possible, the Japanese did their best to secure the supplies they needed by conventional means: by trade. But this was not particularly easy. Economic relations between Japan and the Indies had soured considerably during the Depression, because Batavia had put major limitations on imports of Japanese consumer goods in an attempt to protect local industry. Whether local industry in fact benefited substantially from this move is unclear, but it certainly upset the Japanese.

However, the Japanese did not risk everything on just one strategy. They also undertook preparations to ensure that, if necessary, they would be able to take what they needed by force of arms. A crucial element in any such preparations was intelligence: a knowledge of roads, railways, harbours and the like. This they collected by a variety of means, including the use of intelligence agents, often disguised as tradespeople resident in the Indies: merchants, barbers, tailors, photographers and the like.

The last year or so before the outbreak of the Pacific War saw an intensification of Dutch preparations for war and of tensions between the Indies and Japan.

Recruitment to the KNIL, the colonial army, was extended. In June 1940 a young Javanese, whose only previous work experience had been as a bank clerk, enlisted in the army and was sent for NCO training to a depot just to the west of Yogyakarta. His name was Suharto; just over a quarter-century later he became Indonesia's second President, a position he held until 1998. A militia was established to defend the Indies, over the protests of nationalists in the Volksraad who had wanted to tie the legislation to parliamentary reform.

In January 1941 the colonial authorities arrested Thamrin and Douwes Dekker, on the grounds that they were in contact with the Japanese. In the case of Douwes Dekker, this was hardly surprising, since he was employed as Secretary to the Japanese Chamber of Commerce in the Indies; but the only evidence against Thamrin appears to have been that a Japanese trade delegation in Indonesia in 1940 had made contact with him. When he was arrested Thamrin was seriously ill, and he was to die in police custody five days later.

On the international front, in mid-1941 Dutch–Japanese negotiations on the question of granting Japan priority access to Indies raw materials broke down. In retaliation for the pressure the Japanese had exerted on them, the Dutch followed the American lead and banned the export of iron ore or scrap metal to Japan. Japanese investments in the Indies were also frozen.

For Indonesia, the Pacific War started on 10 January 1942, when Japanese forces invaded Java and Sumatera. Resistance quickly collapsed: the Dutch surrendered on 8 March 1941, their rule over

Indonesia being brought to an end, swiftly and effectively, forever. The Dutch did attempt to reassert their control after the Japanese surrender in 1945, but failed, and by 1949 had acknowledged Indonesian independence.

The reactions of the Indonesian population to the invasion were varied, and in many places very confused. Nowhere was there any active, organised resistance to the Japanese by civilian Indonesians. In some places there was indifference, in others the Japanese were welcomed as liberators, the people who had driven the Dutch out of the country.

The Japanese occupation was to last three and a half years—a very short time compared to the three and a half centuries during which the Dutch held at least some parts of the Indonesian archipelago. But these few years were crucial to the development of an independent Indonesia, seeing fatal damage done to Dutch military and political power and prestige. This damage was probably greatest in the eyes of those who had previously put a good deal of faith in the Dutch. Thus Syafruddin Prawiranegara, a pre-war public servant and advocate of cooperation with the Dutch, later said:

> I believed then that the Dutch really did intend to educate us to a level which would enable us to become independent and handle our own affairs . . . I changed this stand after I saw how the Dutch gave in to the Japanese just like that . . . that was the moment I completely lost faith in their aims.[5]

It also opened up major new opportunities for Indonesians in military, political and bureaucratic affairs, but at the same time led to economic hardship unprecedented at least in living memory.

Japanese administration

The Japanese administration of the Indies differed from that of the Dutch in several crucial ways. First, and perhaps fundamentally, the Japanese administration was a much harsher and more restrictive one. Martial law prevailed throughout the islands. The Kempetai, the secret police, were much more to be feared than their Dutch counterpart, the PID. Those who worked with the Japanese were treated reasonably well, but those who opposed them were dealt with harshly and without even the pretence of fair treatment. Many prominent nationalist leaders, including Sukarno and Hatta, were released from jail or exile, but the downside was that all political parties were banned. The only political institutions permitted were those created by or at the instigation of the Japanese, and which contributed to Japanese war aims and objectives.

Second, whereas the Dutch had rejected mobilisation of the Indonesian population, even when defeat by the Japanese was imminent, the Japanese administration actively sought the mobilisation of the people, though naturally of course in support of Japanese war aims. They established a variety of civil and quasi-military organisations with this end in mind.

Third, whereas the Dutch had ruled Indonesia as a single unit, the Japanese divided the region up into three zones: eastern Indonesia, Java and Sumatera. The eastern zone was under the control of the 2nd Southern Fleet, with headquarters at Makasar. The other two zones were under army control, the 16th Army in the case of Java and the 25th Army in the case of Sumatera, the latter also responsible for Singapore and Malaya until 1943. For a short while, both sides of the Straits of Melaka were again under a single administration.

The commanders of these three military zones took rather different positions on the independence movement. As a general rule, the 16th Army in Java was most favourably inclined towards independence, the 2nd Southern Fleet of the Navy least favourably inclined.

Of course, no commander in the Indies, whether army or navy, had the authority to make final decisions about matters of such great importance as this: ultimately, such decisions were taken in Tokyo. The 16th Army's outlook, combined with restrictions on the movement of people between military zones, strengthened the position in the nationalist movement of the leaders on Java, but weakened efforts to stress the geographic inclusiveness of the movement.

Fourth, from 1941, the Japanese reoriented the economy, especially its international component, away from Europe towards Japan. This had a major impact on commercial agriculture and mining activities. When the tide of war turned firmly against the Japanese, however, by perhaps mid-1943, Indonesia's trading links with Japan became more and more tenuous, leading to severe shortages of imported goods such as cloth and medicines. The archipelago was plunged into economic depression far worse than anything seen in recent decades of Dutch administration.

Finally, the Occupation put the 'seal of approval' on Indonesian as the national language when the Japanese banned completely the public and private use of Dutch. The effect of this was to force the leading nationalists—including the leading nationalist writers—into practising what they preached, using Indonesian in preference to Dutch.

Perhaps the single most important question Indonesians had to answer during the Occupation was reminiscent of the one that had confronted them during the 1920s and 1930s: whether to cooperate with the Japanese. This was a dilemma faced by nationalist leaders in most Asian colonies occupied by the Japanese, and by many political leaders in occupied Europe. However, the situation these Asian leaders faced was rather different from that faced by leaders of European countries overrun by the Nazis. The European countries all had legitimate governments that had been overthrown by the Germans. European leaders who cooperated with the Germans were thus clearly choosing to side with the invaders against their own legitimate governments.

In Asia, the places Japan invaded were mostly not independent countries, but colonies of European powers—indeed, they were already 'occupied' before the Japanese came, by Europeans. Thus the choice facing Asian nationalist leaders was not between collaborating with an invader and remaining loyal to their own legitimate governments, it was between collaborating with the new invader or remaining loyal to the old one. Most rejected firmly the notion that collaboration with the Japanese could be equated with European collaboration with the Nazis.

For some Indonesian nationalists, the collaboration dilemma was relatively easy to resolve. Sjahrir, for instance, was both a committed socialist and an anti-fascist; for him, as a matter of ideological principle, there could be no possibility of collaboration with the Japanese. This certainly did not imply a loyalty to the Dutch—merely rejection of the idea of working with the Japanese. He had connections with what passed for an underground or a resistance during the Occupation, and as a result, at the end of the war he had a favourable image with the Allies.

Hatta, like Sjahrir an anti-fascist, took a rather different view of relations with the Japanese, ultimately deciding to work with them— as an advisor, not an employee—after receiving assurances that they were indeed committed to supporting Indonesian independence.

The most important decision was that taken by Sukarno. In March 1942 a group of Japanese army officers came to see him in Padang, to pass on to him a proposal that he work with the Occupation authorities. In his *Autobiography*, Sukarno relates the story of this meeting, and says he agreed to help the Japanese run Indonesia in return for a Japanese pledge that they would eventually grant Indonesia its independence. He saw the decision as a purely pragmatic one, with no ideological complications.

Other Indonesians resolved the cooperation dilemma in different ways.

For some, the dilemma was less challenging than it was for the politicians. Indonesians in the civil service, for instance, having worked for the Dutch, had already demonstrated a largely apolitical approach

Tradition is evident everywhere in Indonesia, as can be seen in the dress of the soldier from the Sultan's guard at Yogyakarta.

A wood carver in Mas, Bali.

A rice goddess shrine presides over a Balinese rice field. (*Photo Milton Osborne*)

Offerings are still made to the rice goddess, but mechanised farming has replaced more labour-intensive traditional methods.

The Prambaman temple complex near Yogyakarta. Mt Merapi can be seen in the background. (*Photo Milton Osborne*)

Gods of many cultures can be found in Indonesia. This statue of Christ watches over Dili, East Timor.

The streetside hoarding above depicts former President Suharto as the Father of Development, but the anti-Suharto posters below, from Bandung in West Java, label him as a 'multidimensional clown' and a 'king without a people'.

to their jobs: or at least, a view that the best way they could help their compatriots was by ensuring that the colonial administration was as humane as possible. Much the same considerations coloured the attitude of most of them toward the Japanese. The Japanese rewarded those who stayed in the bureaucracy, promoting them to take the places of Dutch civil servants, who were interned, and giving them a degree of influence far beyond that which they had wielded earlier. True, there was no doubt that the Japanese were in ultimate charge, but they needed the civil servants' cooperation in order to manage the country. This experience positioned the civil servants well to take up similarly senior positions in the bureaucracy of an independent Indonesia.

Indonesian members of the Dutch Indies Army, the KNIL, were in a slightly different position again, having fought for the Dutch against the invading Japanese. On the Dutch surrender, many were interned, but most were subsequently released. Some later joined the police force or one of the military formations established by the Japanese, the Peta in Java and the Giyugun in Sumatera. Among the platoon commanders of the Peta was ex-KNIL Sergeant Suharto, now Lieutenant Suharto.

Indonesian artists and writers, many of whom had used their talents to support the pre-war nationalist movement, also faced difficult choices. Some cooperated with the Japanese, working for the Central Office of Culture (Keimin Bunka Shidosho) established in April 1943. The Office's objective was to produce songs, films, poems, slogans and plays carrying the message of the Japanese war aims and what was expected of the Indonesian people in support of those aims.

Others, though, refused to cooperate, attempting to retain their artistic independence in the face of Japanese censorship. The only way of getting around the censor was to hide the real meaning of a piece behind an apparently acceptable façade: the sort of thing that Sukarno and other collaborating nationalists were doing in the political arena. One such writer was Idrus, almost certainly the best short-story writer Indonesia produced during the 1940s and 1950s. In 1943 he published the short story 'Kota-Harmonie', ostensibly about a tram ride between Kota and Harmonie in war-time Jakarta, describing the city through which he was passing as a place where poverty, misery and suffering dominated. At one level, the story was simply a description of a city, but at another level Idrus clearly meant his readers to connect, in their minds, the poverty, misery and suffering he was describing with the Japanese and the Occupation.

Chairil Anwar, Indonesia's greatest twentieth-century poet, published a major poem called 'Diponegoro', ostensibly about the Java War. In part the poem read:

> For your country
> You lit a fire
> Better destruction than slavery
> Better extermination than oppression
> It may come after our death
> But life has to be life
> Forward
> Attack
> Charge
> Strike[6]

Few of Chairil's Indonesian readers would have been in any doubt that he was talking not just about Diponegoro and his struggle against the Dutch in the 1820s but also about their own struggle against the Japanese in the 1940s.

The Japanese, naturally, wanted to draw as many Indonesians as possible into support for their cause. Their first attempt to mobilise popular support was made with the formation in April 1942 of the so-called 'Triple A' Movement. The name of the organisation derived from the three slogans on which it was based: Asia led by Japan; Asia protected by Japan; Asia enlightened by Japan. It is clear from these slogans that this organisation was focused exclusively on Japan: no recognition was given to any Indonesian role, other than the passive one of being led, protected and enlightened.

In a sense, the establishment of the 'Triple A' Movement was a way of testing the resolve of the nationalist leaders who had said they would cooperate with the Japanese. Sukarno and Hatta had both qualified their promise of cooperation with the condition that Indonesian interests would have to be served, not just Japanese ones, and as Indonesian interests seemed to be completely absent in this organisation, both Sukarno and Hatta declined to take any roles within it. Other major nationalist leaders followed suit: as a result, it never got off the ground, and was dead within the year.

Sukarno played the next move in this complex game of political chess. Pushing his old theme of the need for unity in the nationalist movement, he proposed the establishment of an all-embracing political movement representing the nation as a whole. The Japanese saw the advantage of such an organisation: it would give them access to all the elements of the Indonesian political spectrum at one go, though of course there was the risk that it would run according to its own timetable rather than that of Tokyo. Nonetheless, agreement was reached and the Putera was set up on 9 March 1943: the first anniversary of the Dutch surrender.

The title Putera had a double meaning. At one level it was an abbreviation of Pusat Tenaga Rakyat, or Centre of People's Power. But *putera* is also an Indonesian word meaning 'child' or, more commonly and specifically, 'son'. Sukarno, with his usual fine grasp of political showmanship, used this double meaning to emphasise to his listeners that this organisation was one dedicated to Indonesian ends as well as Japanese ones. 'Putera', he said, was a name 'which recalls to each son of Indonesia that he is a Son of his Mother, with the responsibility to honour her so long as blood still flows in his veins and a soul still lives in his body.'

The objective of Putera, as set out in its constitution, was to: '[extend] aid and cooperation to Greater Japan for the purposes of securing the ultimate victory in the Greater East Asia War and harmonizing the operations of military government'. Being established under the auspices of the 16th Army, Putera operated only in Java. Ultimately, organisations like Putera were also established in Sumatera, but only at the level of the Residency, not the island as a whole, and as such had little capacity to mobilise large numbers of people.

Putera provided a major propaganda platform for its leaders, Sukarno and Hatta in particular. Radio was the organisation's favoured medium of communication: the Japanese were very aware of the propaganda value that could be derived from radio broadcasts, and installed public radio sets in even the smallest of villages. For the first time, just about everyone in Java was within reach of the radio, and thus of Sukarno's voice. It was a masterstroke for the nationalists.

Putera sponsored the formation of Peta, the Army of Defenders of the Homeland, in October 1943. Previously, the only quasi-military units the Japanese had permitted were the *Heiho*, a corps of auxiliary troops under exclusively Japanese officers which were to be used mainly for guard duties to relieve Japanese troops of those roles. Peta officers were Indonesian, though they were often chosen on the basis of political rather than military skills and attributes. Peta training placed great emphasis on building up the fighting spirit and national pride of members; these factors were regarded as being of greater significance than purely military skills, in line with the Japanese concept of *bushido*, 'the way of the warrior'.

Military units similar to Peta were also established in Sumatera, where they were generally referred to as Giyugun. When independence was proclaimed in August 1945, Peta and Giyugun had 65 battalions with a total of 57 000 men, of whom 37 000 were on Java.

It was also through Putera that the recruitment of *romusha*, forced labourers for the Japanese, was organised. Sukarno was personally responsible for overseeing this program, which brought hardship and suffering to tens of thousands of people. After the Occupation, and under attack for his role in the romusha program, Sukarno was at pains to argue that his participation in fact alleviated its worst aspects; that if he had not supervised it, the Japanese would have found someone else to take it on, someone much less sympathetic to the interests of the labourers than he was. This is a fairly weak argument, but it is probably the best that could be made.

Although Islamic leaders were also present in Putera, the Japanese felt a need to permit the establishment of a separate organisation to represent specifically Islamic interests. They took the view that the anti-Dutch sentiment expressed by pre-war Islam could be turned into an anti-Allied sentiment during the war, and consciously set out to woo Islamic support.

As noted earlier, before the invasion most of the major Islamic organisations had joined in the formation of a loose federation, the MIAI. In September 1942 the MIAI held its first post-invasion conference where it elected a new leadership reflective primarily of urban Muslims, and in particular the modernist Muslims of the Partai Sarekat Islam Indonesia. For the Japanese this was unfortunate, since their links with the urban modernist community were becoming increasingly tense. On issues such as the Japanese demand that Indonesians bow in the direction of the Emperor's palace in Tokyo, declare a Holy War against the Allies and cease using Arabic in Islamic schools, urban Muslims had led the resistance.

The rural traditionalist Muslim leaders seemed less opposed to Japanese ideas, and more useful too, in that they were in a position to influence a much greater proportion of the Javanese population than were the urban Muslim leaders. Thus the Japanese authorities embarked on a deliberate campaign to bypass urban Muslims and establish direct contacts with rural Muslims. To this end, in late 1943 they disbanded the MIAI and formed a new Islamic association called Masjumi, the Consultative Council of Indonesian Islam. This organisation, although it had representatives of all streams of Islam, was nonetheless clearly dominated by the rural traditionalists. Its first leaders were Kiai Haji Hasjim Ashari (founder of the Nahdatul Ulama) and his son Wahid Hasjim.

Through the Masjumi, Islam in Indonesia was able to acquire a paramilitary force for the first time. In 1944 it was permitted to establish the Hizbullah, the 'Army of Allah'. This organisation had about 50 000 members in August 1945. As with Peta, though, the Japanese ensured that it remained a defensive rather than offensive organisation. Its units had strong local ties, and were usually commanded by local religious leaders who had been given minimal military training. Unlike Peta, however, few if any Indonesian former members of the pre-war KNIL joined Hizbullah.

By early 1944 the Japanese had apparently decided that Putera was not doing enough to support the war effort, or perhaps that it was doing too much for the Indonesian cause. Supporting the war effort was becoming a pressing issue, given the situation prevailing at the time: the war was clearly turning against the Japanese, and thus the need to focus Javanese attention fully on the struggle was greater than it had been previously.

On 1 March 1944 Putera was disbanded and replaced by a new organisation—which was, significantly, known primarily by its Japanese name rather than its Indonesian one: the Jawa Hokokai, or Java Service Association—and headed by the Japanese military commander in Java. Its constitution made no mention of cooperation between Java and Japan: rather, its objectives were:

> to assist in attaining the goals of the Greater East Asia Sacred War, and to advance and execute the policies of the Military Government within a fraternity of all peoples, thereby contributing to the successful completion of the Sacred War which is the mission of the peoples of Java as a link in the Greater East Asia Co-Prosperity Sphere.[7]

Despite these objectives, its leadership brought together a wide range of Indonesians, with backgrounds in Putera and Masjumi, in the public service and the Chinese community. It was the most representative body ever assembled by the Japanese. It was also permitted, in August 1944, to form a paramilitary wing, the Barisan Pelopor (Vanguard Front). Trained for guerrilla warfare, the Front had around 80 000 members at the time of the Japanese surrender.

Even as it was being formed, however, the course of the war meant that the Jawa Hokokai was largely irrelevant to the problems faced by the Japanese in Java; the key local issue now was the Japanese attitude to Indonesian independence if, as seemed increasingly likely, the Allies won the war.

The first indications that the Japanese were considering seriously the question of Indonesian independence emerged in mid-1943, when the tide of war was already beginning to turn against them. On 16 July the Japanese Prime Minister, General Tojo, told the Japanese parliament that the government intended to find ways of 'associating the local population [of Java] more directly with the processes of government'. He reiterated this message when he visited Jakarta later in the month.

In September 1943 the Japanese established the Chuo Sangi In (the Central Advisory Council) to advise the Commander of the 16th Army on matters to do with the administration of Java. Sukarno was appointed its Chairman.

How useful this Council was to the nationalists is a matter of judgement. On the positive side, the Council's membership was entirely Indonesian. This was the first time that any quasi-governmental organisation in the Indies had been constituted in this way. On the negative side, the Council's role was purely advisory, and its membership either directly nominated by the Army commander or elected on the basis of a very limited franchise. Moreover, it covered only the island of Java. A similar organisation was eventually set up in Sumatera a year later, but none elsewhere. The Sumateran Council met only once, from

27 June to 2 July 1945. There was certainly no Advisory Council for the Indies as a whole.

In November 1943, in his capacity as Chairman of the Council, Sukarno was invited to visit Tokyo, the first time he had ever been out of Indonesia. He used the occasion, and the four meetings he had with Prime Minister Tojo, to press strongly his expectation that in return for supporting Japan in the war, Indonesia would get its independence soon. Tojo appears to have remained unmoved, and Sukarno returned to Indonesia empty-handed.

During the first half of 1944, the Japanese suffered further setbacks in Indonesia and in the Pacific. The effects of rice requisitioning had already begun to be felt in Indonesia in 1943, with instances of malnutrition and even starvation beginning to be reported. First in February 1944, and then later in the year, riots broke out in a number of parts of rural Java in protest against this policy. Japanese efforts to control these disturbances through their influence with rural Islamic leaders were unsuccessful.

In the cities, educated young people were beginning to see that with the war going against the Japanese, the time was coming when they might have the opportunity to take up arms against them. It is ironic that these young people were the very ones on whom the Japanese had expended so much propaganda effort in an attempt to bind them more closely to Japan. In fact the reverse happened; all that the Japanese propagandising and martial training had done was to strengthen their resolve to fight for Indonesian independence. The Japanese had had as little success with this part of their policy as the Dutch had had a generation earlier with the Ethical Policy. Both policies had been based on the belief that if only the young people of the Indies could come to know the occupying culture—Japanese or Dutch—more closely, they would become attracted to it, and forget about nationalism.

In June the first American bombing raids were made on Tokyo; in September American forces landed on Morotai, the first of the

Indonesian islands to be recaptured by the Allies. These reverses were sufficiently drastic to lead to the downfall of Prime Minister Tojo and his replacement by Koiso.

Koiso was much more inclined than Tojo to consider favourably Indonesian claims for independence. On 9 September 1944, he made a momentous statement to the Diet on the subject, which has become known as the Koiso Declaration. He said:

> the natives of the various areas have thoroughly comprehended the Empire's true intentions and consistently continued their tremendous efforts towards the successful climax of the Greater East Asia war; moreover, their cooperation with local military governments has been truly something to behold. In response to these circumstances and in order to ensure the permanent welfare of the East Indies, the Empire here states that their independence will be sanctioned in the future.[8]

The statement is cautious, imprecise. But for the first time since the Indies fell under Dutch control, a colonial power was acknowledging that, at some time in the future, they would be independent. Significantly, the Declaration referred to Indonesia as a whole, not just Java. Sukarno greeted the Declaration as a thorough vindication of all that he had done during the Occupation. If the nationalist movement played its cards right, independence could be achieved.

In March 1945 a somewhat clumsily named body, the Committee to Investigate Preparations for Indonesian Independence (Badan Penyelidik Usaha Persiapan Kemerdekaan Indonesia), was established, and began meetings—with a fine touch of irony—in the Jakarta building which formerly housed the Volksraad. The Committee included virtually all the established nationalist leaders: Agus Salim, Ki Hajar Dewantoro, Soetardjo, as well as Sjahrir, Sukarno and Hatta. In proportional terms, the membership of the 60-strong Committee favoured the religiously neutral nationalists; Muslims were comparatively under-represented, as were young people. Communists were absent altogether.

The job of the Committee was to draw up a Constitution for an independent Indonesia. In undertaking this job it considered a whole range of questions, some of them of great import, others relatively minor.

A few issues were quickly resolved. It was determined that the state would be a republic, not a monarchy. It would be a unitary state, not a federation—a rather more difficult question, but one where Sukarno's influence was probably felt quite strongly. To have opted for a federation, with its division of powers between a central government and the governments of the states or provinces, would have been an affront to his quarter-century of struggle to bring unity to the nationalist movement. The boundaries of the state were set as those of the old Netherlands India. There was some debate about this question, with a few Committee members arguing for the inclusion of Portuguese Timor and the states of the Malay peninsula, and a few for the exclusion of New Guinea, but these views were quickly voted down.

The one issue on which agreement was difficult to achieve was that of the position of Islam in the state. Many Muslim politicians on the Committee argued that, since the vast bulk of the Indonesian population was Muslim, the state should formally be an Islamic state. Sukarno argued against this point most vigorously. A move in this direction, he said, would be fatal to national unity. It would almost certainly have meant the secession of those parts of the archipelago in which Islam was a minority religion, places such as Bali and the Catholic and Protestant parts of east Indonesia.

Sukarno proposed that the state should simply recognise the importance of religious belief for its citizens, without specifying any particular type of religious belief. He summed up this position in a speech he made on 1 June 1945 outlining what he called the Five Principles of the Indonesian state—the *Pancasila*. The fifth of these principles was belief in God: the others were nationalism, humanitarianism, social justice and democracy. The Committee accepted this formulation. Belief in God was subsequently elevated to first position, and the Pancasila took on the status of a state philosophy.

There was one issue, though, on which the Muslims did seem to win the day. They managed to have inserted in the Preamble to the draft Constitution a requirement that Muslims obey Muslim law. The victory was, however, a short-lived one: when the provisional Indonesian parliament met later to adopt formally the draft constitution, this clause was dropped.

A proposal to incorporate a Bill of Rights in the Constitution was also rejected. Sukarno argued against the proposition on the grounds that any statement of human rights would represent a concession to individualism, and thus ought to be rejected. It was agreed that individual freedoms, such as rights of assembly, the right to work and to education, would be regulated by laws enacted by Parliament, rather than enshrined in the Constitution itself.

Finally, though the Constitution was primarily concerned with political matters, Article 33 dealt explicitly with economic issues, in ways that reflected the influence of Hatta and Sjahrir. This article required that the economy be organised cooperatively, and in accordance with what it termed 'the principle of the family system'. Quite what this meant has never been satisfactorily explained, although it probably reflects rejection of the western notions of capitalism and communism in favour of the rather romantic view of indigenous Indonesian society held by many nationalist leaders and based on the paternalistic rural village.

Other parts of Article 33 provided that nationally important branches of production, and land, water and natural resources, would be regulated by the state: 'regulated', not 'owned', reflecting the ideological mix of the nation's political leaders. Among them were Marxists and socialists who believed that land and natural resources and the means of production ought to be nationalised. A more important section of the nationalist elite consisted of members of the indigenous petty bourgeoisie: the small traders, the manufacturers of cigarettes and batik cloth, the rural landowners. Clearly these people were not going to support nationalisation of natural resources or the means of production: rather, they wanted them to be brought under benevolent government control, which (they believed) would be in their interests.

By early July 1945, the Committee had agreed upon the text of the Constitution. The only real question remaining now was exactly under what circumstances independence would be proclaimed. In late July, the Japanese authorities announced that they would recognise Indonesian independence in September, or shortly thereafter. The dropping of the atomic bombs on Hiroshima and Nagasaki on 6 and 9 August changed the complexion of events in Indonesia. On 15 August, Japan surrendered unconditionally to the Allies, presenting the Indonesian leaders with a sensitive problem. They wanted independence as soon as possible, on their terms and no one else's, but the surrender agreement with the Allies required the Japanese commanders in the Indies to maintain the political status quo until Allied forces could land and re-establish an administration.

Sukarno, Hatta and most of the other established nationalist leaders were wary of taking any unilateral step which might provoke the Japanese forces into taking action against them. The danger here seemed very real. The Japanese forces in Java and Sumatera were still intact; no one really knew how they were reacting to the news that, despite there not being any Allied soldiers on either island, they had nonetheless surrendered. It was a quite reasonable fear that any untoward incident might provoke the Japanese into taking out their frustrations on the Indonesians, with deadly consequences. Thus these leaders wanted to proceed cautiously with the proclamation of independence, ensuring that it was done according to a timetable that the Japanese were aware of well in advance.

But radical young people, the *pemuda*, disagreed strongly. In their view, independence had to be seized as soon as possible, in order to show the world that the proclamation of independence was actually made by Indonesians, and not something tainted in the post-war world by having been undertaken in collaboration with the Japanese. On 16 August Sukarno and Hatta were kidnapped by a group of pemuda who wanted to force their hand and declare independence immediately. Sukarno and Hatta refused to do this, but did negotiate an arrangement whereby the proclamation would be made the following day, after the Japanese commander had been informed unofficially about what was going to happen and had agreed not to intervene.

Thus it was that on the morning of 17 August 1945, in front of his house in Jakarta, Sukarno read the following proclamation:

> We the people of Indonesia hereby declare our independence. Matters concerning the transfer of power, etc., will be attended to in an orderly fashion and as speedily as possible.
> In the name of the People of Indonesia.
> Sukarno and Hatta.

7
FROM REVOLUTION TO AUTHORITARIAN RULE 1945–1957

In little more than a decade, from the proclamation of Indonesian independence to the demise of the system of parliamentary or constitutional democracy late in the 1950s, Indonesia went through perhaps the most turbulent years of the century. It started out having to fight off the Dutch, who were determined to return to their colony and re-establish their authority there. Once this had been achieved, the much more difficult task began: that of trying to give substance to the nation's independence, and in particular to devise political and economic systems which would satisfy the expectations of the citizens of the new Indonesia. It was to prove to be a task beyond the capabilities of the nation's first generation of political leaders.

To declare independence was a relatively easy task; to give substance to that proclamation was far harder. We have already seen that the pre-war nationalist movement was divided (among other issues) on the question of whether to cooperate with the Dutch. Those who did co-operate argued that the most effective way to pursue the cause of independence was through negotiation, that the Dutch were too strong to confront directly, and in any event open to persuasion through rational argument. The non-cooperators, in contrast, believed that provided they were united in anti-colonial mass action, the Indonesian people could make the Indies ungovernable for the Dutch, and eventually drive them out. Thus confrontation was for them the only way of securing true independence. Supporters of the non-cooperation principle included Hatta, Sjahrir and most notably Sukarno.

During the Occupation much the same question arose with respect to the Japanese, though now Sukarno and Hatta were leading cooperators; Sjahrir and members of the underground, including its putative leader Amir Sjarifuddin, remained firmly in the non-cooperation camp.

By late 1945 the issue had surfaced once again, and this time caused a breach in Indonesian political ranks which was to remain a characteristic of national politics at least until the late 1950s. There were in fact two questions to be asked here: What were the nation's objectives in the struggle against the Dutch? and What were the best strategies to be followed in pursuit of those objectives?

One group of leaders saw the goal of the nationalist struggle as being primarily the achievement of political independence: removing the Dutch colonial administration and replacing it with an Indonesian one. The latter would clearly be more democratic than the former because it would be based on the consent of those it governed, and would ultimately be legitimised through national elections. Major social and economic changes would take place only gradually, avoiding any unnecessary interruptions to national life. The most prominent of the politicians in this camp were Hatta and Sjahrir.

In the other camp were those who saw the struggle as having much broader immediate objectives. Certainly political independence was essential; but so was social and economic independence. What use was it to have Indonesians in control of the national parliament, for instance, if foreigners still controlled the economy and society was still governed by old, feudal hierarchies? Sukarno fell into this camp, though in the early months of the revolution a more prominent exponent was Tan Malaka, the communist leader from the 1920s who had slipped back into Indonesia from exile in 1942. He popularised the catch-cry '100 per cent Independence!' to capture what he saw as the fundamental objective of the anti-colonial struggle.

The second question—of the methods to be used in the struggle —also saw a binary divide in the political elite.

One group, in which socialists and communists were well represented, along with radical youths and many former members of Peta, argued that the Dutch would only surrender the Indies if forced to do so: the old non-cooperation argument. This meant that every opportunity had to be taken to put pressure on the Dutch, through military force and popular mass action. Dutch forces, they argued, were far weaker than they had been during the colonial era, exhausted by the effort of fighting the war in Europe and in the Pacific, and thus could be defeated. Some members of this group also argued that military force and mass action would need to be directed not just against the Dutch but also against those Indonesians who wanted to retain the existing social and economic order. As a result, places such as Aceh, north Sumatera, Banten and the northwest coast of central Java in 1945–46 were to see violent intra-Indonesian clashes instigated by local radicals aimed at the elimination of indigenous power holders. In the case of Aceh, for example, the outcome of this conflict was the almost complete extirpation of the traditional aristocracy (uleebalang) by religious officials and scholars (ulama) and their youthful supporters. A major clash also took place at Madiun in east Java in 1948, between leftist radicals and the Indonesian army. Between 1945 and

1949 more Indonesians were to die in clashes with other Indonesians than in the fighting with the Dutch.

The second group took the view that, weak as the Dutch might be, they had powerful backers, especially in Britain and the United States (and in the early months of the revolution, Australia as well). Moreover, the Republic's own military forces were not strong in any conventional sense. Their greatest strength lay in small-scale guerilla warfare: fighting in this way, the Indonesians certainly could not be defeated by the Dutch, but neither could they drive the Dutch out of Indonesia. Moreover, to encourage mass action against the Dutch would be to invite not only huge casualties but also anarchy. The way to weaken the Dutch was not to challenge them militarily, but rather to negotiate with them and, in particular, to try to swing foreign support away from them and towards the Republic. Hatta and Sjahrir were prominent members of this group.

In practice, of course, the dichotomy was by no means as clear-cut as this, as most political leaders drew on both camps, to a greater or lesser degree, for support. Nor was membership of the groups static: there was movement between them as circumstances changed. But for virtually the entire period of the revolution, the balance of political power was in the hands of leaders who favoured negotiation, or diplomacy, over military struggle against the Dutch.

However, these questions were still in prospect when independence was declared on 17 August. In Jakarta, following the proclamation the leadership moved quickly both to consolidate their own positions and to begin the process of establishing the organs of state. The PPPKI formally adopted the Constitution previously agreed upon (less the requirement for Muslims to obey Islamic law), appointed Sukarno and Hatta President and Vice-President respectively, and established a system of regional administration based on a division of the Republic into seven provinces each headed by a nominated governor. Twelve government ministries were set up, and plans laid for the appointment of members to an interim parliament, the

Indonesian Central National Committee or Komite Nasional Indonesia Pusat (KNIP).

These moves were all clearly of major importance. But there was an air of unreality about them in that, for the moment anyway, the government actually had little to govern.

The authority of the Republican Government was limited, in part as a result of the different policies applied in different parts of the country by the Occupation authorities. Thus its position was strongest in Java, and much weaker on the other islands. But it was also limited by the fact that it was extremely wary of taking any action that would bring it into conflict with the Japanese authorities which, although formally defeated, were in fact in control of much of central and western Indonesia. With the exception of eastern Indonesia, Japanese forces remained intact and undefeated by the Allies after their surrender. Jakarta, for instance, was not re-occupied by the Allies until late September, six weeks after the Japanese surrender and the proclamation of independence. How Japanese troops would react to the proclamation of independence and the establishment of an Indonesian government was unknown. Most would probably have little on their minds other than repatriation to Japan, but others might well support either the Republicans or the returning Dutch. Certainly the Allies had instructed them to maintain the status quo until their own troops could be assembled and landed in Indonesia.

After the independence proclamation, some Japanese troops were sympathetic enough to allow Indonesians to seize weapons and equipment from them, with or without token resistance, but few were willing to jeopardise their futures for the Republican cause. Republican leaders thus had to ensure, so far as possible, that there were no clashes between Indonesians anxious to seize control of the state and its apparatus, and the Japanese.

News of the proclamation of independence filtered out of Jakarta only slowly. Except for some of the better-informed, mostly urban groups, for some time at least it was treated with caution as people sought to weigh up just what it might mean. But once the news did sink in, it provoked a variety of reactions.

Thus in Bukittinggi, the centre of the Japanese administration of Sumatera, local young people took the initiative to show their support for the Republic, in the absence of any official representatives of the new government. Their actions were primarily symbolic: raising the Indonesian red and white flag, scrawling nationalist slogans on public buildings and distributing pamphlets explaining the meaning of the proclamation of independence. In Aceh, young people also took the lead in promoting the cause of the Republic, but here they were aligned with religious leaders, the ulama, who had spearheaded the resistance to Dutch colonialism.

In eastern Indonesia the situation was more difficult, both because during the Occupation the Japanese authorities here had been much more restrictive of the nationalist movement than their counter-parts in Java and Sumatera, and because the progress of the war had seen many parts of the region fall to Allied troops, mostly Australian. These forces were preparing to hand their regions over to returning Dutch troops who, of course, were intent on preventing any displays of Republican sentiment. There were demonstrations of support for the Republican cause in these areas, but they were muted. Only in south Sulawesi and in Bali were representatives of the central government in reasonably secure control of their regions.

In Java, the news travelled more swiftly than in Sumatera and the eastern islands, but the reach of the central government was not much greater. By mid-September, the news of the proclamation had reached all the major cities, and produced a series of demonstrations to indicate support for the Republic. Major rallies were held in Surabaya on 11 and 17 September, but by far the biggest was held in Jakarta on 9 September, when a crowd estimated at 200 000 gathered in what is now Medan Merdeka (Freedom Square) in the centre of the city. These rallies were all organised by local people, quite outside the formal structure of government.

These 'unofficial' activities presented a real dilemma for the government because of the danger that they would get out of hand and provoke clashes with the Japanese. In trying to avoid this possibility, the government was well served by having Sukarno as its leader. He was a known quantity to the Japanese, someone they had dealt with in the past and, at least to some extent, someone they trusted. He had widespread support among Indonesians: he was the country's best-known leader, and a superb communicator. It was Sukarno who, after a brief speech, persuaded the 200 000 demonstrators in Medan Merdeka to disperse peacefully, preventing a clash with the heavily armed Japanese troops surrounding the square. But even Sukarno was unable to prevent clashes between Japanese troops and radical youth groups in Bandung, Semarang and Surabaya, which left substantial casualties on both sides.

Dealing with the Japanese was not the only external challenge the Republican government faced. It knew that Allied forces would eventually land in central and western Indonesia, and attempt to reassert control. The first such landings, by British and Indian troops, were at Jakarta on 30 September; Medan and Padang were reoccupied in mid-October, and Semarang, Surabaya and Palembang later that month. From around this time on, the Republican government had to deal with the Allies rather than the Japanese. Sukarno was now a liability rather than an asset.

For all his protestations of having worked with the Japanese only to further the cause of Indonesian independence, the Allies saw Sukarno as a Japanese collaborator and thus at best an undesirable person to deal with, and at worst someone who should be tried for complicity in Japanese aggression and war crimes. For those leaders who saw negotiation as the key to defeating the Dutch, this was a major problem.

The Indonesian leader most acceptable to the Allies was Sjahrir, who was not tainted in any way by collaboration with the Japanese. In October–November 1945, largely in reaction to these considerations, the provisional government appointed Sjahrir Prime Minister—a post not mentioned in the recently adopted Constitution—and in effect reduced Sukarno's status to that of figurehead. He was still head of state, but no longer head of government, making it more difficult for the Dutch to argue that the Republican government was in the hands of former collaborators with the Japanese. Although the Prime Ministership changed hands several times during the revolution, this political system was maintained; indeed, it was only replaced in 1957 when Sukarno reasserted Presidential authority.

This shift in political power was not enough to prevent clashes breaking out between Allied troops and Indonesian fighters. The heaviest fighting was in the East Java capital of Surabaya in November 1945, where Indonesians fought a determined street battle against Allied troops supported by British aircraft and warships in Surabaya harbour, eventually being worn down by sheer weight of numbers. The Battle of Surabaya, as it came to be called, convinced the British that they should withdraw from Indonesia as quickly as possible. Having just emerged from six years of world war, British public opinion was in no mood to see British lives lost in a colonial conflict in which British interests were, at best, only peripherally involved. Moreover, given that the bulk of the troops under British command in Indonesia were actually Indian, London came under increasingly heavy pressure from New Delhi to ensure that these troops were not involved in fighting against what was seen as a fellow nationalist movement.

The international attention paid to the battle, and particularly to the strong resistance the Indonesians put up against the British, confirmed the views of those Indonesians who had been arguing that the Republic needed not only politicians and diplomats to negotiate with the Dutch, but also an army to back those negotiators up.

When independence was proclaimed, the government had been reluctant to establish an army for fear of provoking a clash with the Japanese; not until 5 October did they establish the People's Security Army, Tentara Keamanan Rakyat (TKR). At this time Indonesia had two groups of men available to it with some military training. First, there were the soldiers who had been pre-war members of the KNIL; they had had good professional military training, but were tainted in the eyes of many Republican leaders because they had served the Dutch cause. Second, there were those who had been members of the wartime Peta; their military training might have been somewhat lacking, but their devotion to the revolutionary cause was undoubted.

In addition, any number of para- or quasi-military groups had sprung up to fight the Dutch, often with few weapons and little if any formal military training. Some were associated with Islamic groups such as the wartime Hizbullah, linked with the Masjumi; others had links with various radical youth groups; others still were little more than bandits taking advantage of the disturbed times to win for themselves an element of respectability, while seizing whatever opportunities were available to enrich themselves.

The TKR was placed under the command of ex-KNIL Major Urip Sumohardjo, the highest-ranking Indonesian ever to serve in the colonial army. Urip's job was to fashion a Republican army primarily out of former members of the KNIL and Peta; a particularly difficult task, given the degree of mistrust between these two groups. Indeed, it very quickly became evident that in one important sense at least the job was beyond his capabilities. In November 1945 senior officers of the TKR met in Yogyakarta and, in a reflection of the kind of democratic spirit which was to characterise the army for much of the revolution, decided that they would elect their own commander. Urip was defeated in this election by Sudirman, a former Peta member, and relegated to the position of Chief of Staff; he died in November 1948.

By the end of 1945, the Republican army was led primarily by ex-Peta officers.

Meanwhile the two-pronged diplomatic-military strategy for dealing with the Dutch was coming under strong challenge from a radical nationalist group focused on Tan Malaka, the former communist leader. This group argued that Sjahrir and his colleagues had underestimated the fighting will of the Indonesian people; that if the Republic undertook a radical program of social and economic reform, aimed at eliminating Dutch interests and influences, then the Indonesian people would flock to the independence cause, exerting irresistible pressure on the Dutch. Diplomatic compromise was unjustified. Tan Malaka assembled a broad coalition of forces supporting this cause.

By early 1946 this movement, called the Persatuan Perjuangan, or Struggle Union, had achieved enormous popularity, leaving Sjahrir so isolated that he felt compelled to resign as Prime Minister. His opponents, however, although united enough to achieve his removal, were not united enough to replace him. As soon as he had resigned and the Persatuan Perjuangan seemed poised to initiate a program of radical reform, the coalition behind it began to crumble. The political process was stalemated and Sukarno intervened to reappoint Sjahrir as Prime Minister. Sjahrir in turn exploited the divisions among his challengers to construct a somewhat broader government and in this way survived the challenge. Once reinstated, moreover, he had Tan Malaka arrested and detained without trial until September 1948.

With Sjahrir confirmed in power, negotiations with the Dutch became the government's first priority. Eventually, under pressure from the British who desperately wanted a means of withdrawing from the Indies, the two sides reached a grudging agreement at Linggajati in West Java in November 1946. This agreement provided that by 1 January 1949 Indonesia would become independent as a federation joining the Republic (on Java and Sumatera) and two still-to-be-created states of Borneo and the Great East (Sulawesi, Nusa Tenggara, Maluku and West New Guinea).

Federalism was a principle strongly supported by the Dutch, and in particular by the Lieutenant Governor-General, van Mook. He argued that federalism would accord the best degree of protection for the non-Javanese peoples of the archipelago, while still allowing Jakarta to retain full and appropriate sovereignty over national issues such as defence, currency, foreign relations and the like. His proposals attracted a good degree of support outside Java, especially in those regions where sympathy with the Dutch had traditionally been strong, including some (though by no means all) of the Christian areas. But the Republican government saw the proposal as simply another Dutch tactic to 'divide and rule' Indonesia. It believed that the federal states to be set up outside Java would be simply Dutch puppets, independent in name only and still heavily dependent on the Netherlands for political and economic decision making. To form a federation with such bodies would have implied a quite unacceptable diminution of the sovereignty of the state. It was a measure of the Republic's determination to achieve recognition of its independence almost at any price that, despite very clear reservations, it was prepared to sign the Linggajati Agreement, though it was not formally ratified by the KNIP until March 1947.

The agreement served one of its purposes: it provided the British with an exit from the Indies. But neither of the main protagonists, the Indonesians and the Dutch, was ever fully supportive of it, each seeing it as giving too many concessions to the other. The tempo of clashes between the two sides, temporarily reduced, picked up again. Eventually, in July 1947, the Dutch launched a military invasion of the Republic, alleging Republican violations of the agreement.

In this so-called 'police action' the Dutch secured a series of military successes, seizing half the Republic's territory on Java as well as its richest territories on Sumatera. Politically, however, they failed to destroy the Republic and may indeed have strengthened its resolve. The action also brought the United Nations directly into the dispute for the first time, and indirectly sparked off what was to be a crisis of enormous significance for the future of the Republic.

In response to the Dutch action, India and Australia brought the situation to the attention of the UN Security Council in July; the Council then established a three-member Good Offices Committee (GOC) to help find a peaceful resolution to the conflict. The Committee consisted of Belgium (chosen by the Dutch), Australia (chosen by the Indonesians) and the United States (chosen by the other two members). Under GOC auspices, negotiations between the two sides took place in January 1948 and produced the Renville Agreement, named for the American ship on which the negotiations had taken place. Under the agreement, the Republic conceded to the Dutch the territories that it had lost in the attack, in return for another Dutch promise of eventual independence.

The conclusion of this agreement caused great division within Republican ranks, many of the more radical political leaders, both Muslim and left-wing, seeing it as a sell-out to the Dutch. Popular opposition to the agreement was such as to force the resignation of the government which had signed it. Sukarno then appointed Vice-President Hatta as the new Prime Minister.

The Republic which Hatta now led, however, was facing very considerable economic difficulties, particularly given the loss of the fertile food and export producing territories which had fallen under Dutch control. The government's response was an austerity program which included reducing the numbers of civil servants and disbanding army units that were surplus to its requirements. All of this contributed to a growing sense of grievance in an increasingly tense political environment.

These moves were quickly exploited by the government's opponents. The Communist Party, growing rapidly in strength following its emergence from a shadowy underground existence in late 1945, for the first time adopted a program of radical social reform and uncompromising confrontation with the Dutch. Its new radicalism took on greater sharpness with the return from the Soviet Union of Musso, who had been a party leader at the time of the abortive 1926-27 uprisings. The party's cadres began a determined campaign to drum up support among the workers and peasants of the Republic.

Tensions between the government and its opponents culminated in the East Java city of Madiun in 1948 with a coup by the local PKI supported by leftist army units, and the formation of a communist government. The Hatta government denounced the coup as an uprising against the state. Faced with a choice between denouncing his supporters and confronting Hatta, Musso sided with the rebels, accused the Hatta government of betraying the ideals of the revolution and announced a full-scale communist uprising. Brutal civil war followed. Within a month, however, the left was defeated. Musso was killed and other leftist leaders arrested; some were later to be summarily executed by government forces in December 1948. The Madiun Affair left communism with a taint of betrayal which made it permanently suspect in the eyes of the army leadership. The memory of this 'betrayal' is still strong today, and is frequently cited when Indonesians want to point to the untrustworthiness of the PKI.

The Madiun Affair had one very important international consequence. The United States, which up to this point had remained largely neutral in the Indonesian–Dutch conflict, now came down on the side of the Indonesians. The Republic had, after all, just put down a communist rebellion, at a time when in Asia and Europe communism seemed to be surging forward. This American sympathy for the Republic was to be crucially important at the end of the year.

In December, taking advantage of what was seen to be the military weakness of the Republic, the Dutch launched a second military attack, this one designed to eliminate the Republic altogether. The Republic's provisional capital at Yogyakarta in central Java was captured, along with Sukarno, Hatta and most of the Cabinet. However, the army held out against the Dutch, the only instrument of the Indonesian state to do so, and in this way ensured that the state would survive as an independent and non-communist entity.

The Dutch were thus unable to secure a quick military victory, the one thing which might have caused the United States to ignore their actions. As it was, Washington was concerned that an extended period of guerilla warfare would give the communists and their military allies the chance to stage a comeback, something which it obviously saw as highly undesirable. Strong American diplomatic pressure, including the threat of cutting off the post-war reconstruction assistance being supplied to the Netherlands through the Marshall Plan, was thus exerted on the Dutch. This pressure, together with the realisation by the Dutch that they were ill-prepared militarily or politically to fight a long guerilla campaign, eventually forced a change of policy on the part of the government in The Hague. They restored Sukarno and Hatta to Yogyakarta and began yet another round of negotiations at what was called the Round Table Conference, which led this time to a formal Dutch recognition of Indonesian independence in December 1949.

Indonesians could justifiably claim that theirs was the first Asian nation to proclaim its independence, and the first to successfully defend that independence in the face of armed resistance by the former colonial power. Pride in this achievement remains at the centre of Indonesian political consciousness today.

The Indonesian army ended the revolution in a relatively strong political position. Its top-level leadership had by now passed firmly into the hands of officers who had received their initial military training in the KNIL: both the Chief of Staff of the Armed Forces, General Simatupang, and the Chief of Staff of the Army, Colonel Nasution, had been trained at the Dutch military academy at Bandung. The army's continued and, to an extent, successful resistance to the Dutch at the time of the second attack on the Republic, when the members of the civilian cabinet had allowed themselves to be arrested, had encouraged army members to believe that the major contribution to the success of the revolution had been theirs.

But the army had identified two enemies during the revolutionary period, enemies that were to remain part of the military's mythology for decades to come. One was communism. The other was Islam.

Most politically active Muslims were prepared to accept the religious compromises implicit in the 1945 Constitution, at least during the revolution. However, one group did not: those who wanted to see

Indonesia made into an Islamic state, with the consequent application of Islamic law to all Indonesian Muslims. In 1948, a group of such Muslims had formed the Indonesian Islamic State, usually called the Darul Islam (literally 'Abode of Islam'), based in West Java and South Sulawesi. The Indonesian army soon found itself fighting not just the Dutch but also the troops of the Darul Islam. To many in the army leadership, the actions of the Darul Islam represented a fundamental betrayal of the state. The Darul Islam was never a serious military threat to Indonesia, but its continued existence was a constant reminder to Jakarta that the problem of the position of Islam in the state had still not been resolved.

The ethnic Chinese community came out of the revolution in a rather mixed position. During the revolution, some prominent ethnic Chinese sided with the Republic. A few became members of the Republican parliament, representing parties as diverse as the PKI, Indonesian Socialist Party, the Partai Sosialis Indonesia or PSI, the Catholic Party and the Christian (that is, Protestant) Party. A very few—noticeable, perhaps, precisely because there were so few of them—were elected to parliament to represent Muslim parties such as the Masjumi and, after 1947, the Partai Sarekat Islam Indonesia or PSII. Four became Cabinet ministers, including one from the PSII. Other Chinese gave financial support to the Republican cause. Certainly more Chinese supported the Republic during the revolution than had ever supported the nationalist movement in the late colonial era.

However, the extent of this support was overshadowed, in the popular Indonesian view at least, by the fact that many other Chinese did not support the Republic. Some formed the Pao An Tui, or Peace Protection Corps, an armed militia aimed at protecting Chinese property from attacks by Indonesian guerrilla fighters. Although this militia had no formal connections with the Dutch, for obvious reasons it was seen by many Republicans as giving support to the colonialists' cause. Other prominent ethnic Chinese gave support and funds to the Dutch.

At the end of the revolution, the political position of the ethnic Chinese was thus ambivalent. The community had not sided enthusiastically with the Republic, as the Arab community for instance had done. Certain individual Chinese had rendered strong, public and valuable service to the Republic; but they were generally seen as having acted as individuals, not as representatives of their community. Thus, while individual ethnic Chinese might have emerged from the Revolution with honour in Republican eyes, the same was not true of the community as a whole, which was regarded with suspicion by many—perhaps most—indigenous Indonesians.

Ironically, the politicians who had led the revolution were also in an ambivalent position. Their leadership of the Indonesian nation was now internationally recognised—but the price of this recognition had been significant concessions to the Dutch, which weakened their domestic position, especially with respect to their critics, on both the left and the right.

At the political level, it was not the unitary Republic of Indonesia whose independence had been recognised in December 1949, but rather the federal Republic of the United States of Indonesia, the Republik Indonesia Serikat or RIS, of which the Republic was just one of sixteen member states. Moreover, the RIS was a partner with the Kingdom of the Netherlands in the Netherlands–Indonesian Union, headed by the Dutch monarch. Even more serious, the Dutch retained control of the western half of the island of New Guinea, previously regarded as an integral part of the Netherlands Indies and thus also of Indonesia.

The deal the Republic's representatives negotiated in the economic field was no more favourable to Indonesian interests. The Round Table Conference Agreement provided that the Republican government would continue to recognise all the rights, concessions and licences which had been granted by the colonial government, and which were still valid in 1949. In effect, this meant that the Indonesian government agreed to honour all the agreements under

171

which Dutch capital had been able to exploit the resources of the Indies. This meant that in 1950:

- the Indonesian banking system was dominated by seven banks, all foreign-owned;
- the nation's central bank, the Java Bank, which held the country's foreign exchange reserves and issued the nation's currency, was a private Dutch-owned company;
- inter-island shipping was the virtual monopoly of the Dutch-owned KPM line;
- in 1952, the first post-war year for which reasonably reliable data are available, just four Dutch firms handled 50 per cent of all consumer goods imported into Indonesia.

The Agreement further provided that there was to be no nationalisation or expropriation of Dutch-owned enterprises except under very limited circumstances, and then only provided appropriate compensation was paid. Finally, the Republic agreed to accept responsibility for the repayment of the public debt of the Netherlands Indies, which amounted in 1949 to some f.4300 million, or approximately US$1125 million. Of this sum, 30 per cent was to be repaid in hard foreign currency.

In the military field, Indonesia agreed to accept a Dutch military mission of 600 men to assist with the training of the Indonesian armed forces. Almost to a man, the top leadership of the armed forces was opposed to this provision. They believed that the Dutch could teach them very little about military matters—had they not just defeated the Dutch army during the revolution? Their opposition was largely responsible for the mission's withdrawal in early 1953.

The Agreement also required the Indonesian armed forces to accept as members any Indonesian individuals or units which had served with the KNIL or any other Dutch military unit. Since the alternatives to joining the Indonesian armed forces were repatriation to the Netherlands or demobilisation and the prospect of facing a long period of unemployment, a relatively large number of such men opted to join the Indonesian army. Many, though, had served a lifetime with the KNIL, and had borne the brunt of the Dutch military efforts against the Republic. Not surprisingly, there was a great deal of suspicion and doubt on both sides about how successfully these units could be integrated into the regular Indonesian military, whose enemies they had been until recently.

Not surprisingly, the fact that the country's political leaders had agreed to these provisions confirmed, in the minds of many military men, that those leaders were at best naive when it came to defending the country's interests, and at worst thoroughly incompetent. This impression, like the suspicion of communism and Islam, was to remain with the leadership of the military in the ensuing decades, down to the present day. Much of the military's subsequent behaviour can only be explained by reference to its experiences during the revolution. The period shaped not only its professional doctrine and tactics, but also its political alliances and prejudices.

By January 1950, while Indonesia was politically independent, the questions posed at the outset of the revolution concerning its aims and its methods remained largely unresolved in the eyes of many Indonesians. For some national leaders, the revolution had meant a change of regime, a change from Dutch rule to Indonesian rule, but little else. These leaders considered that the revolution was over, and the task now facing the government and the state was one of rebuilding Indonesia's political, economic and social bases. Much of the detail of those bases had to be changed. Thus, for instance, great emphasis was now to be laid on extending educational and health facilities, with the object of improving the welfare of all Indonesians. There was agreement on the need to see control of the economy fall into Indonesian hands. The basic parameters within which the society would operate were to be similar to those operating in many western European countries at the time. The economic system was to remain mixed, a substantial degree of government intervention leavening a generally capitalist base. Foreign capital might be limited, but was not to be eliminated. The political system was to be parliamentary, and ultimately to be legitimated by general elections. Civilian authority was to be exerted over the military. Freedom of the press and of trade unions was to be respected. The arts were to be free of overt government influence. It was this group of leaders who had argued for acceptance of the 1949 Round Table Conference agreements, not because they were ideal for Indonesia, but rather because they represented the best that could be achieved without further, damaging prolongation of the war with the Dutch.

On the other hand were those leaders who believed that the revolution had not achieved its goals by December 1949; that the process of struggle against foreign domination and for Indonesian independence had not ended, but merely entered a new phase. The struggle from 1945 to 1949 had been against the formal institutions of colonialism. The struggle now was against the colonialism of ideas, the colonialism of the mind. These leaders believed that independence would only have been achieved when all unwanted foreign influence had been driven out of the country: political, economic, cultural. An economic system had to be created which served Indonesian interests, not foreign ones; in particular, a system which served the interests of Indonesian peasants and factory workers. The arts had to serve a social cause. The political system had to reflect Indonesian political values, not Dutch ones. These leaders had been dissatisfied with the 1949 agreement with the Dutch, believing that the government had compromised far too much.

This picture is, to some extent, an exaggerated one; there were very few national leaders whose ideas fell wholly into one camp, with no leakage to the other. And there were some issues—Irian Jaya was one—on which the two camps were united. And for a small number of leaders, the revolution was seen to have virtually no meaning at all—this was true especially of the leaders of the Darul Islam movement, for whom the Dutch and the Republicans were equally unacceptable. But among the mainstream Indonesian leadership there were these two clear loci of national opinion.

People such as Hatta and Sjahrir epitomised the first group; gradually Sukarno and the PKI came to represent the latter. For perhaps the first seven years of the 1950s, it was the first group which determined the course of national development. But as the decade wore on, more and more people drifted away from this camp toward the other, so that when Sukarno moved to seize power in 1957 there was no effective opposition.

The first major political issue the Indonesian state faced after the recognition of its independence was its formal structure: specifically, whether it would remain a federal state, with power shared between the central and provincial governments, or revert to a unitary format, in which the power of the central government was unchallenged. The Republic of Indonesia established in 1945 had been unitary, but it was the federal Republic of the United States of Indonesia (RUSI) whose independence the Dutch had recognised in 1949. The Republic of Indonesia, with its capital now at Yogyakarta, had become just one of fifteen provinces that constituted the RUSI.

On this issue there was little difference between the political leaders. Federalism was widely seen in Jakarta as something which had been inflicted upon Indonesia by the Dutch, with the deliberate intention of making the central government weak and the provinces strong. This, it was believed, would prolong Dutch influence by ensuring there would be divisions within the Indonesian state which could be exploited by Dutch sympathisers, especially in the eastern islands of the archipelago. Immediately after Dutch acknowledgement of Indonesian independence, a carefully orchestrated campaign began to see the federal state abolished and replaced by a unitary one.

The campaign was very successful. During the first seven months of 1950, the governments of the federal states one by one were persuaded to amalgamate their territories into the Yogyakarta-based

Republic of Indonesia. Only in the southern Maluku islands was there any serious and prolonged opposition to the idea. But on 17 August 1950, the fifth anniversary of the proclamation of independence, Sukarno announced that the federal system had been abandoned and the unitary republic restored. A temporary Constitution was drawn up and adopted, on the understanding that a Constituent Assembly would shortly be elected to undertake the task of writing a permanent Constitution for the country.

There was widespread recognition that full economic independence was still some way off. In particular, it was acknowledged that Dutch and ethnic Chinese interests effectively controlled all the important aspects of the national economy. The problem was to work out how this stranglehold on the economy could be loosened and eventually removed.

As noted earlier, before the Dutch arrival in the Indies, and for some time afterwards, indigenous Indonesians had been active commercially as producers and traders of a wide range of commodities. During the eighteenth century these Indonesian entrepreneurs had been overwhelmed at the level of international trade and investment by Dutch commercial power, and at the local level by the Chinese, whose immigration to the Indies, and business activities, the Dutch encouraged. In 1950, as a result, indigenous business was particularly weak.

To many Indonesian policy-makers it seemed that the only way that they could assert Indonesian control over the national economy was through state intervention: the indigenous private business sector was simply not strong enough to undertake this task on its own. Through to the present day successive Indonesian governments, of various political persuasions, have retained the view that government intervention was needed in order to liberate the economy from foreign control.

A second effect of colonialism had been to give private capitalism a bad name. Political colonialism was seen as being backed by an economic system that Indonesians characterised as capitalist. Since colonialism was regarded by Indonesian nationalists as unquestionably a bad thing, so capitalism was tainted as well. Thus even had there been a substantial indigenous capitalist class present in Indonesia in 1950, it is still likely that the government would have sought to regulate and to curb its activities.

To the present day, the word 'capitalism' or the phrase 'economic liberalism' carry discomforting overtones in Indonesia. A nationwide public opinion poll conducted in 1999 found that while Indonesians were enthusiastic about democracy, they were ambivalent at best about a free-market economy. Forty-one per cent said they would prefer an economic system which is essentially controlled by the government, while only 31 per cent favoured one with little government control.

In order to try to redress these perceived inequities, all governments in Jakarta between 1950 and 1957 proclaimed that it was a major objective of their programs that control of the economy would be taken out of foreign hands—often meaning ethnic Chinese as well as Dutch—and put back into the hands of Indonesians. In fact, though, at best only piecemeal efforts were made to achieve these economic goals.

Commercial agriculture would have seemed to have been an obvious place to start, given the extent to which this sector of the economy was dominated by foreign capital: Dutch, other European, American and, to a lesser extent, Chinese. During the revolution a number of Dutch-owned estates, especially on Sumatera, had been occupied by local squatters, who began to cultivate them for themselves, producing food rather than commercial crops. With the recognition of sovereignty in 1949, the Dutch lessees of these estates called on the government in Jakarta to take action to clear their lands of these squatters.

Here was an almost classic case of conflict between foreign companies and indigenous peasants, a situation where one might readily have expected to see government firmly rejecting Dutch pressure and stepping in on the side of the peasants, perhaps buying, perhaps even nationalising, the estates and dividing the land up among the squatters. But up to 1957, governments in Jakarta not only did not take this step, they actively opposed the squatters and deployed their security forces on the side of the lessees.

In other Dutch-controlled areas of the economy, too, little action was taken to strengthen Indonesian control. In 1955, Jakarta did unilaterally abrogate the financial and economic conditions of the sovereignty recognition agreements, much to the chagrin of the Dutch. But in other respects the position of Dutch capital in Indonesia was protected. The whole emphasis in economic policy was on restoration of the economy to the prosperous position it had enjoyed in the days before the depression, two or more decades ago.

Efforts to reduce the importance of Chinese capital in the economy were pushed ahead with perhaps slightly greater fervour, though not necessarily with any more positive results. Especially under the Prime Ministership of the PNI politician Ali Sastroamidjojo (1953–55)—Hatta's fellow-accused in The Hague 20 years earlier—governments in Jakarta tried to institute policies to restrict the economic activities of Chinese entrepreneurs and strengthen the position of indigenous businesspeople. The standard means used to achieve this end, one which would have been familiar to the 1930s Dutch colonial bureaucrats, was through a system of licences and permits available only to firms controlled by indigenous Indonesians. But all that the system of licences and permits did was to create a new industry—evading the system. This era saw the emergence of firms in which the majority of the shareholders, or the majority membership of the Board of Directors, were ostensibly indigenous Indonesians; the firms could thus benefit from the government licences or credits or what-have-you, which had been reserved for indigenous-owned enterprises. In reality, the real power and authority in these firms was still held by Chinese, who simply used the indigenous Indonesians as fronts for their activities. As Ali himself was later to acknowledge in his autobiography, his policy initiatives here ran into problems. The speed with which this policy was implemented:

> resulted in a lack of detailed examination and in the issuing of commercial licences to people who had no experience in trade and commerce. The result was that many Indonesians sold their licences to Chinese businessmen, and became scornfully known as 'briefcase businessmen'.[1]

The general picture of the economic policies pursued during most of the 1950s, then, was that they were remarkably similar to the kinds of policies which had been followed before the war, before independence. Private Dutch and Chinese capital was still in a commanding position. No substantial or effective moves had been made to nationalise any of the major enterprises run by Dutch or Chinese interests, with the one major exception of the Java Bank, which became Bank Indonesia in 1952. The government was still in the position of being the supplier of the economic and administrative infrastructure to private capital.

The reasons for these policy decisions on the part of the government are not particularly difficult to find. In general, governments in Jakarta believed that some limits on the nation's economic sovereignty were the price that had to be paid for restoration of the economy. Those in command were, after all, in the main western-trained, often with degrees from Dutch universities, whose outlooks on matters political and economic were remarkably similar to those of their Dutch counterparts.

These policies were not, however, successful in their chief ostensible objective: restoring the national economy to the degree of stability and profitability it had enjoyed 30 years earlier. During the early to mid-1950s the economic situation deteriorated badly. Food production, despite government efforts to increase it, declined to the point where in 1956 rice accounted for 13 per cent of the country's total imports, up from zero per cent at the end of the 1930s. Inflation was on the rise; imports were up and exports down. And by the middle of the decade the rebellion in the Outer Islands was proving to be a major drain on the country's financial reserves.

Given the policies pursued, this economic failure was probably inevitable, and the efforts to recreate the profit-producing conditions of the pre-war period doomed from the start. The world of the 1950s was vastly different from the world of the 1920s. Markets had changed, the balance of economic power had altered, new demands had been created and old commodities supplanted. Trying to make the Indonesian economy go forward by recreating the past was not a particularly useful idea.

Similarly, attempts by government to reduce the number of people on the public payroll, to raise efficiency and to reduce the drain on the national budget, were ultimately just as unsuccessful. In the case of the bureaucracy, it was not just that public servants themselves resisted the cutbacks. The bureaucracy in the early 1950s had become heavily politicised; most of the major political parties had actively sought recruits in the public service, and many had succeeded in converting one or more departments into their own little fiefdoms. The PNI commanded the Home Affairs Department, the NU the Department of Religious Affairs, the PSI the Department of Defence. These Departmental strongholds were important sources of political power for the parties. Not surprisingly, they resisted attempts to see the public service streamlined—this would have been a direct attack on their power bases.

The army presented an even greater problem. Attempts to reduce its size and raise its professionalism meant retaining in military service only the best trained and educated officers and soldiers. In effect, this meant retaining those who had received formal training from the Dutch; most Japanese-trained or Indonesian-trained men simply could not compete with them. Some of the Dutch-trained men had joined the Republican army in 1945, but others had fought with the KNIL *against* the Republicans during the revolution, only transferring to the

Indonesian army in 1950. Naturally this did not sit very well with those revolutionary army officers and men who believed—almost certainly correctly—that they were likely to be demobilised or passed over for promotion because, in comparison, they had little formal military training. They thus mobilised all their resources, including their bureaucratic and political allies, to fight off government attempts to implement its plans.

The net result of these pressures was that, despite their best intentions, governments in the 1950s achieved little by way of restructuring the economy and rationalising the infrastructure of the state.

In the political field, the lack of change is also striking. In the absence of general elections, membership of the Indonesian parliament in the early 1950s was determined by negotiation between the leaders of the political parties. The parties themselves were heavily focused on the personalities of their leaders, rather than on ideologies or ideas. These factors, together with the multiplicity of parties represented in the parliament, meant that governments could only be formed on the basis of multi-party coalitions, and that those coalitions were inherently unstable. In the period 1950–56, for instance, Indonesia was led by no fewer than five different Prime Ministers—one of them twice—with the average lifespan of a Cabinet being about a year. Since virtually all parties had a chance of coalition membership, and thus of accessing the political, financial and other rewards which came with participation in government, few of them had any interest in fundamentally altering the political system.

The one major exception was the PKI, the only significant party which rejected the status quo, with or without minor amendments. For this very reason the other major parties collaborated to ensure that the PKI was never invited to join a coalition government.

The PKI did not direct all its energies to the parliamentary sphere, however. More than any other political party, it sought to build up a strong base of popular support, both through individual membership and through support for social and industrial organisations. It was,

181

for instance, active in the trade union movement, and among peasants, fishers, rural labourers and artists.

The major political issues of the first half of the 1950s were the holding of national elections, and the recovery of the territory of Irian Jaya from the Dutch. The latter issue had wide support through the political community. The Round Table Conference Agreement had recognised that the Indonesian and Dutch sides remained in dispute over the territory, but required a resolution to be found within twelve months. Such a resolution was not found. From the Indonesian perspective, the region was part of the Republic, both because it had been included in the 1945 independence proclamation, and because the Dutch in 1949 had recognised Indonesian sovereignty over the whole of the Netherlands Indies, without exception. The only point remaining in dispute with the Dutch was the process by which Indonesian sovereignty in the territory would be established. When no agreement was reached by December 1950, Jakarta took the position that Irian Jaya was a legitimate part of its territory, illegally occupied by the Dutch.

From 1950 to 1953, Indonesian governments continued to negotiate with the Dutch, but without success. In 1954, Ali Sastroamidjojo became Prime Minister. Ali's policies were somewhat different from those of his predecessors; more radical, and less cautious or conservative. Rather than emphasising economic rationality and recovery, he pressed instead for the assertion of full Indonesian political and economic sovereignty, even if there would be economic costs attached to such a policy. He was hardly a radical revolutionary; but he was rather further along the axis towards the second group referred to earlier than his predecessors had been.

Ali decided to internationalise the Irian Jaya issue by taking it to the United Nations. A resolution supporting the Indonesian position was supported by more than half the members of the General Assembly, but not by the two-thirds majority necessary to commit the UN to taking action, and thus the resolution failed. It was, however, an important moral victory for Indonesia, and certainly drew the attention of the international community to the dispute.

Reflecting further his recognition of the linkage Indonesia could make between national and international affairs, Ali also took the initiative in the formation of the Asian-African bloc of states—now known as the Non-Aligned Movement. By the middle of the 1950s, a growing number of Asian and African countries had achieved their independence. In April 1955, at Indonesia's invitation they came together in Bandung, West Java, for their first-ever conference, which attracted a plethora of distinguished delegates: Nasser, Nehru, Zhou Enlai, Tito. Ali and, of course, Sukarno were at the centre of things. The conference marks the beginning of a decade in which Indonesia was to play a major role in world affairs.

The chief political issue facing the country was undoubtedly the holding of national elections. Among the political public, there was a belief that the chronic political instability Indonesia had experienced since 1950 would be cured by the holding of elections. The elections were eventually held in 1955, and were well organised and honest. But instead of stabilising politics by producing a clear result, with one party or firm coalition of parties getting a clear majority of the vote, the reverse happened: the popular vote was widely dispersed among no fewer than 28 parties. The Nationalist Party of Indonesia (PNI) proved the most popular, securing 22 per cent of the vote. This was followed by two Islamic parties, Masjumi (21 per cent) and Nahdatul Ulama (NU, 18 per cent), and the Communist Party of Indonesia (PKI, 16 per cent). It would have taken a coalition of three of these four major parties to command a simple majority of the vote and thus claim a mandate to govern—a most unlikely occurrence.

The elections not only failed to produce any single winner; they also starkly revealed the extent to which regional divisions were politically powerful. The ethnic Javanese heartlands of central and east Java were the strongholds of the PNI, the NU and the PKI, which between them controlled 141 of the 257 seats in the parliament. The regions outside central and east Java—the western third of Java and the other islands in the archipelago—had only one major party to represent their views: the Masjumi. Many non-Javanese feared that this would mean that their interests would be subordinated to those of Java. This consternation was made worse the following year, 1956, when Hatta resigned as Vice-President. Being a Sumateran, Hatta had long been seen by non-Javanese as an important guarantor of the political balance in Jakarta.

Rather than uniting Indonesia, the elections merely confirmed the divisions in the country. From this point onwards, Indonesian politics moved rapidly towards conflict and crisis.

8
GUIDED TO PANCASILA DEMOCRACY 1956–1998

For the next 30 years, Indonesia was ruled by two quasi-dictators, Sukarno (to 1967) and Suharto (1967 to 1998), men who came from very different social, ideological and economic backgrounds and in power followed very different formal political ideologies and practices.

Yet both saw strong, centralised rule as the best way to manage the country. Neither tolerated open opposition to their rule, neither saw the liberal democratic process as being relevant to Indonesia's political and social needs. They were agreed on the need for Indonesia to be a religiously neutral state. And neither was a particularly efficient dictator, with the result that their periods of rule were never quite as thoroughly repressive as they might have been, or indeed as they might have wished them to be.

For these reasons, we will here be dealing with the Sukarno and Suharto periods together.

For the Indonesian state, and more particularly its leadership, the crisis faced in the late 1950s had perhaps two main elements. One was political: the increasingly obvious collapse of the parliamentary system and the absence of any powerful figures who seemed prepared to stand up for it or to fight for its survival. Among the sceptics, none was more vocal than Sukarno himself. Sukarno had never made any bones about the fact that he rejected parliamentary democracy, with its competing political parties and its emphasis on reaching decisions by majority votes. To him, this system was inherently divisive, alien to Indonesian political culture and the prime cause of the country's political instability. The political parties, in particular, were in his sights. In October 1956, he made a speech strongly critical of the parties, and calling for the establishment of a new form of democracy. He explained:

> [T]he democracy I crave for Indonesia is not liberal democracy such as exists in Western Europe. No! What I want for Indonesia is a guided democracy, a democracy with leadership. A guided democracy, a guided democracy, something which is guided but still democracy.[1]

Just exactly what he meant by 'guided democracy, a democracy with leadership' was not entirely clear. But he subsequently urged a return to what he described as the traditional Indonesian values reflected in the nation's villages. In the villages, he said, decision making was a cooperative process, involving all adult members of the community, under the leadership or guidance of the village head. Proposals or suggestions for action were discussed at length (*musyawarah*), until eventually consensus (*mufakat*) was reached. In this way harmony within the village was maintained. And what was good for the village was also good for the nation.

Sukarno made two specific proposals to give effect, at least in part, to his ideas: the formation of a Cabinet in which representatives of all the major political parties would sit, and the establishment of a National Council, its membership based on what he termed 'functional groups'. These included farmers, women, artists, religious leaders and the military. Both these proposals were aimed at reducing the power of the political parties, in one case by requiring them all to work in cooperation, and in the other by creating a national political institution in which the parties did not hold a monopoly over participation.

The political parties were divided in their responses to these proposals. Support came chiefly from the PKI and the PNI, with opposition from the Muslims, especially of the reformist stream. The latter were particularly concerned that the effect of these proposals would be to give the communists access to much greater power than they had ever previously had; up to this point, despite their strong electoral showing, the other parties had always kept the communists out of the cabinet. Clearly, if Sukarno's proposals were to be accepted, this situation could not continue.

The second element to the crisis was regional. For many living in the Outer Islands—effectively, outside Java—estrangement with Jakarta was growing almost daily. They saw the central government coming under increasing influence from the left, and in particular the PKI; Outer Islanders tended to be politically more conservative. The government's economic policy was seen to be increasingly protectionist, and concerned with looking after the interests of consumers in Java; many Outer Islanders were entrepreneurs, often exporting their product to Singapore and Malaya. Secularism was seen to be on the rise in Jakarta, along with moral and ethical decay; religious observance, whether Islamic or Christian, was still a crucial part of life for many Outer Islanders.

The results of the 1955 elections had illustrated the extent of this geographical divide; the resignation of Vice-President Hatta in 1956 confirmed it. In response, in late 1956–early 1957 a group of regional military commanders in Sumatera and Sulawesi seized power from the local civilian administrations appointed by Jakarta, and set up their own administrations.

These developments posed a major challenge to the authority of the central government. It was a challenge that Prime Minister Ali Sastroamidjojo—in office for a second time—was simply unable to meet. Ali resigned his office on 14 March 1957, immediately after which Sukarno accepted the advice of Army Commander General Nasution—himself a Sumateran—and proclaimed a state of martial law across the country. This move, however, failed to dissuade the Outer Island dissidents: on 15 February 1958 they proclaimed the establishment of the Revolutionary Government of the Republic of Indonesia, the Pemerintah Revolusioner Republik Indonesia (PRRI) in west Sumatra. Two days later they were joined by rebels in Sulawesi. As the title of their government suggests, the rebels were not seeking separation from the Indonesian state, but rather its reform.

This action effectively split Indonesia in two, the sides being divided by political ideology, religion and economic philosophy as well as geographical location.

The rebel move demanded a direct and forceful response from Jakarta. Sukarno authorised Nasution to take military action: the ensuing military campaign was not very costly or bloody as such campaigns go, though it was damaging enough. The end result, however, was a clear victory for the central government.

On the one hand, this victory strengthened Sukarno's position. He no longer had to worry about the political and economic repercussions which would have followed from either a protracted civil war or, worse, victory by the rebels. Moreover, victory brought him the opportunity to move forcefully against his opponents in Jakarta. The Masjumi and the Indonesian Socialist Party, two of the parties which had expressed the strongest opposition to his proposals for a reorganisation of the country's political system, had been compromised by the involvement with the rebel cause of many of their most prominent leaders, and in 1960 Sukarno banned them both. They had certainly opposed what he was doing, but it was no coincidence that the Masjumi was closely associated with former Vice-President Hatta, and that the leader of the Socialist party was Sjahrir. Sukarno had finally struck back at the politicians who had pushed him out of power fifteen years earlier.

The other major victor was clearly the army under Nasution, who argued strongly that without its assistance the central government would have been defeated and the unity of Indonesia broken. The army was now firmly established as a major political actor. In 1958 Nasution set out a political doctrine for the armed forces, which he termed the 'Middle Way'. He argued that the Indonesian armed forces had a unique role to play in society:

> We do not and we will not copy the situation as it exists in several Latin American states where the army acts as a direct political force; nor will we emulate the Western European model where armies are the dead tools [of the government] or the example of Eastern Europe.[2]

In Nasution's view the army stood in the middle, having both a military and a civil–political role to play in the life of the nation, just as it had done during the revolution. But the army could not play this role unless the political system were altered: parliamentary democracy had no place for an army wanting to wield direct political influence. Sukarno's emerging guided democracy did offer such an opportunity, so long as it could be moulded in the right direction. Nasution thus had an interest in the establishment of guided democracy; he and Sukarno were drawn into an alliance, though on both sides it was one of convenience rather than conviction.

His position now relatively secure, and with Nasution's support, Sukarno moved to put in place his guided democracy and to secure the wide-ranging changes in Indonesia's political, social and economic makeup that he had been seeking, with increasing determination, since 1945. A crucial element was the reinstatement of the 1945 Constitution, which gave the President far greater powers than the Provisional Constitution of 1950. The Constituent Assembly, since its election in 1955, had been trying unsuccessfully to agree on a permanent Constitution. On 22 April 1959 Sukarno formally proposed to the Assembly that, rather than continue its attempts to draft a new Constitution, it simply re-adopt the Constitution of 1945. In light of their experiences, there was a good deal of sympathy for Sukarno's proposal among Assembly members, but one major and long-standing problem loomed over the issue: the question of whether the state should be based constitutionally on Islam or on the Five Principles of the state philosophy, Pancasila.

Three times in mid-1959 the Assembly voted on whether to accept the 1945 Constitution, which makes no formal reference to Islam; three times a simple majority of members favoured this course of action, but the two-thirds majority required to make a decision binding was never achieved. Finally, on 5 July 1959, his political patience exhausted, Sukarno stepped in and unilaterally declared that the Constitution of 1945 had been reinstated.

Many politicians protested at this action, arguing that it was illegal and unconstitutional. Formally, it may well have been both those things. But in practical terms, Sukarno had made the decision, and he could enforce it: he was able to secure the active support of sufficient people to ensure that his decision stuck. With this decisive, albeit rather risky, action he had seized the political initiative and ushered in the era of guided democracy.

Guided democracy was a system of government in which the parliament was to play a relatively small role, as were most political parties, with the increasingly important exception of the Communist Party. It was a system that saw the Indonesian army consolidate its position as a major political force. It was a populist political system, in the sense that political leaders—Sukarno in particular—encouraged mass popular participation in political rallies, parades and so forth, something early leaders had assiduously avoided. Perhaps most importantly of all, the system was one in which Sukarno played a pivotal role.

Many of the features of guided democracy can be seen in the campaign to force the Dutch to relinquish control over Irian Jaya. We have already noted that Ali Sastroamidjojo had adopted a more activist line on this issue than his predecessors, giving up bilateral negotiations with the Dutch in favour of internationalising the dispute through the United Nations and the Asian-African Movement. Four times the matter went before the UN General Assembly; four times it secured the support of a simple majority of members, but never the two-thirds majority required for adoption. The campaign certainly raised international awareness of the Indonesian position, but it still left the Dutch in control of the territory.

In late 1957, after the General Assembly had once more failed to give its full support to Indonesia, Sukarno announced that Indonesia would now follow a new course of action in trying to recover the territory, putting direct pressure on the Dutch. This meant, first of all, a campaign against Dutch business interests in Indonesia. Major Dutch businesses were taken over, in most instances by their employees, although all eventually came under government or military control. Dutch nationals were subjected to public harassment, and most were finally expelled from the country. Mass rallies and parades were held in cities, towns and villages across Indonesia, demanding that the Dutch get out of the territory.

The next step in this new approach was taken at the end of the decade, when Indonesian troops and volunteers were landed in Irian Jaya, by boat and by parachute, to challenge the Dutch militarily. In one sense these military actions were a defeat for the Indonesians: the vast bulk of their troops were quickly either captured by the Dutch or killed. But the Dutch soon found that their military victory was being won at enormous political and financial cost. It was easy enough, and cheap enough, for the Indonesians to infiltrate small groups of soldiers into the territory at places and times of their own choosing. But for the Dutch to defend adequately a territory situated literally half a world away from the Netherlands was vastly more difficult and more expensive.

Domestically, no political group of any substance opposed Sukarno's policy, and the PKI was particularly active in supporting it. This was both because it was ideologically most committed to the cause of anti-imperialism and colonialism, but also because it gave the party the opportunity to bring its members and sympathisers out onto the streets, to mobilise them in a clear public demonstration of its growing popularity and strength. The issue also enabled the party to demonstrate how external powers stood on the issue. Indonesia had support for its cause from the Asian–African Movement and—importantly—from the communist bloc, including the USSR but also from China. This fact was played up by the PKI to show that international communism supported Indonesia, while the Americans and their allies opposed it.

Early in the 1960s, under the presidency of John F. Kennedy, the United States began to take a more active interest in the situation. Its primary concern, as it had been at the time of the Madiun Affair more than a decade earlier, was Indonesia's position in the Cold War. Under Sukarno, there seemed to Washington to be a real likelihood that Indonesia would throw in its lot with the communists, especially—and most dangerously—with China, with potentially disastrous consequences for American strategy in Asia. Sukarno thus had to be diverted from the communists, to be shown that he had more to gain from friendly relations with Washington than with Beijing. Supporting the Indonesian position on Irian Jaya was an opportunity to do this; at the same time it would weaken the political position of the PKI and strengthen those army leaders who, while committed to the recovery of the territory, were nonetheless anti-communist in their ideological orientation.

In 1962, with the assistance of a retired American diplomat, Ellsworth Bunker, the Dutch and the Indonesians came to an agreement under which control over the territory would be transferred to Indonesia in 1963, via a United Nations Temporary Executive Authority. The one condition placed on this agreement was that by 1969 an 'Act of Free Choice' had to be undertaken, to give the people of Irian Jaya the opportunity to say whether or not they wanted to remain within the Indonesian Republic. This condition was duly met, though under conditions which gave strong reason to doubt the authenticity of the results of the polling. From the Indonesian perspective, the Act of Free Choice was of little significance: it was simply the condition that the international community had imposed on Indonesia to enable the country to secure control over a territory which it regarded as rightfully its own.

With his new approach to the Irian Jaya issue, Sukarno had given the people the sense that they were participating in a great crusade against colonialism; a crusade not just national but also international in its reach. The campaign was also important in cementing the unity of the Indonesian nation, so recently under challenge in Sumatera and Sulawesi. Virtually no identifiable group in the community opposed it: communists, Muslims, military leaders and politicians of all persuasions participated in the struggle. The contrast with the divisive politics of the parliamentary democracy period was striking.

Sukarno was to try the same strategy between 1963 and 1965, in his campaign against the formation of the Federation of Malaysia. This time he was spectacularly less successful.

In the early 1960s, in collaboration with the leaders of the Federation of Malaya and of Singapore, the British had worked out a plan for the formation of a new state of Malaysia, to be made up of the already independent Federation of Malaya and the British-controlled territories of Singapore, Brunei, Sabah and Serawak.

At first this proposal aroused little interest in Indonesia. However, in January 1963, Foreign Minister Subandrio announced Indonesia's opposition to the plan, proclaiming:

> The President has decided that henceforth we shall pursue a policy of confrontation against Malaya . . . we have always been pursuing a confrontation policy against colonialism and imperialism in all its manifestations. It is unfortunate that Malaya, too, has lent itself to become tools of colonialism and imperialism. That is why we are compelled to adopt a policy of confrontation.[3]

Sukarno's argument was that the Malaysia proposal was an attempt by the conservative leadership of Malaya on the one hand, and the British on the other, to preserve the regional economic and political status quo after the withdrawal of formal British colonial and military power. As such, the scheme was a classic illustration of the global conflict between what Sukarno called the New Emerging Forces and the Old Established Forces; that is, between those seeking radical change in the world and those who stood for conservatism and colonialism.

Not all observers accept that these were Sukarno's real motives for opposing Malaysia. Some have seen his position as reflective of an adventurist and aggressive foreign policy, or an attempt to divert the attention of the Indonesian people away from increasing internal economic and political turmoil and towards another foreign issue, even a reflection of his pique at not having been consulted on a major regional political issue. There is undoubtedly at least an element of truth in all these suggestions. By the same token, Sukarno's own explanations for his actions are clearly consistent with his general political reasoning at this time, and should be taken seriously as comprising, at the least, an important part of a rather complex story.

On 16 September 1963, despite Sukarno's opposition, the new Federation of Malaysia was officially established. This brought an immediate reaction in Indonesia: diplomatic relations with Malaya were severed, the British embassy in Jakarta burned down and British firms seized. On 25 September, Sukarno formally announced that Indonesia had embarked on a campaign to 'crush Malaysia'.

This 'crush Malaysia' campaign attracted widespread popular support, with political and other groups manoeuvring to align themselves with the president. The PKI, the political party with the clearest ideological objection to Malaysia, was once again the most active in supporting, organising or participating in scores of mass rallies and parades, and leading the way in the seizure of British-owned business enterprises.

The army was in a much more difficult position. On the one hand, like the PKI, it needed to be seen to be supportive of the President. On the other, many of its anti-communist leaders felt politically threatened by the campaign, given the mileage being obtained from it by their opponents, the PKI. Thus, while giving public support to Sukarno, the army leadership maintained clandestine contacts with the Malaysians and the British, and ensured that elite troops were kept away from the main battlefront in Kalimantan and close to Jakarta.

Malaysia, however, turned out to be no Irian Jaya. Its internal political cohesion and strength were considerable, its military backing clearly more than a match for the Indonesians and its degree of international legitimacy high. Outside Indonesia, Sukarno's position was supported only by China and a handful of like-minded states, such as North Korea. At the end of 1964, Sukarno withdrew Indonesia from the United Nations in protest at Malaysia's election to a seat on the Security Council. By the time the first major blow fell against the Sukarno regime in 1965, despite having been in progress for two years the 'crush Malaysia' campaign was to all intents and purposes stymied. When the military came to power under the leadership of General Suharto, one of its first acts was to end confrontation, and to establish friendly relations with Malaysia.

On economic matters, Sukarno's position was the complete reverse of that of the nation's leaders in the early 1950s. No economist himself, Sukarno was critical of those who were. He took the view that political reform was a higher priority than economic development;

indeed, without political reform there could be no meaningful economic development. In particular, it was more important to raise the people's political consciousness and morale, to make them proud of themselves and their nation, than to worry about mundane things such as the reform of the bureaucracy and making manufacturing industry more efficient. Thus guided democracy saw the erection around the country—but most particularly in Jakarta—of numerous statues, skyscrapers, stadiums and other buildings symbolising the greatness of Indonesia and its peoples. Sukarno described critics of his expenditure on such monuments as 'chicken-hearted souls with a grocer's mentality'. Unfortunately, while it might indeed have been important to raise the self-esteem of the people after decades of colonial rule, the economic cost to the country was high. By the mid-1960s, Indonesia's annual inflation rate was over 650 per cent, and the nation's coffers all but empty.

Indonesia's ethnic Chinese population experienced decidedly mixed fortunes during the guided democracy period. Sukarno himself was not anti-Chinese. Indeed, in a country where anti-Chinese outbursts from national leaders were distressingly commonplace, he stands out as having supported full membership of the Indonesian national community for citizens of ethnic Chinese descent. And the increasingly close relations between Indonesia and China, especially in the 1960s, meant that, at least at the public political level, being of ethnic Chinese descent was not a handicap. A Dual Nationality Treaty had been negotiated between China and Indonesia in 1955, the object of which was to resolve once and for all the question of the nationality of ethnic Chinese in Indonesia. For the first time, China accepted the principle that someone of ethnic Chinese descent could renounce their Chinese nationality, opening the way for Chinese in Indonesia to adopt Indonesian nationality.[4] Chinese community schools were largely free to operate, and newspapers and magazines could publish in the Chinese language. Chinese festivals such as New Year were widely observed. Baperki, a major organisation representing ethnic Chinese interests, contested the 1955 general elections, and had members in both the elected parliament and Sukarno's largely nominated parliament after 1960.

On the other hand there were still many obstacles in the way of the realisation by ethnic Chinese of the opportunities formally open to them. Resentment against their role in the economy was still strong, leading to the issuing of Government Regulation 10 of 1959 that effectively banned them from the retail trade in rural areas. There were outbreaks of anti-Chinese violence, the worst in Sukabumi in West Java in 1963. Illustrating the extent to which many ethnic Chinese felt uneasy at their situation in Indonesia, at the end of the 1950s and the early 1960s several tens of thousands chose to migrate to China. This movement in turn caused other Indonesians to question the commitment to Indonesia of the ethnic Chinese community as a whole.

The rise of the New Order government

The end for the Sukarno regime came in the mid-1960s, largely as a result of the rising conflict between the two political forces which—apart from Sukarno himself—had gained most from guided democracy: the communists and the military.

During the early years of guided democracy, while martial law was still in force, the army was probably more powerful than the PKI. When martial law was lifted in 1963, and most of the restrictions on civilian political activity were subsequently removed, the balance of power began to shift.

Theoretically, all political groups could have taken advantage of the opportunities the ending of martial law offered; in practice, though, only the PKI had the organisational capacity, the discipline, the ideological training and the popular support to take full advantage of it. By the early 1960s it was the largest political party in the country, with about three million members.

The army did establish a number of civilian functional groups or associations under its de facto leadership, to operate on its behalf after the ending of martial law. It also established a secretariat to co-ordinate the activities of these functional groups, known as Sekber Golkar. By and large, however, the leadership of these functional groups showed far less flair for propaganda and organisation than did the leadership of groups affiliated to the PKI.

By the mid-1960s, the conflict between the army and the PKI had become the dominant theme in Indonesian politics, the political system heading for a major clash between two powerful but contradictory political forces. Just such a clash did take place, starting in the second half of 1965. It saw a shattering of the PKI, its leaders killed or imprisoned or in exile; it saw Sukarno on a steady downward slide from office; and it saw the army firmly entrenched in power.

The catalyst for these developments emerged on the night of 30 September–1 October 1965 when squads of troops and members of PKI-affiliated youth and women's organisations kidnapped six of the country's most senior army officers and killed them. Though he was on the murder list, General Nasution managed to escape his would-be assassins. Other troops seized control of the centre of Jakarta and broadcast a statement in the name of what they termed the '30th September Movement', saying that they had acted to protect the President from a *coup d'état* being planned by right-wing generals in the pay of the CIA.

The troops failed, however, to capture General Suharto, the commander of the Strategic Reserve, a sizeable, well-trained and well-equipped force stationed in the capital. Suharto used these troops to confront the rebels; by nightfall on 1 October, Jakarta was firmly in his hands. Although there were demonstrations of support for the 30th September Movement in a number of cities and towns in central and east Java, the movement was effectively dead by 2 October. The PKI itself was banned on 12 March 1966.

Suharto moved cautiously but firmly to take over authority from Sukarno and to establish what he called his 'New Order' government.

He secured a mandate to exercise temporary authority in Sukarno's name on 11 March 1966. He became Acting President in 1967 and finally displaced Sukarno as President in 1968. By the end of the 1960s, the ousting of Sukarno was virtually complete. Held under house arrest, and in bad health, he eventually died in Jakarta on 21 June 1970.

To describe these events in the bald terms we have just used is quite easy; to do so, however, is to gloss over the huge human tragedy which they represent. In the aftermath of the victory of the forces led by Suharto, perhaps half a million people were killed in an orgy of violence in which people died for a variety of political, social and economic reasons—and for no apparent reason at all. In some cases the army was directly responsible for the murders; in many others it took no meaningful steps to halt the violence. Hundreds of thousands more were imprisoned, on the grounds that they were allegedly supporters of the 30th September Movement. Most of those imprisoned without trial were freed by 1979; some, who had been sentenced to long terms of imprisonment, or to death, were not released until Suharto's fall from power in 1998.

The conflict which brought Suharto's New Order government to power involved not only the army and the PKI. The army was supported in its fight against the communists by a loose coalition of at least two major civilian groups, and a host of minor ones.

One important group consisted of politically active Muslims, especially from the reformist stream of Islam. They included former leaders of the strongly anti-communist Masjumi party, banned since 1960. Some traditionalist Muslims also rallied to the support of Suharto; indeed, in many parts of central and east Java, killings of Communist Party members were carried out primarily by members of Ansor, the youth wing of the conservative and traditionalist Muslim party NU.

The second major group supporting Suharto consisted of students and intellectuals. In the early weeks after the coup attempt, university and high school students formed action groups which launched massive street demonstrations in support of what they called the 'Three Demands of the People': the lowering of prices, the banning of the PKI and the purging of PKI members and sympathisers from the Cabinet. Student groups were also involved in violent attacks on a number of public buildings, including the Department of Foreign Affairs; student demonstrations and attacks also spread to other cities, including Surabaya, Ujung Pandang (Makasar) and Medan.

While there is no doubt that these demonstrations genuinely reflected the views of their participants, it is equally clear that they were carried out with at least the tacit approval of the army leadership. Indeed, some authors have suggested that the army leadership was the key element in their organisation, seeing them as a convenient and effective way of mobilising popular civilian opinion in their struggle against the PKI, and ultimately against Sukarno.

For the students and the Muslims, the Sukarno regime had come to represent moral, intellectual and economic bankruptcy; the New Order government was seen as offering a way out of that bankruptcy. By and large, however, these groups did not see the military solution as a long-term solution. Rather, they saw it as a short-term expedient, something that would facilitate a return to what they saw as normalcy and order, after which the army would return to its barracks and leave politics to the civilians once more. On this issue they were to be sorely disappointed. Although the country was not a military dictatorship in the normal sense of the term, the military continued to play an important role in Indonesian politics through to the end of the New Order period, and arguably beyond.

Once consolidated in power, Suharto's New Order government set the achievement of political and economic stability, and then economic development, as its major broad policy objectives.

In the search for stability, the identification of enemies was of crucial importance—and here the military was nothing if not consistent. We have already noted that during the 1950s, it had seen two primary political enemies: communism and Islam. The New Order government systematically went about eliminating the first and domesticating the latter.

The physical destruction of the Communist Party and its membership has already been described. But the government went further than that in proscribing anything that could in any way be described as politically leftist. Pramoedya Ananta Toer, probably Indonesia's greatest post-war prose writer, was imprisoned or exiled for ten years on the grounds that he had been a communist sympathiser. More than that, all his writings were banned: this was the first time that an Indonesian government had banned an author's entire oeuvre, rather than specific works. The ban on his work remained until 1998, though it was fairly porous: the books were always reasonably available for anyone who really wanted to read them. Some universities even made a point of setting them for reading by students of Indonesian literature.

The anti-communist crusade did not stop at those who were accused of direct involvement with the Communist Party or its affiliates. Candidates for employment in the public service, for example, had to show not only that they were not involved with communism, but also that none of their relatives was so involved.

Although to the very end of the New Order period the government continued to warn of the danger of resurgent communism, to all intents and purposes the party and its ideology had disappeared from Indonesia long before. This was not just the result of the anti-communist policies of the Suharto government; the changed world environment also had a role to play. Yet the spectre of communism continued to play a useful role for the government in justifying restrictions on personal liberties, and the repression of opposition forces.

The suspicion of Islam was, ironically, founded on much the same basis as that of communism. Indeed, one of the slogans promoted by the government during the 1970s and 1980s was 'Beware the dangers of the Extreme Left and the Extreme Right'—the former referring to communism, the latter to a form of Islam. Both were seen as a danger to the New Order government because they proposed sets of values and morals which were at variance with those the government was wanting to promote, and answered to a leadership which was outside the control of the New Order. In some respects Islam was the more dangerous of the two, given that some 85 per cent of the Indonesian population was in some sense Muslim.

This all came as something of a surprise and a disappointment to at least some Muslims. Having been part of the coalition that brought Suharto to power in 1965–66, many—especially from the modernist community—felt that their political fortunes would be on the rise again.

Former members of the Masjumi Party, for instance, banned by Sukarno in 1960 for its alleged involvement in the Outer Islands rebellions and its anti-communism, expected that they would be permitted to re-form the party, but the government quickly made it clear that this would not be permitted. The most that the government would allow was the formation of Parmusi, a new party generally representative of modernist Islam, but on the condition that no former members of Masjumi took any leadership roles within it.

Clearly, in government eyes being anti-communist was not sufficient reason to allow Masjumi to re-emerge. Masjumi's anti-communism was outweighed by its apparent support for the separatist rebellions. Since the maintenance of the territorial unity of the state was for Suharto an issue of primary importance, any individual or organisation challenging his concept of Indonesian unity could expect short shrift.

In 1973, Suharto took explicit action against the four Muslim political parties then still in existence, including the long-standing Partai Sarekat Islam Indonesia and the Nahdatul Ulama. These four parties were required to amalgamate in the United Development Party, the Partai Persatuan Pembangunan (PPP), which was, however, denied the right to use Islamic symbols or even to call itself an Islamic party: its philosophical base was to be the Pancasila with its non-sectarian commitment to belief in one supreme god.

If there is a symbol of what many Muslims saw as Suharto's

attempts to crush their religious aspirations, and to favour Christians, it is the riots in Tanjung Priok, the very poor harbour region of Jakarta, in September 1984. As with so many cases of communal or religious conflict in the New Order Indonesia, the precise details of what happened are unclear. What is certain is that, for whatever reason, a group of Muslim demonstrators in Tanjung Priok came into conflict with the local military garrison; the latter opened fire on them, killing (according to government sources) eighteen people or (according to Nahdatul Ulama leader and later fourth President Abdurrahman Wahid) several hundred. The commander of the armed forces at this time was General Benny Murdani, a Catholic.

Later in the New Order period Suharto seemed to be reconciling himself to Islam, seeking to get closer to it. At a personal level, in 1991 he made the pilgrimage to Mecca, and on his return took 'Muhammad' as his given name. Politically, in 1990, and clearly at Suharto's behest, B. J. Habibie—later Indonesia's third President—established an organisation called the League of Indonesian Muslim Intellectuals, the Ikatan Cendekiawan Muslim se-Indonesia (ICMI). Under Habibie's chairmanship, the ICMI emerged as a kind of surrogate Islamic political party, generally supportive of the government.

Just why Suharto appeared to reverse his position on Islam is a matter of considerable conjecture. On the one hand, it was clear that Islam in Indonesia, as in many other countries, was undergoing something of a revival in the late 1980s. As many writers have observed, a rising group of educated, largely middle-class Muslims were seeking new forms of expression for their faith. They were offended by the ways Suharto had tried to limit the role of Islam in the state, and by the favouritism he was accused of displaying towards the non-Islamic, and particularly the Christian, communities. There was an ethnic edge to this feeling among some Muslims: Sino-Indonesians were singled out in particular as having benefited from the years of Suharto rule.

This was a new form of political Islam, one that could not be ignored. Rather than confront it, Suharto may have concluded that the best approach was to try to accommodate it, at least to some extent, in the hope of preventing it taking on an even more challenging and radical form. Other observers have suggested that the key to Suharto's changed attitude lies in the widening rift between the President and his traditional allies, the military. In earlier times, the support of the military had been crucial to ensuring that Islam would not develop an independent and possibly critical political voice, which might challenge Suharto's grip on power. But this gave the military considerable power over Suharto. By switching his position on Islam, Suharto may have been creating a political counterweight to the military. Certainly the late 1980s and the early 1990s saw a series of changes in military leadership which reduced the influence of theso-called 'Red-White' faction in the military—made up largely of Muslims fairly relaxed about their faith and Christians, named for the colours of the Indonesian flag—and increased the influence of the 'Green', or Islamic, faction. Thus the Catholic General Benny Murdani was moved out of power; generals such as Try Sutrisno and Feisal Tanjung, much more sympathetic to Islam, were promoted to leadership positions.

Whatever combination of factors was responsible, it is clear that by the early 1990s Islam was playing a more influential role in Indonesian politics than at any other time since the establishment of the New Order in the mid-1960s.

Let us turn now to the political structure that Suharto put in place.

While in political terms Suharto may have differed from Sukarno on many issues, one thing they shared was the belief that western political systems would not work in Indonesia. Suharto set out to create his own political system, which maintained a fine balance between allowing a degree of public debate on political issues and at the same time ensuring that his government's control over political power was not threatened.

The key to this system was the depoliticisation of the population through the application of what was called the 'floating mass' principle.

Politics as it had been practised to this time, the Suharto government argued, had been disruptive: it had certainly disrupted economic development, because of the way it had diverted resources, and people's energies, away from productive activities and into party politics. To remedy this situation, the government proposed that popular participation in politics should be limited to voting in five-yearly general elections. Further, political parties would be allowed to establish branches only in the major cities, not in the villages and small towns where the majority of Indonesians lived. In this way, it was said, the people would be insulated from, or protected from, the demands of party politics, and as a result would be able to devote their energies to more productive activities and thus improve their economic condition.

Neither the non-communist nor anti-communist political forces which initially allied themselves with the military in 1965 were likely to accept these propositions, having been expecting that they would be able to take over the reins of government and reassert civilian control over the nation. For the government, countering these groups would not be easy; certainly the brutal and repressive measures used against the PKI and its members could not be used against them. Two major strategies were evolved.

First, a political machine had to be established to mobilise support for the government, in competition with the existing political parties. In fact, the shell of such an organisation already existed: Sekber Golkar. Initially it had not been particularly effective. The late 1960s and early 1970s, however, saw the government make enormous efforts to boost Golkar's fortunes.[5] Many civilian supporters of the government were coopted into its leadership, and civil servants were required to give it their support. Massive amounts of government funds and other resources were channelled in to it. These efforts were rewarded in 1971 when, at the first elections held post-1965, Golkar won over half the votes cast, and well over half the seats contested (Table 8.1 gives voting details). Although there was clearly an element of manipulation in this election, there is also little doubt that the government had been remarkably successful in turning Golkar into a slick vote-gathering machine. In subsequent New Order elections, held at five-yearly intervals from 1977, Golkar continued to capture the majority of the popular vote. In the last elections held during Suharto's Presidency, in 1997, Golkar is recorded as having won 74.3 per cent of the popular vote.

Table 8.1: Election results, 1971–1997 (% of popular vote)

	1971	1977	1982	1987	1992	1997
Golkar	63	64	64	73	68	74
PPP	27	28	28	16	17	23
PDI	10	8	8	11	15	3

Note: the PPP and the PDI were not formed until 1973. Here, the results recorded for the constituent elements of each party at the 1971 elections have been aggregated for the sake of comparison.

Second, Suharto moved to ensure that his political opponents' activities be strictly circumscribed. After the 1971 elections, the government announced that a rationalisation of the opposition parties was to take place—their numbers, then standing at nine, were to be reduced to two. One party, as we have already noted, was to be vaguely Muslim, formed by amalgamating all four Muslim parties; the other was to be secular, encompassing all other parties. The reasoning offered for this action was that the plethora of parties operating in Indonesia unnecessarily complicated the political process and made it less efficient and less capable of reflecting the wishes of the people.

The various parties naturally objected to this amalgamation, but individually had nothing like the popular support required to successfully defy the government's plans. In 1973 the two new parties were inaugurated: the United Development Party, the Partai Persatuan Pembangunan (PPP) formed from the Muslim parties, and the Indonesian Democratic Party, the Partai Demokrasi Indonesia (PDI) from the others.

In the first elections it contested, in 1977, the PPP managed to attract around 30 per cent of the popular vote, but this share later fell. In 1987 it failed to win a majority of the vote in any province—even the most strongly Muslim ones such as Aceh. In the last elections held under the Suharto Presidency, in 1997, support did rise considerably, from 17 per cent in 1992 to 23 per cent, but this was more the result of a collapse in the PDI's vote than of any increase in the PPP's own strength.

The other party, the PDI, for a long time seemed politically irrelevant, struggling to maintain sufficient votes to retain any kind of popular legitimacy. To the surprise of many observers its support went up noticeably in the 1992 elections, to around 15 per cent. This may not seem much, but it was nearly twice what many had expected it to be. The PDI had campaigned very strongly on a range of moral issues: anti-corruption, rights of the individual, the environment and so forth. In December 1993, the PDI elected Megawati Sukarnoputri as its Chair. The daughter of Indonesia's first President, Megawati was a high-profile and popular leader; popular in particular with younger, educated Indonesians attracted by the kind of nationalism she and her father represented.

The government clearly became worried about the potential of the PDI under Megawati to be a powerful focus of discontent with its leadership; not powerful enough to topple the government, but certainly enough to make political life difficult. Thus, in June 1996 the government heavy-handedly engineered a congress of the PDI in Medan at which Megawati was ousted from the Chair and replaced by Soerjadi, her immediate predecessor. Megawati and her supporters rejected this development, asserting that they represented the real PDI. There followed a series of clashes between the two PDI camps over control of party facilities, culminating in Jakarta in July 1996 when Megawati supporters were physically removed from the party's national headquarters. This move, clearly organised either by or with the active support of the government, led to two days of rioting in which at least five people died.

The electoral laws in force at the time permitted only authorised parties to stand candidates in elections. As Megawati's PDI was not recognised by the government, it could not contest the 1997 elections. It is a mark of the support retained by Megawati, however, that the PDI of Soerjadi managed to win only 3 per cent of the vote, down from 15 per cent five years earlier.

New Order foreign policy

In foreign affairs, as much as in domestic politics, Suharto was keen to draw a clear dividing line between his government and that of his predecessor. Sukarno's foreign policy had been activist and global in its scope and, in the later years of guided democracy, increasingly aligned with China. Sukarno saw himself as a world figure, the leader of Southeast Asia.

Suharto's foreign policy was much less visible, and regionally rather than globally directed. Soon after taking power in 1965–66, the new directions in Indonesian foreign policy were made clear. We have already noted that the Suharto government ended confrontation with Malaysia. It also froze diplomatic relations with China, alleging that Beijing had supported the PKI's coup attempt. Relations with China were not normalised until August 1990.

In 1967 Indonesia joined with Malaysia, Thailand, Singapore and the Philippines to form the Association of Southeast Asian Nations (ASEAN). Brunei, Burma, Cambodia, Laos and Vietnam subequently joined the group. There is little doubt that most Indonesian politicians saw their country as the natural leader of ASEAN; nonetheless, the government went out of its way on most issues to avoid the appearance of dominating the association.

One issue, however, seemed to bring seriously into question the New Order's determination to be seen as a responsible, peaceful state in its relations with its neighbours: the invasion of the former

Portuguese colony of East Timor in 1975, and its incorporation into the Republic as its twenty-seventh province in 1976.

The New Order and East Timor

The history of the incorporation of East Timor is both confused and complicated. By mid-1975, the two major political forces in East Timor, União Democrática Timorense (UDT) and Fretilin, were struggling for control of the territory, the Portuguese colonial authorities having virtually abandoned it following the 1974 coup in Lisbon which brought an anti-colonialist government to power. Although it is simplifying a complex situation, we may characterise UDT as favouring East Timor's incorporation into Indonesia and Fretilin as wanting full independence. Fretilin was clearly the more popular party. There is no doubt that Indonesia was contributing to the conflict between these two parties by infiltrating troops into the territory in the guise of 'volunteers' supporting the UDT. On 16 October 1975 some of these troops, in company with East Timorese irregulars, probably shot and killed five Australia-based journalists at Balibo, near the border with West Timor.

Despite this covert assistance to the UDT, by late 1975 the Fretilin forces were getting on top of their opponents. On 28 November, Fretilin proclaimed the independence of the Democratic Republic of East Timor. Nine days later, on 7 December, Indonesia officially landed troops in the territory. On 17 December pro-Indonesian forces established the Provisional Government of East Timor on board an Indonesian warship, and six months later, on 31 May 1976, the Indonesia-nominated regional assembly formally applied to have the territory incorporated into Indonesia.

This incorporation did not go unchallenged, either in East Timor or outside it. Forces loyal to Fretilin continued the armed struggle against the Indonesians, and the United Nations continued to regard

Portugal as the legitimate authority in the region, as did the Portuguese themselves. Other countries came to accept that the territory was Indonesian, though they frequently expressed reservations at the way in which it was incorporated into Indonesia, and in particular at the horrific loss of life this process entailed.

Indonesia's motives in invading and incorporating East Timor can be variously interpreted. Jakarta was certainly concerned that an independent East Timor would be politically unstable, and liable to domination by a leftist, if not communist, regime which might in turn unsettle neighbouring parts of Indonesia or even encourage latent secessionist movements. Some critics of Jakarta argued that the Indonesians had strategic and economic reasons for wanting to incorporate East Timor, including the desire to control the seas around the territory, which are strategically important because of their depth, and may prove economically important as sources of oil and gas. Others have drawn parallels between East Timor and Irian Jaya, seeing in them both evidence of some deep-seated Indonesian expansionism, which might later threaten Papua New Guinea. This latter fear seems most ill-founded; Indonesia has never evinced any interest in absorbing Papua New Guinea, nor does it have the military, economic or administrative capacity to do so.

In the two decades or so until the independence referendum of 1999, Jakarta never succeeded in persuading any significant proportion of the East Timorese population to accept its rule over the territory. Certainly it made major infrastructural investments in East Timor, towards the end of the period spending US$100 million annually in the province. Even critics of Indonesian rule acknowledged that it built roads, bridges, ports, schools and hospitals. But what Jakarta failed to do was to treat the East Timorese as genuine and equal citizens of the Republic. To use the cliché, Indonesia lost the battle for the hearts and minds of East Timorese. It treated East Timorese as quasi-colonial subjects and was viewed accordingly by most East Timorese.

If there was one event which symbolised this failure of the

Indonesian administration to win acceptance, it was the Dili Massacre of 12 November 1991. What started out as a memorial service for a murdered young man turned into a demonstration of support for Fretilin, the party of independence, and its imprisoned leader Xanana Gusmao. As the funeral procession wound its way from the Motael Church towards the Santa Cruz Cemetery, there were clashes between the mourners and the troops guarding the route. At the cemetery itself, the military opened fire, killing over 200 people. Similar incidents had happened in the past, but never in front of foreign journalists and their cameras; within hours of the massacre, the events were being shown on international television. Jakarta did make some half-hearted attempts to discover and punish those responsible, but from this point on it was virtually impossible for Jakarta to maintain the line that its rule in East Timor was acceptable to the East Timorese, at least with respect to the international community.

Domestically, most Indonesians probably thought little about East Timor. The government had been assiduously promoting the message that the only people dissatisfied with the region's status as part of Indonesia were a few malcontents, who were communist sympathisers anyway. But the massacre does seem to have had an impact on the political elite in Jakarta. There was a growing recognition that policy on Timor needed to be reviewed, and perhaps completely reversed. This position was rarely based on high moral principles, such as the inherent right of the Timorese to settle their own affairs themselves, but much more commonly resulted from a calculation that the cost to Indonesia of retaining Timor was simply far higher than any benefit. Some felt that the Timorese were having large sums of money thrown at them, for which they were totally ungrateful. At least figuratively, they were taking Indonesia's money, then thumbing their noses at Jakarta. This being the case, the consensus seemed to be that Indonesia should send them packing, and let them survive on their own resources, thus saving Indonesia the money and the trouble. Others, however, had wearied of the international opprobrium suffered by their country for a policy which they, along with the vast majority of their fellow citizens, had had no hand in shaping.

But ultimately, nothing was to come of this sentiment. Suharto himself was behind Indonesian policy on East Timor. Any significant changes in policy could only come about either with his support—which was most unlikely—or after he had vacated the presidency.

Separatism in Aceh

Suharto considered threats of regional separatism—attempts to break the territorial integrity of the state—just as dangerous and just as subversive as communism or extremist Islam. The case of Aceh illustrates this point well.

Aceh is a strongly Islamic region, arguably the most Islamic in the country. This has always given the Acehnese a strong sense of their own identity, manifested sometimes in demands for substantial local autonomy, and sometimes for full independence.

The Dutch war against Aceh formally ended in 1903, although some Acehnese argue it never really ended at all, an argument not as fanciful as it might seem. Many Acehnese never accepted that the Dutch had defeated them, merely that they had secured a temporary military advantage. When the Japanese invaded Indonesia in 1942, some Acehnese took advantage of the situation by rising up against the Dutch again, in February and March 1942: the last campaign, perhaps, of the Aceh War.

The Japanese reversed the earlier political relationship between the uleebalang and the ulama in Aceh, siding with the ulama. They were, in other words, playing the same political game as the Dutch, but taking the opposite side.

During the Occupation, the Japanese had represented central power and authority, though they were rarely able to exercise it in any meaningful way, but after their surrender in 1945 central authority virtually ceased to exist. The Republicans and the Dutch were in open conflict for control of the Indies: neither was able, even had it been willing, to intervene in Acehnese affairs. The result was a bloody civil war between the uleebalang and the ulama. By 1946, it was clear that the ulama had won; probably half the leading uleebalang in the region were killed.

The leaders emerging from this conflict declared Aceh's support for the Indonesian Republic. Indeed, individuals in Aceh subscribed funds to enable the central government to purchase its first aircraft, which was used to break the Dutch blockade of Republican areas. However, the capacity of the Republican government to influence day-to-day affairs was very limited, for Aceh exercised a high degree of local autonomy.

In 1947 a leading Acehnese religious figure, Daud Beureueh, was appointed the Republican military governor of the province of North Sumatera—in effect the region of Aceh, since the rest of the province was in Dutch hands.

The alliance between the Acehnese and the Republican government was never more than one of temporary convenience. Between the two sides was a deep ideological gap resulting from the perennial issue of the role of Islam in the state. The Republican government in 1945 had determined that the basis of the state would be not Islam but the Pancasila. While the first principle of this was Belief in the One Supreme God, it was not meant to imply any special status for Islam, or indeed any other religion. For many Acehnese, including Daud Beureueh, this position could never be accepted—in their view, politics and religion could not be separated, and thus ultimately the state had to be based on Islam.

Nearly two years later, in late 1948–early 1949, Aceh under Daud Beureueh demanded formal recognition of the region as a province. The Republican government at this time was operating on a temporary, emergency basis from Padang in West Sumatera, its headquarters in Yogyakarta, most of its key personnel having been captured by the

Dutch. In such a weakened political position, it had little choice but to accede to the Acehnese demand. Daud Beureueh, not surprisingly, was appointed Governor.

The Republican government might not have been happy with arrangements in Aceh, but Aceh was distant from the centre of power—as long as the Republic was still fighting the Dutch, it had neither the capacity to do much about the situation there, nor did it see an overwhelming political necessity to do so.

But West Java was a different matter. Here, as we saw in the previous chapter, in 1948, a small group of Muslims had declared the establishment of Darul Islam—the 'Land of Islam'—and the formation of the Indonesian Islamic State. The Republican government felt that it had to take action against the Darul Islam, even though it was short of men and materiel, and engaged in armed struggle against the Dutch, because West Java was close to the heartland of the Republic, and to Batavia, the Dutch colonial capital. Its location was of great strategic and political significance. Thus Republican forces quickly took the field against the forces of Darul Islam, though with little immediate success. By the mid-1950s, however, it had worn the movement down to the point where it was no longer a significant threat, although it was still capable of hit-and-run raids on government facilities until the early 1960s.

Once the revolution had been brought to an end and the independence of the Republican government internationally recognised in 1949, Jakarta had the civil and military resources available to conduct a campaign in Aceh, with the aim of reversing the central government's earlier decisions and downgrading Aceh's quasi-autonomous status. In achieving this aim, the territorial and political unity of the Republic would be put beyond question.

Jakarta's first moves were primarily political. Playing a game remarkably reminiscent of that played in earlier times by the Dutch, the Jakarta government began to give political backing to some of the uleebalang who had survived the Acehnese civil war of 1945–46. Thus a member of an uleebalang family was appointed military governor of the region in early 1950, though following sharp local protests his nomination was withdrawn. Later that year Jakarta announced that Aceh's special status was to end, and that the region was to be reincorporated into the province of North Sumatera.

This event marked a turning point in Jakarta's relations with Aceh. The central government had won this round of the battle, and moved to consolidate its power via the uleebalang. The religious leaders, however, moved further away from the central government, and deeper into Islamic rural society. From the safety of this position they struck out against Jakarta. The latter was portrayed as a hotbed of corruption: political, moral and economic. Gambling and the drinking of alcohol in Aceh were said to have increased greatly following the assumption of direct control by Jakarta. Aceh's economy, a major earner of foreign exchange for the Republic, was said to have suffered considerably through Jakarta's imposition of bans on direct trade across the Straits of Melaka with the ports of the west coast of the Malay Peninsula, a traditional trade route for the Acehnese. Furthermore, it was alleged, the central government was treating Aceh shabbily in terms of funding public works such as roads, irrigation systems and educational facilities. But the crucial issue was still, of course, Islam.

In early 1953 Sukarno visited Aceh, to be greeted by large crowds demonstrating against the Pancasila and in favour of Islam. Later during the same year the central government alleged that its forces had turned up evidence of clandestine communications between Daud Beureueh and the Darul Islam in West Java. In this light, it is perhaps not surprising that in September 1953 the formal break between Aceh and Jakarta was finally made, with the proclamation by Daud Beureueh of Aceh's secession from the Republic of Indonesia, and its adherence to the Indonesian Islamic State of the Darul Islam. The proclamation was marked by a series of attacks on army and government posts by Islamic guerrilla groups. The Indonesian government

215

was faced with a situation very similar to that which the Dutch had had to face 60 or 70 years earlier.

Daud Beureueh's revolt clearly had a degree of local support, and the natural environment of Aceh was such that relatively small numbers of guerrillas were able to tie down much larger government forces with comparative ease. The leaders of the revolt against Jakarta were men with impeccable revolutionary credentials, men who had led the local struggle against the Dutch. The only significant group in Acehnese society which was opposed to these Islamic groups, and which could thus have served as a useful base on which to build an opposition, was the uleebalang: the very people the Dutch had used to spearhead their own anti-Islamic activities.

During 1954–56 the central government tried to defeat Daud Beureueh's forces by military means. Troops were sent to the region, and extensive military operations undertaken. Again, it is difficult to avoid the comparison with the approach taken, at least initially, by the Dutch.

By around mid-1956 the Jakarta government came to the conclusion that it was just not going to win a military campaign in Aceh, and began serious attempts to find a negotiated settlement to the dispute. In March 1957, a cease-fire was arranged, though its enforcement was patchy and sporadic for some time. It was not until two years later, in May 1959, that formal negotiations involving representatives of the central government and Daud Beureueh finally took place. A compromise was reached under the terms of which Jakarta recognised Aceh's status as an autonomous region, with the administrative status of a province.

Daud Beureueh remained at large until 1962. When he finally returned to his home village, he was accorded formal recognition for his services to the Republic during the revolution, and granted a government pension. This marked the virtual ending of the revolt in Aceh, at least in a form that posed any serious threat to central power and national cohesion, for the time being.

Islam remained the dominant force in Acehnese political life. But under the Suharto government, there was some evidence, albeit slight, that its significance was starting to decline. In elections from 1971 to 1982, Aceh voted for Islamic parties. In 1977, of all the provinces in Indonesia, only Jakarta and Aceh gave a majority of their votes to the PPP. In 1982, Jakarta fell to Golkar, leaving only Aceh. In 1987 Aceh itself fell to the Golkar juggernaut. Certainly we have to treat election results with a modicum of caution given the extent to which vote-rigging took place, but even the fact that the Jakarta government was prepared to release results which show PPP gaining fewer votes than Golkar says something about its increasing confidence that it was winning the struggle against Islam.

But at another, less immediately obvious, level developments were taking place in Aceh which showed clearly that the battle against separatism was far from won. In 1976 a small group of Acehnese separatists calling themselves the Aceh Sumatera National Liberation Front proclaimed the independence of Aceh. They were led by Hasan di Tiro, a descendant of the remnants of the Acehnese aristocracy who was (in his terms) the forty-first ruler of Aceh since 1500. He had been in exile from Indonesia since the 1950s, living first in New York where he worked as a stockbroker and then in Stockholm in Sweden.

Jakarta reacted to the challenge to its authority by bringing Daud Beureueh out of Aceh and setting him up in a house in the capital, clearly with the objective of preventing his being used as a focal point for this new group. This initial revolt seems to have been crushed fairly quickly and easily; there is little reliable evidence of its having any active existence after 1977, except for a few hit-and-run raids on local economic infrastructure, and especially at foreign-owned—often American—oil and gas industry installations. In 1983, in the most daring of these raids, two American oilmen were killed in an attack on an oil pipeline.

By the late 1980s the organisation was beginning to make its presence felt in more concrete ways. Renamed the Free Aceh

Movement, or Gerakan Aceh Merdeka (GAM), it stepped up its military activities, carrying out an increasing variety of raids on government and commercial installations. Conflicts between government forces and rebels gradually escalated until in 1989 Jakarta proclaimed the province a Military Operations Area, or Daerah Operasi Militer (DOM), giving it a virtually free hand in dealing with the problem. Once again, Jakarta was resorting to military means to tackle the problem of regional discontent, an approach that clearly had the opposite result of the one hoped for: it stirred resentment of the central government, and encouraged support for the rebels, rather than eliminating that resentment, and those rebels.

The reasons for this are painfully obvious. The methods the military used in attempting to defeat the GAM were those of violence and of terror. Aceh was a distant province, safe from the gaze of the international community and news media; in also fearing nothing from the heavily controlled domestic media, the military clearly felt it could act in Aceh in whatever way it thought fit. Its actions were probably no different from what it was doing in East Timor at this time. Although press censorship allowed little informed public discussion of developments in Aceh over the next several years, there is little doubt that by 1998 Jakarta was facing a full-scale armed revolt.

Economic developments under Suharto

Let us turn now to a discussion of economic developments under the Suharto government.

Guided democracy had been disastrous for the Indonesian economy. The annualised inflation rate in mid-1965 was around 1000 per cent; foreign exchange reserves were adequate to cover only a few weeks' worth of imports; and physical capital was in a state of disrepair or complete breakdown. If inflation could not be brought down, and prices and wages stabilised, the country would very quickly be literally bankrupt. Suharto moved rapidly to arrest and then turn around this situation. Public-sector expenditure was cut, foreign investment attracted back with generous financial and other incentives, and the collection of taxes revitalised. Investments were made in the productive, revenue-earning sectors of the economy, such as commercial agriculture and mining, to boost export earnings. Wages were controlled and strikes, if not formally outlawed, were at least strongly discouraged. In a clear reversal of Sukarno's policy, foreign aid was actively sought. In 1967 a group of Indonesia's major western creditors, including Japan, the United States and Australia, formed the Inter-Governmental Group on Indonesia (IGGI), an organisation aimed at coordinating the flow of aid to Indonesia.

In combination, these policies had the desired effect, with the national inflation rate falling to single figures by the start of the 1970s. Over the quarter-century from 1965 to 1990, Indonesia's annual rates of economic growth averaged 4.5 per cent: well in excess of the average for middle- and low-income countries (2.2 per cent and 2.9 per cent respectively), and in excess even of the rates recorded in the other high-growth Southeast Asian economies of Malaysia and Thailand. In the 1990s growth rates were higher still: in 1996 it was about 7.5 per cent.

Rising growth rates led to substantial inroads being made into poverty, especially in rural areas. While poverty measures are notoriously difficult to produce, and even more difficult to operationalise, there is little doubt that by 1997 there were vastly fewer Indonesians living below the poverty line than there were 25 years previously.

A 1996 World Bank report went further and concluded that the gap between the top 20 per cent of income earners in Indonesia and the bottom 20 per cent was extremely narrow—one of the narrowest in Asia. This implied a fairly even distribution of income. This conclusion provoked a great deal of debate among observers of the Indonesian scene, many arguing that the data simply did not accord with what they saw around them. The critics argued that the distribution of income and wealth had almost certainly become worse in the past 25 years rather than better; that the gap between rich and poor was now wider than at any time in the recent past. Developments since 1997 add weight to this argument. There seems little doubt that one of the key causes of much of the violence in Indonesia since 1997 has been precisely this gap between rich and poor.

In parallel with its quite spectacular growth rate, the Indonesian economy also underwent massive structural transformation, particularly in the late 1980s and early 1990s. One of the most spectacular shifts was out of agriculture and minerals exploitation into manufacturing. By 1997 agriculture produced only about 19 per cent of GDP, while industrial activities had grown to produce about 41 per cent, of which manufacturing accounted for about 21 per cent. The manufacturing sector was growing at about twice the rate of industry as a whole, and making a sizeable contribution to exports. Manufactured exports grew from US$501 million in 1980 to US$2.5 billion in 1986, and a massive US$29.4 billion in 1995. Whereas oil and gas exports as recently as 1988 accounted for 41 per cent of export revenues, by 1995 the proportion had fallen to 23 per cent.

Foreign direct investment (FDI) poured in, especially in the 1990s. In 1993, $8.1 billion of FDI was approved. The figure jumped to $23.7 billion in 1994, and in 1995 reached a record $39.9 billion, representing an increase of 68.4 per cent over the previous year. Total approved FDI up to 1996 reached $171.6 billion in value, spread over 4806 projects. At the time this capital inflow was taken as a mark of the increasing strength of the Indonesian economy; today it looks like one of the most critical reasons for the country's economic crisis.

One feature of this expanding economy, which marked both its success and yet also its weakness, was its domination by a relatively small number of very large firms. Many, commonly referred to by the generic term 'conglomerate', were owned by Indonesians of ethnic Chinese descent. Major players here included Sudono Salim, Mochtar Riady, Mohammad Hasan and Ciputra; their groups include Astra, Sinar Mas and Lippo. Their conglomerates were a major presence in banking, real estate development, manufacturing and import-export, and a number of them established, and benefited from, close political connections with Suharto and his family. Salim and Riady in particular were very close to Suharto. The conglomerates were later to be the target of much public ire, provoked in part by their connections with Suharto, in part by the ethnicity of their owners and in part by a belief that their managers had deliberately sought to crush the small and medium-sized business sector in Indonesia, the area where indigenous Indonesians, many of them Muslim, were most likely to be found.

There were major firms owned by indigenous Indonesians as well. Achmad Bakrie, for instance, sometime chair of the Indonesian Chamber of Commerce and Industry, Kamar Dagang dan Industri (KADIN), headed the then-powerful Bakrie group with interests in plantations, construction and trade. Other major players include several of the children of President Suharto, among whom Bambang, Sigit, Tommy and Tutut were the most prominent. The companies they owned in many respects ought to be compared with the Sino-Indonesian conglomerates in terms of their size and their spread of interests and activities—and, of course, their association with holders of political power.

State-owned enterprises dominated the plantation sector and the supply of electricity, and were very powerful in mining, banking, transport and telecommunications, and petroleum. Most of these businesses were run by public employees, and had the same problems with achieving efficient operating patterns as their counterparts in most western countries. There was another group of companies which were not, strictly speaking, owned by the state, but rather by an arm of the state: the military. Military firms were generally smaller than the mainstream state-owned firms, and were often active in areas such as transport, the hospitality industry and food processing, although some of the larger ones were involved in manufacturing. Many could trace their origins in military hands to the seizure of Dutch-owned enterprises in the late 1950s. Their activities were crucially important for the funding of military activities. It has been calculated that the state budget met only about 30 per cent of the armed forces' financial needs. Much of the rest came from these commercial enterprises. Without them the military would have demanded a much greater share of state resources.

There were also many major foreign-owned firms operating in Indonesia, though legislation kept them out of such strategic sectors of the economy as transport, communications, the media and retailing.

One result of this growing economy was the emergence of an urban middle class. Although measuring the size of the middle class is very difficult, it is often estimated that by mid-1997 perhaps 15 million people were enjoying what we would recognise as a middle-class lifestyle. In many Asian countries, the emergence of such a class was taken as a sign that political liberalisation would follow, that a middle class would not long tolerate the denial of individual political rights, and would eventually mobilise in support of political change. In different kinds of ways, this seems to have been the experience of Thailand, Korea and Taiwan. But this did not happen in Indonesia. For most of the New Order period the middle class wielded little political clout.

This was partly for ethnic reasons: many middle-class Indonesians were members of the ethnic Chinese minority, and thus politically vulnerable to pressure from the government, exerted either directly or indirectly. It would be unfair—and incorrect—to characterise this community as being either uniformly well off or uniformly disinclined to take on political causes, but many of its members did fit both categories.

A second important reason for the general political quiescence of the middle class was that many of them were civil servants; as a group they too were disinclined to challenge the authority of the state under whose auspices they were enjoying unprecedented prosperity.

The one section of this middle class which was probably an exception to this general rule of non-involvement in politics was the urban, educated, Islamic-oriented elite. Dissatisfied with what they saw as a long-standing bias in the Suharto government against Islam, many of these people started to take on more overly political roles. By the 1990s the group had grown in size and influence to the point where

Suharto found it more profitable to try to coopt them into the state through the ICMI than to keep them in the political cold.

There was a downside to these apparently positive economic developments, one long recognised as problematic: the persistence of corruption, the use of official position or resources for private gain. A 1995 survey of expatriate businesspeople in Asia gave Indonesia a corruption rating of 7.4 out of 10 on a scale where 0 represented the absence of corruption. This score put Indonesia on a par with India; only China was (slightly) worse. By way of comparison, Malaysia scored 4.3 and Singapore 1.0. Corruption was particularly prevalent in state-owned enterprises and in certain government departments, especially the Taxation Office, closely followed by Public Works and then the Police Service.

There is little doubt also that Indonesian labour productivity was not high by regional standards. A survey of expatriate managers in ten countries of East and Southeast Asia carried out in 1995 ranked Indonesia ninth in terms of labour skills: once again, only China was worse. Even government ministers readily conceded that this was an issue that had to be tackled. Abdul Latief, then Minister for Labour and a businessman himself, noted in 1995: 'Foreign investors came for cheap labour, but now we are talking about competitive workers, and we must increase training and productivity. There is no more cheap labour in Indonesia'.[6]

In summary, the Indonesian economy up to the middle of 1997 was apparently moving ahead rapidly, dominated by politically well-connected businesses and characterised by massive inflows of foreign capital. But it was also a fairly high-cost economy, much of these costs resulting from corruption and low labour productivity.

Restraints on the exercise of power

Finally, we might consider what kinds of restraints there were on the exercise of power by the political elite. Realistically, there were very few.

The courts certainly did not play this role. Theoretically, a citizen with a grievance against, for instance, the police force or a government bureaucrat could take them to court to seek redress. And occasionally this did happen. But there were no significant cases where any court ever found for the plaintiff under such circumstances. This was partly because judges were—and remain—civil servants, not independent judicial officers, but also because corruption among the judiciary was rife. Court cases were routinely resolved in favour of those with the deepest pockets.

Nor did the Parliament act as an effective brake on arbitrary action by the government—even though it had the formal authority to do so. The primary reason for this was that the government, and specifically the President, had a major hand in deciding who would sit in Parliament, both through the control of the electoral process and through the President's right to nominate half the members of the Upper House and, with the military, 20 per cent of the members of the Lower House.

The press was no independent watchdog over government either. Although there were periods of relative openness, the last one being in the early 1990s, under the New Order the press operated under very tight government constraints. Open censorship was relatively rare; more commonly, editors would exercise their own censorship of stories on the basis of what they believed the government wanted to see reported.

Thus, although Indonesia was far from being a political dictatorship, the degree of pluralism the New Order system permitted was severely constrained.

Overall, Suharto was remarkably successful in controlling Indonesian political life, reducing civil society to a position of weakness and dependency on the state and preventing the emergence of any viable alternatives either to him as President or to the New Order system of government. By the mid-1990s, though, as Suharto aged, the government was facing the greatest challenge it had known to date: managing the transition to the third Presidency.

9
REFORMASI: THE POST-SUHARTO ERA?

The years since Suharto's resignation have been marked by riots, civil conflict, renewed separatist violence, the secession of East Timor, three different Presidents, an upsurge of religious-based political activities and a massive downturn in the economy. The origins, development and implications of these events will be considered here, particularly in terms of how they have impacted on ordinary citizens, and on the very concept of Indonesia itself. Many observers have predicted that the break-up of the Indonesian state is imminent. Yet this has not happened; the chapter concludes by suggesting that, although the question of whether Indonesia will survive is still a valid one, the state's collapse is now looking increasingly unlikely.

How Suharto might have handled the transition to the third Presidency will now never be known. By the end of 1997, Suharto—and indeed Indonesia—had been overwhelmed by the greatest political, social and economic challenges facing the country since 1965–66.

In August 1997 Indonesia was hit by the Asian financial crisis which had begun in Thailand the previous month. Despite—some would say because of—negotiating two rescue packages with the International Monetary Fund (IMF), in October 1997 and January 1998, the Indonesian rupiah slid from its mid-1997 rate of 2400 to US$1 to over 17 500 in March 1998, after B. J. Habibie was nominated as Suharto's Vice-President. Among all the Asian countries hit by the crisis, Indonesia was by far the worst affected, economically, politically and socially. There were several reasons for this.

First, for most of the 1990s the exchange rate for the rupiah against the US dollar had been held too low, and Indonesian interest rates too high. This meant that for many businesses it was cheaper to finance domestic projects using borrowed US dollars than the local currency. So long as the exchange rate was reasonably stable, this practice was sustainable. But as the exchange rate began to fall following the collapse of the Thai economy in July 1997, dollars became more expensive to buy in terms of rupiah. This started a panic buying of dollars, as businesspeople tried to buy that currency before the price in rupiah got even higher—the logical and inevitable outcome was that the price of US dollars got even worse than it had been previously: in other words, the exchange rate was pushed further and further out, until it hit 17 500 rupiah to US$1.

Second, Indonesia's world competitiveness in exports was low and had begun to decline over the last few years. What really hit Indonesia's exports was the falling dollar cost of wages in China, one of its main international competitors. In 1996, China had devalued its currency by 45 per cent, enormously increasing its competitiveness on world markets. Even during the good times, Indonesia's had been a relatively high-cost economy, the result of corruption and low labour productivity. Added to the falling exchange rate, the Chinese devaluation helped put an unsustainable burden on the economy.

Third, much of the foreign and domestic investment made in Indonesia in the years just before the crisis was in speculative and essentially non-productive activities, the best example of which was commercial property. By 1997 the property markets in Jakarta and several of the other major cities, especially Surabaya, were grossly overvalued, exhibiting all the classic characteristics of a bubble economy. Once the money stopped flowing, the bubble burst, to the point where today the Jakarta skyline is dotted with half-finished skyscrapers, their skeletons quietly rusting into oblivion.

Fourth, the banking system, which had grown so rapidly following substantial deregulation in the early 1990s, failed to cope adequately with the challenges of growth. In particular, many of these banks were owned by or had close connections with major business conglomerates, and it was common practice for the banks to make substantial loans to their parent companies or their affiliates, with minimal collateral, if any. When the parent companies experienced difficulties and were unable to repay the loans, the lending banks themselves were in trouble.

Fifth, once the crisis began to hit in the third quarter of 1997, Indonesia took what was at the time widely considered to be an extremely wise step: it called in the IMF. But this move backfired. The IMF rescue package negotiated in late October 1997, which was intended to stabilise the rupiah at about 3000 to US$1, failed to have the desired effect. Indeed, far from helping to stabilise the situation, the package contributed to the economic problems Indonesia is facing today by directing attention away from the real problems and focusing on relatively minor issues. In particular, it treated the Indonesian situation as if the real problem was one of an excess of state spending, and therefore mandated major cuts to the government budget. In fact, the major problem lay in private indebtedness, which was largely untouched by the package. Six weeks after the package was concluded, the rupiah plunged for a second time, falling from around 4000 to the dollar down to 12 000 to the dollar between mid-December and early January. A second reform package negotiated in January 1998 did nothing to halt the slide.

Sixth, Indonesia had become increasingly dependent on Japan and Korea as markets for its exports and as sources of investment capital; as these two countries got into economic difficulties themselves, they slashed both their imports from Indonesia and their investment of capital in the country.

Seventh, Indonesia's natural environment was experiencing conditions unfavourable to the economy. The year 1997, for instance, was extremely dry. Apart from helping along extensive forest fires in Kalimantan and Sumatera, the dry weather caused a substantial drop in rice production. Output in 1997 was about 38 million tonnes; substantially less than consumption. Had the exchange rate remained reasonably stable, this would not have been a major problem, any shortfall being made up by imports. But once the rupiah had devalued, rice imports became very expensive, pushing up prices at home.

And finally, the whole issue of political leadership had an enormous and negative effect on the situation. In 1997 and early 1998, when foreign governments and financiers were looking for strong and effective government in Indonesia, they saw instead a 76-year-old President, not in good health (there is little doubt that Suharto had a mild stroke in early December 1997) and with no obvious successor except for B. J. Habibie—who actually made prospects look worse rather than better. There was a massive flight of confidence from the government: no one believed that Suharto had the will or the capacity to pull Indonesia out of the developing crisis. As the IMF itself acknowledged, the enormous depreciation in the rupiah from October 1997 'did not seem to stem from macroeconomic imbalances. [Rather, it] reflected a severe loss of confidence in the currency, the financial sector and the overall economy'.

But it was not just Indonesia's economy that was being rapidly eroded. At a different level, the effect of the three decades of authoritarian rule by Suharto was that civil society was paralysed as well. Virtually no political or social institutions of any standing were operating independently of government. Organisations ranging from political parties to sporting associations had enjoyed, and become reliant upon, government patronage. This meant that as the government foundered these institutions foundered as well, tearing at the very fabric of Indonesian society. There were very few non-government leaders who enjoyed any substantial, nationwide, popular support, and virtually none who had had any experience of government. There was no loyal opposition, ready to take over from the Suharto government in any smooth or organised way.

From early in 1998, as the economic crisis worsened, student-led demonstrations against Suharto were mounted with increasing frequency in the major cities. Radical student movements, challenging the existing social order, have a long history in modern Indonesia. There have been at least three times when they have played major roles in helping to initiate political change, most dramatically—and in many senses most ironically—in 1965–66, when they spearheaded the movement which resulted in the downfall of the country's first President, Sukarno, and the rise to power of then-General Suharto. For weeks at that time, student groups had held rallies and demonstrations in Jakarta and other major Indonesian cities demanding the resignation of Sukarno, the banning of the then-powerful Communist Party of Indonesia and the lowering of consumer prices.

Twenty years earlier, in 1945, students had been at the forefront of Indonesia's independence movement, urging the established nationalist leaders, including Sukarno, to proclaim the nation's independence after the Japanese had surrendered, before the Dutch and their allies had had a chance to return to reclaim the Indies.

Before the war, it was students and recent university graduates that formed the backbone of the nationalist movement directed against the Dutch colonial authorities. In 1908, medical students in

Jakarta had formed Budi Utomo, the precursor to the modern Indonesian nationalist organisations. Sukarno himself first began to play an active role in nationalist politics while an architecture student in Bandung, a pattern followed by many nationalist leaders.

Thus in their activism in Jakarta in 1997 and 1998, Indonesia's students were following a well-established political tradition of opposing those in authority. That they emerged as the cutting edge of opposition to Suharto should not have been surprising to anyone with any knowledge of Indonesia's recent history.

Student-led opposition came to a head in May 1998 when troops shot and killed four students at Trisakti University in west Jakarta. There followed two days and nights of vicious rioting, worst in Jakarta but bad also in Solo, in central Java, which saw around 1200 people killed. Most of the victims were trapped in shopping centres which had been deliberately set on fire. Over 100 women, most of ethnic Chinese origin, were systematically raped. At the same time, there was a large movement of people out of the country, particularly foreigners and Indonesians of Chinese descent, and of a large amount of capital as well.

On 21 May 1998, Suharto formally resigned the Presidency.

The student-led demonstrations, the public face of the movement that brought Suharto down, certainly had the effect of convincing many former Suharto loyalists, civilian and military, that they should consider abandoning the sinking ship. However, the key to Suharto's fall was not the demonstrations but the economic crisis.

Suharto had built his claim to political legitimacy on Indonesia's economic development. Many Indonesians had probably accepted the limitations on their personal freedoms inherent in the Suharto style of government as the price to be paid for rising economic prosperity—but once that prosperity was threatened, that political accommodation collapsed. By the evening of 20 May, even long-time political allies of Suharto were telling him that he had to go.

Suharto's successor as President was his hand-picked Vice-President and long-time confidant, B. J. Habibie. German-educated, an aeronautical engineer by profession, Habibie had been elected Vice-President in March 1998, in a move which had drawn widespread criticism. He was seen as having secured the position simply by reason of his long political alliance with Suharto. His political experience was limited to having been the Minister for Research and Technology for over twenty years, and holding the Chairmanship of ICMI. His ideas on economic development, focusing on the role to be played by high-technology industries such as aircraft production, were rejected by the bulk of the country's economists. Financial markets greeted his election by driving the rupiah down to its lowest levels ever against the US dollar.

In taking on the Presidency Habibie was confronted with a Herculean task: to keep one step ahead of the reformist movement which had led the charge against Suharto, his former boss and political sponsor, and which was now demanding radical changes in the way in which Indonesia was run. For a while, against all the odds, it seemed that he might just be able to pull it off.

His first few months as President saw the implementation of a raft of important policy initiatives, including the freeing of political prisoners, the almost complete removal of political censorship of the press, the lifting of restrictions on the formation of political parties and trade unions and, the most important developments of all, planning for the holding of free general elections, which took place on 7 June 1999, and for a referendum on independence in East Timor, held on 30 August 1999.

The downside of Habibie's Presidency outweighed the upside in the eyes of most Indonesians, however. In political terms, he failed to distance himself sufficiently from his predecessor. Most importantly, he failed to meet widespread public demands for action to be taken against former President Suharto, and his associates, for corruption. He failed to take firm action against those who perpetrated the riots, rapes and arson in Jakarta in May 1998. He failed to prevent further

231

outbreaks of violence around the country. Indeed, inter-communal violence in 1998 was worse than anything seen in the previous year.

Even several of Habibie's apparent successes had major political costs associated with them. There was a firm expectation on the part of many Indonesians that the June elections would help resolve the crisis in national leadership by establishing which politicians or political parties had the support of the majority of the electors. The elections were largely honest, fair and peaceful, and in that sense met one of the short-term objectives, but in the longer term were not so successful. When the results were eventually declared, after a long delay while the votes were laboriously tallied, no one party had won enough seats to control the parliament. By far the most popular party was the Indonesian Democratic Party of Struggle, or Partai Demokrasi Indonesia Perjuangan (PDIP), the party of Megawati Sukarnoputri, populist politician and daughter of Indonesia's first President, which scored 34 per cent of the vote. Golkar, the party of Habibie and Suharto, ran second, a long way further back, with 22 per cent of the vote. Then there was quite a gap to the next biggest party, the National Awakening Party, Partai Kebangkitan Bangsa (PKB), with 13 per cent: this is the party with which Abdurrahman Wahid is associated. And so on through the rest of the 48 parties which contested the elections.

Though some observers profess to have been surprised that Golkar's vote was as great as it was, to its long-time members and supporters the view was rather different. They saw that Habibie had led them to defeat. Indeed, the party's leadership had indicated its lack of confidence even before the ballot by refusing to confirm that Habibie would be its chosen nominee in the Presidential elections due for November. Supporters of other parties would have seen the election results as confirming their view that Habibie was on his way out.

By contrast to the elections, the referendum campaign in East Timor was a violent and bloody affair. Quite why Habibie, not known for his political nous, approved the holding of the referendum in the first place, to the surprise of virtually all observers and apparently to many of his political colleagues as well, remains a matter of debate.

Habibie might possibly have thought the referendum would result in victory for the pro-autonomy position. He might also have seen it as a way of making his political mark independent of his erstwhile sponsor, Suharto. Indonesia's East Timor policy was very much Suharto's policy; breaking with Suharto meant breaking with that policy. But what is absolutely clear is that significant sections of the political elite, both civilian and military, did not agree with his position.

The referendum, in which voters were asked whether they wished to remain with Indonesia under a special autonomy package offered by the government, was held on 30 August 1999. The result was a sweeping victory for the opponents of the package, led by Xanana Gusmao (newly released from prison in Jakarta). Nearly 80 per cent of the electoral roll voted against special autonomy and thus, by implication, for independence.

Ultimate responsibility for the murder, arson and forced movement of people across the border into West Timor that preceded and followed the independence ballot can properly be sheeted home to the military, and in particular to its commander, General Wiranto. The links between the militias, which wreaked much of the havoc, and the military have been sufficiently well documented as to leave no doubt that they were the key to the violence. Whether Wiranto directly ordered the violence may still be a matter of conjecture; what cannot be doubted is that, as commander of the armed forces, Wiranto was ultimately responsible for the actions of the troops under his command.

In a political sense, and a moral one as well, President Habibie must share this responsibility. Constitutionally, he was not only Head of State but Supreme Commander of the Armed Forces as well. He was also seen by many Indonesians—including senior military officers—as being responsible for a degree of national humiliation the country had not previously experienced. The extent to which many ordinary

Indonesians had become convinced that the bulk of the East Timorese were accepting of the region's status as an Indonesian province should not be underestimated. Nor should the extent to which many believed that the results of the referendum were the product of manipulation by the United Nations Assistance Mission in East Timor (UNAMET), which was responsible for the conduct of the ballot, and by foreign countries, notably Australia. The establishment of the International Force for East Timor (INTERFET) commanded by Australian General Peter Cosgrove, and the Australian triumphalism which accompanied its position in the region in mid-September, were all seen as part of the humiliation of the nation. Blame for all these developments was sheeted home to Habibie.

On the economic side, too, Habibie's ineffectiveness was evident. Under his Presidency the economy went further into decline. Inflation in 1998 was 78 per cent, compared with around 11 per cent in 1997. Economic growth during the year was negative 14 per cent, compared with 6–8 per cent per annum in the first half of the 1990s. Unemployment was at least 20 million, and underemployment at least that much again. Probably as many as 90 per cent of Indonesia's major companies became technically bankrupt, many banks were closed, and building construction came to a standstill.

The combination of continued economic decline, humiliation in East Timor and defeat in the elections meant that the Parliament's vote of no confidence in Habibie in October could hardly have been unexpected. But who his likely successor would be was by no means clear.

The dispersion of the vote in the June elections meant that the workings of the new Parliament would be dependent on there being a working coalition involving at least two parties, and probably more. As many observers pointed out, this situation was worryingly reminiscent of the results of the 1955 elections, and illustrative of the difficulty of trying to govern a country as politically and socially diverse as Indonesia through political devices which are difficult enough to manage even in much more homogeneous societies.

Together with representatives of the provinces, functional groups and the military, the parliamentarians elected in June constituted the People's Consultative Assembly, or Majelis Permusyawaratan Rakyat (MPR), which was to elect the President and Vice-President. That election was held in November.

Although in the run-up to the election half a dozen would-be Presidents threw their hats into the ring, on the day it came down to a contest between Megawati Sukarnoputri and Abdurrahman Wahid, popularly known as Gus Dur. In the end, Wahid defeated Megawati reasonably comfortably, by a margin of nearly 40 votes out of 700. The following day, in the election for Vice-President and with the support of Wahid, Megawati easily defeated her sole rival.

Wahid came to office with a high reputation for personal integrity and for a commitment to a pluralist and democratic society. Long-time leader of the Nahdatul Ulama—with over 35 million members, the largest Muslim organisation in the world—he nonetheless argued strongly against making Indonesia an Islamic state. He made strenuous efforts to assure the country's Christian and ethnic Chinese minorities that he respected and valued their membership of Indonesian society. And although his views on economic policy were not well known, the financial markets greeted his election warmly, strengthening the rupiah to around 8000 to the US$1. The one major cloud on the horizon was his health: he had suffered two major strokes in recent years, was suffering from diabetes and virtually blind.

Why did Megawati not win the Presidency, given her party's success in the general elections? Her gender was undoubtedly a factor working against her. Some Indonesian Muslim leaders argued that Islam did not permit a woman to be head of state—including Hamzah Haz, in 2001 to be elected her Vice-President. But there were at least as many Muslim scholars who argued the contrary case. There were others who said simply that women in general were not intellectually or emotionally equipped to be national leaders.

Megawati had a bigger handicap than her gender, however. Simply, she was not a particularly effective politician. In terms of political ideas she appeared to many to be something of a policy-free zone. Her associates and advisers were left to indicate what she might do in government. Moreover, she showed a poor sense of political priorities. She steadfastly refused, for instance, to take part in any of the debates for presidential candidates held in 1998.

Perhaps her biggest political blunder occurred in October, in the run-up to the Presidential elections. While other candidates were out wheeling and dealing, trying to cement-in support coalitions, Megawati stood aloof, giving the impression that she thought others should come to her—not the other way around. Gus Dur gave no such impression. He was extremely active in trying to lock-in support for his candidacy, all the while publicly wavering about whether he was in fact a candidate at all.

For all of that, though, Megawati remained a powerful symbol to many Indonesians, a symbol of the fight for justice and freedom, a symbol of all those Indonesians who have personally paid the price of that fight. And symbolism can be a very powerful force in politics.

The combination of Wahid and Megawati in the Presidential and Vice-Presidential positions was not one that many observers had predicted. Even Wahid himself acknowledged its unusual nature. At his inauguration he said that the pairing was fitting: he himself, he said, could not see and Megawati could not speak, in reference to his own near-blindness and Megawati's reluctance to make definitive pronouncements on anything policy related. Whether Megawati appreciated his wry humour is not known.

For perhaps the first six months of his Presidency, Wahid seemed to be fulfilling his promise. His first Cabinet, though having its share of debt-repaying appointments, also had some members of real standing in the Indonesian and international communities. The rupiah began to strengthen, and peace negotiations were opened with the Free Aceh Movement. Economic growth turned positive, reaching

5 per cent in 2000, albeit with considerable pain for ordinary Indonesians. Civilian control was gradually being exerted over the military. A start was being made on working out the details of the decentralisation program commenced by the Habibie government, and promising the regions much greater control over their own resources, and greater independence of control from Jakarta.

By late 2000, the cracks were beginning to appear in the political façade and the economic one.

The primary political problem confronting Indonesia was that of preserving the unity of the state. A multicultural, multi-ethnic country, Indonesia has always faced a degree of tension between the central government and minority populations, and indeed between different ethnic and religious groups in society. This tension was not always handled very well, but it had been kept under a degree of control. This was no longer the case.

The situation was worst, and the challenge to the unity of the state greatest, in the province of Aceh at the northernmost tip of Sumatera.

When the Suharto government fell, both domestic and international attention was turned on Aceh in ways not previously possible. Of primary importance here was the role of the newly freed press. The Military Operations Area condition, which had prevailed since 1989, and under whose auspices the military had felt free to act in the ways they did, was lifted in August 1998. Almost overnight, leaders of GAM (the Free Aceh Movement) began to appear in the newspapers and on television. It seemed almost childishly simple for journalists, both Indonesian and foreign, to find and to interview GAM leaders—curious, given that the Indonesian military had in the past ostensibly found it so difficult to locate and capture these people. The electronic media even began to carry live interviews with GAM officials.

Yet under Habibie, after an initial degree of euphoria, the situation in Aceh seemed to be getting steadily worse. By late 1998 there were officially just under 100 000 internal refugees in the province:

people who had fled their home villages and sought refuge in mosques, community halls and schools in regions where they felt, at least, safer than at home. The total population of the province at the time was only four million.

A new law on the division of revenues between the provinces and the central government, introduced by the Habibie government in April 1999, attracted little positive reaction from government critics in Aceh, being seen as a case of too little, too late. In August 1999, the commander of the National Police announced the deployment of an additional 3100 riot police and 2000 troops to the province to hunt down the GAM fighters. He further said that he expected to have the problem resolved by the New Year. He did not quite say that he would have his forces home by Christmas, but there was that element of un-reality in the way that Jakarta was dealing with the problem.

Habibie's replacement by Wahid seemed to suggest that there was hope for a rather different kind of response from Jakarta, and that there would be genuine attempts by both sides to find a peaceful resolution to the conflict. One of the first things that Wahid said after becoming President was that if the people of East Timor deserved a referendum, how could the people of Aceh be denied a similar choice. He very rapidly changed, or perhaps reinterpreted, that statement, though, explaining that in the referendum he envisioned the Acehnese would be allowed to decide only whether to apply Islamic laws inside their province, not whether to withdraw from the republic. Independence would not be an option.

The referendum theme was quickly taken up by many in Aceh, and especially young people, students, and urban dwellers. This was a particularly important development. Up to this time, the Free Aceh Movement had been largely, although not exclusively, rurally based, drawing its membership largely from what we might term the less modern or modernising elements of society: the remnants of the aris-tocracy, the graduates of rural Islamic boarding schools and the like. The freeing up of the debate about Aceh's future, and in particular the lure of holding a referendum, brought out urban and middle-class support for the cause. The main organisation bringing together such people was the Acehnese Centre for Referendum Information, the Sentra Informasi Referendum Aceh (SIRA).

Massive demonstrations of support for the referendum cause began in late 2000, especially from about November, in the run-up to what was expected to be a massive show of support on 4 December, the 24th anniversary of GAM's proclamation of Acehnese independence. Ultimately, the anniversary passed off rather more peacefully than many had predicted. At the central mosque in Banda Aceh, the GAM flag was not raised, in compliance with police instructions, though it was paraded through the mosque. In other locations, though, low-level clashes took place between military or police units and GAM fighters.

One of the reasons for this relative lack of violence was that during 2000 a strikingly new element had entered the political arena. Under Suharto there had never been any question of negotiations with the separatists. Wahid, however, quickly took the initiative to initiate a dialogue with GAM, a dialogue that took place in Geneva in Switzerland under the auspices of the Henri Dunant Centre. On 12 May 2000, representatives of the two sides signed a three-month ceasefire agreement officially called 'The Joint Understanding on Humanitarian Pause in Aceh'. The aim of this agreement, as its name suggests, was not actually to broker a settlement of the conflict, but rather to arrange a temporary halt to hostilities to allow the two parties some breathing space in which to seek some more permanent resolution of their differences. The initial agreement was extended in September 2000 to January 2001.

In January 2001, however, the two parties were unable to agree on a further three-month extension of the agreement, and violence again increased. The prospects for a peaceful resolution of the conflict suffered a major setback.

What drives the resentment of Jakarta in Aceh today?

There is no doubt that Islam is an element central to the cause, having been for centuries a primary measure of Acehnese identity. The implementation of Islamic law, or Shariah, in Aceh has been a consistent demand of the separatist movements for the past half-century. Wahid conceded this point, and allowed legislation establishing Islamic law in Aceh to be presented to the national parliament.

Islam has also been useful in gaining a degree of international support for the cause of Acehnese independence. It seems fairly clear, for instance, that some Acehnese fighters have received limited military training in Libya, and received some weapons from the Libyans. Others fought with the Mujahadin in Afghanistan against the Soviet Union during its occupation of that country.

The significance of Islam is far from being unproblematic, however. Over 80 per cent of Indonesia's 200 million people are also Muslim, and some of them—a minority, but an important minority—are as firm in their belief as are the Acehnese. Islam is thus not a clear marker of Acehnese—as opposed to Indonesian—identity. And the bulk of the countries of the Islamic world, both in the Middle East and closer to home, Malaysia, have rejected GAM's calls for Islamic solidarity, and maintained their support for Indonesian sovereignty in Aceh. Thus Islam's significance is perhaps more symbolic than real, though none the less powerful for many Acehnese as a result.

So what are the more important factors at work here? At least three other issues need to be considered. First, there is a very clear sense of economic deprivation in Aceh. The province is rich in natural resources, particularly liquified natural gas and bauxite. These resources contribute greatly to the revenues of the Indonesian state, but very little to the revenues of the province. The bulk of the employment associated with the processing of these resources has gone to people from outside Aceh, thus again providing little local benefit.

Second, there is a strong sense of moral outrage at the way in which the central government, and in particular its armed forces, has dealt with what was until very recently a rather minor insurgency. In the past decade over 2000 people were killed by the military in what they termed security operations against armed separatist guerillas. Many others have been raped, tortured and imprisoned. This moral outrage has been expressed more vigorously since Suharto left the Presidency, not because violations of human rights in the region have necessarily become worse, but ironically because the political reforms put in place by Habibie and confirmed by Wahid made it possible to express publicly views which previously would have landed you in jail. Despite Jakarta's often-repeated commitment to finding a peaceful solution to the problem, the military in the region still clearly takes the view that the only way to deal with the independence movement is by repression.

And third, there is a strong consciousness of an Acehnese identity here, hard perhaps to define precisely but powerful nonetheless, and drawing heavily on a history of opposition to outsiders: Dutch, Japanese, Indonesian.

What are Indonesia's interests in retaining Aceh as part of the Republic? Answering this question is difficult, because it depends of course on what we mean by 'Indonesia'.

For many Indonesians, the issue here is nothing less than the very existence of the nation state of Indonesia. The key to this problem lies in how Indonesia is defined. It is clearly not defined in an ethnic way, nor a religious way. Nor is it based on a great and glorious history in days gone by, although some nationalists do attempt to portray it in this way. For most Indonesians their country is defined in terms of its more recent history as a Dutch colony. It is the common suffering experienced by people right around the archipelago, and the common struggle against colonial oppression, these people argue, which defines the state. At a symbolic level, this belief is summed up in the popular phrase *Dari Sabang sampai Merauke*: 'From Sabang to Merauke'. Merauke is a city at the very southeastern reaches of the Republic, in Irian Jaya. Sabang is at the other end of the archipelago, on an island off the northern tip of Aceh.

Among civilian politicians, Megawati was a strong supporter of this line. Since becoming President, though, while not resiling from this position she has shown some awareness of the fact that some consideration has to be given to the expressed interests of the Acehnese: that retaining the region as part of the Republic by military force alone will simply not work.

And here is where East Timor and Aceh are fundamentally different. East Timor never had a crucially important defining role in the Indonesian nation state. It could be excised from the nation state without calling the idea of Indonesia into question. Indeed it could be argued that, other things being equal—which of course they never are—removing East Timor would actually strengthen the idea of Indonesia, by getting it back to its historical roots.

Indonesia's current leaders largely reject the idea of a federal state in which Aceh might have a very high degree of local autonomy. Among them only Amien Rais has in the past come out in favour of federalism.

At a more pragmatic level, the economic wealth of Aceh is another reason why many central politicians want to keep Aceh in the Republic. And for some military officers, the continued retention of Aceh is important, both to stress the important role they have played in defending the republic against the threat of separatism, and also because an independent Aceh—once again, like an independent East Timor—might well demand an accounting for the violence perpetrated there in the past two decades.

A similar situation to that in Aceh has arisen in the easternmost province of Irian Jaya, or Papua. Here, too, economic deprivation, exacerbated by moral outrage at the way the military has conducted itself, has encouraged support for the Free Papua Movement, or Organisasi Papua Merdeka (OPM). Rather than being the instrument for unity that many of Indonesia's founders saw as its greatest strength, the military has become one of the most important forces encouraging the break-up of the state.

One important difference between Irian Jaya and Aceh is demographic. Although reliable data are hard to come by, it seems likely that indigenous Papuans today make up only perhaps half the population of the province. There is no clear ethno-political divide —indigenous Papuans supporting independence from Indonesia, non-indigenous Papuans opposing it—but it is by no means clear that a referendum would produce a majority in favour of separatism. And indeed most leaders of the separatist movement do not demand a referendum as the intermediate stage on the road to independence; they demand independence without any preliminaries.

Wahid proved unable to control the actions of the military in Aceh and Irian Jaya. Nor was he able to do much to control the Christian–Muslim violence in Maluku and central Sulawesi, or the anti-Madurese violence in Kalimantan, all of which tear at the very existence of the multi-religious and multi-ethnic nature of Indonesian society. His failure to cut off the development of the Laskar Jihad movement in mid-2000, and to prevent it moving its fighters to Ambon, may turn out to have been one of his most expensive miscalculations.

Attempts to bring Suharto to trial have also ended in failure. After many delays, his son Tommy Suharto was finally brought to court in late 2000, convicted of embezzlement and sentenced to eighteenth months' jail. But he absconded before he could be imprisoned and, in a farce worthy of a B-grade thriller, remained on the loose. In September 2001 the Supreme Court overturned his conviction, on grounds which raised serious doubts about the probity of the judgment. Rather sensibly perhaps, in light of the charges apparently pending against him—including complicity in the murder of a judge who had found against him in the earlier proceedings—Tommy did not immediately emerge from hiding. He was finally recaptured late in 2001 and was subsequently sentenced to fifteen years' jail.

In the longer-term issue of relations with East Timor, and in particular the question of bringing officers of the military to court for crimes allegedly committed there in 1999, Wahid also did not fulfil his early promise.

On the personal front, Wahid was accused of corruption for his alleged involvement with financial scandals involving funds from the Sultan of Brunei for use in Aceh, and the embezzlement of funds from Bulog, the State Logistics Agency. The evidence for Wahid's malfeasance in these two cases is thin; what does seem beyond doubt, though, is that he has proved to be a poor manager of government affairs, and a poor judge of his personal assistants—although few who knew him before his election to the Presidency can have been surprised at this development. There is little if anything in his personal or professional background which would have prepared him for the sheer complexity of the job of presiding over Indonesia, or even for delegating important aspects of that job to his associates.

This was the key to many of Wahid's problems. It was not that he was personally dishonest. Rather, he proved himself unable to meet the many demands being made on him as President and, as a result, he paid the price, in June being dismissed from office by the Parliament and replaced by his deputy, Megawati. Elected as the new Vice-President was Hamzah Haz, a Muslim politician from Kalimantan. Ironically, Haz had been one of those arguing in 1999 against Megawati's Presidential aspirations on the grounds that Islam did not permit a woman to become Head of State.

Whether Megawati will make a better fist of running Indonesia than Wahid is, of course, yet to be seen, but few Indonesians greeted her election with any great degree of enthusiasm. In contrast to the euphoria that greeted the results of the 1999 general elections and Wahid's election to the Presidency, Megawati's ascendancy was greeted—if 'greeted' is the word—more with a yawn. Despite breathless predictions to the contrary, the dismissal of Wahid and election of Megawati went off with a whimper, not a bang. Large numbers of Indonesians have acquired a very modern, Australian approach to their political leaders, a cynicism that assumes they are only in it for themselves, so one cannot expect much from them by way of advancement of the public good. This is probably no bad thing for Megawati: public expectations of her in Indonesia are so low that all she has to do is to keep the ship afloat and she will be a hero.

On the other hand, however, we should not underestimate her political capacities. Despite all predictions to the contrary, she produced a credible Cabinet which is clearly hers, one where Suharto-era civilian and military figures are few in number, and where non-party technocrats are very much in evidence. She has been criticised over the appointment of the Attorney-General, but thus far has exhibited a remarkable degree of control over the appointment process, which suggests she is going to be her own woman while in power.

However any complacency she might have felt would have been shattered by the bombings in Bali on 12 October 2002. These bombings posed the biggest challenge to Megawati's leadership to date, combining as they did the issue of Indonesia's relations with foreign countries, especially Australia, with the place of Islam in the state. The former has always been difficult for Indonesian leaders to manage. Indonesian nationalism has a strong tendency towards xenophobia, often seeing foeigners as (at best) wanting to interfere in Indonesia's domestic affairs or (at worst) plotting to bring down the state. That so many Indonesians, many of them quite well-educated and experienced, believed that the Bali bombings were perpetrated by the United States in an attempt to prevent a resurgence of the Indonesian economy, or to discredit Indonesia, or Islam, or both, is an indication of how far this nationalist thinking can go. But the fact that Megawati was prepared to invite police and intelligence officers from Australia, the United States and Britain to Bali to assist in the investigation of the bombings says something about her preparedness to take a stand against this narrow form of nationalism. Perhaps more important still was her preparedness to challenge radical Islam by having Indonesia vote in the United Nations to declare Jama'ah Islamiyah (JI) a terrorist organisation, and then to allow the arrest of Abu Bakar Ba'asyir, the alleged spiritual leader of JI.

Contrary to the predictions of many observers, these moves did not produce a massive Islamic-based backlash against Megawati, although they did show up splits within her Cabinet. Defence Minister Matori Djalil, for instance, was blunt about his belief that JI and Al Qaeda were behind the Bali bombings, Vice-President Hamzah Haz was much more circumspect.

Megawati has been put under considerable pressure from countries such as the United States and Australia to react forcefully to the bombings. But her preparedness to act in the way she did indicates a strength of character many of her critics believed she did not have. However there is a sense in which we should not spend much time over worrying about whether Megawati is the best presidential choice for Indonesia right now. The institution of the presidency in Indonesia has been substantially weakened over the past four years, although it remains an important post. Political power in Indonesia is now much more dispersed than at any time since the 1950s.

The future of Indonesia remains, of course, unknown. The unity of the state is under greater challenge than at any time since the regional rebellions of the 1950s. The country is clearly not well served by its current leaders. Yet despite economic and political crises, for most Indonesians life goes on, despite the manoeuvrings of those in positions of political leadership. Ultimately the future of the 'nation' and the 'state' will be determined by whether ordinary Indonesians feel sufficiently committed to the principles these terms represent to be prepared to work to ensure that they remain alive. For all its faults, Indonesia still offers the majority of its citizens a better and more enlightened future than any of its potential successor states could offer. The break-up of the state would not only be a strategic disaster for the country's neighbours in Southeast Asia, including Australia but, more importantly, it would be a human rights disaster for its citizens, for no such break-up is likely to occur peacefully. But to survive the nation must adjust and making those adjustments is the challenge now facing the national leadership. The next few years will show how successful they are in meeting that challenge.

BIBLIOGRAPHICAL ESSAY

Some years ago a student, surveying the collection of books on Indonesia in my office, commented that I must have every book that had ever been published on the country. I quickly disabused him of that idea. Today the volume of material available on Indonesia is huge, both in the numbers of books published, and the many more articles in academic journals and magazines. Here I can only hope to skim the surface of this resource.

General works

Of the existing histories of Indonesia, the most comprehensive is Merle Ricklef's *A History of Modern Indonesia*, Macmillan, London, 2002. John Legge's *Indonesia*, Prentice-Hall of Australia, Melbourne, 1980, is also valuable, though now needing updating. For the more modern period, see Robert Cribb and Colin Brown, *Modern Indonesia: A History Since 1945*, Longman, London, 1995.

Two reference books by Robert Cribb are very useful: *Historical Dictionary of Indonesia*, Scarecrow, Metuchen, 1992, and *Historical Atlas of Indonesia*, Curzon, Richmond, 2000.

There is now a substantial volume of Indonesian novels, plays, short stories and poems that have been translated into English. Indonesia's leading prose writer in the second half of the twentieth century was Pramoedya Ananta Toer. His best-known works are the tetralogy he composed while a prisoner on Buru Island, following Suharto's seizure of power in 1965–66. These novels, translated by Max Lane and published by Penguin, are *This Earth of Mankind* (1981), *Child of All Nations* (1982), *Footsteps* (1990) and *House of Glass* (1992). *The Weaverbirds* by the late Y. B. Mangunwijaya and translated by Thomas M. Hunter, published by Lontar Foundation, Jakarta, 1981, is also definitely worth reading.

For Indonesian poetry and short stories see Burton Raffel (ed.), *The Complete Poetry and Prose of Chairil Anwar*, SUNY Press, Albany, 1970; Iem Brown and Joan Davis (eds and trans.), *Di Serambi—On the Verandah: A Bilingual Anthology of Modern Indonesian Poetry*, Cambridge University Press, Melbourne, 1995; Jeanette Lingard (trans.), *Diverse Lives: Contemporary Stories from Indonesia*, Oxford in Asia, Kuala Lumpur, 1996, and Harry Aveling (trans.), *Secrets Need Words: Indonesian Poetry, 1966–1998*, Research in International Studies, Southeast Asia Series, No. 105, 2001.

Tineke Hellwig, *In the Shadow of Change: Images of Women in Indonesian Literature*, Centers for South and Southeast Asia Studies, University of California at Berkeley, 1994, deals with this often neglected subject.

J. J. Fox (ed.), *Indonesian Heritage: Religion and Ritual*, Editions Didier Millet, Singapore, 1998, is also very useful, and well illustrated.

There are many coffee-table books presenting visual images of Indonesia. Two particularly striking ones are Ian Charles Stewart, *Indonesians: Portraits from an Archipelago*, Concept Media, Singapore, 1984, and Co Rentmeester, *Three Faces of Indonesia*, Thames and Hudson, London, 1974.

A superb set of 20 compact discs of Indonesian music is the *Music of Indonesia* series, recorded, compiled and annotated by Philip Yampolsky and produced by Smithsonian/Folkways, SFW 40055–40057, 40420–40429, 40441–40447. These recordings were released between 1991 and 1999. For details see <www.si.edu/folkways>

Chapter 1

The best writer on pre-historic Indonesia, and Southeast Asia more generally, is Peter Bellwood. See, for instance, his 'Southeast Asia before history' in Nicholas Tarling (ed.), *The Cambridge History of Southeast Asia*, Vol. 1, Cambridge University Press, Cambridge, 1992, pp. 55–136, and *Prehistory of the Indo-Malaysian Archipelago*, Academic Press, Sydney, 1985.

Russel Jones, 'Earl, Logan and "Indonesia"', in *Archipel*, 16, 1973, pp. 93–118, is an interesting discussion of the origins of the word 'Indonesia'.

There is no good, up-to-date geography of the Indonesian archipelago, though there is much useful information in Cribb's *Historical Atlas of Indonesia*.

For those interested in the ways in which interpretations of Indonesian, and Southeast Asian, history have evolved, by far the best work is John Legge, 'The writing of Southeast Asian history' in Tarling (ed.), *The Cambridge History of Southeast Asia*, op. cit., pp. 1–50.

Chapter 2

Three chapters in Tarling's *The Cambridge History of Southeast Asia*, Vol. 1, provide a very good grounding in the emergence of states and societies in Southeast Asia in the period covered by this chapter. They are Keith W. Taylor, 'The early kingdoms' (pp. 137–82), Kenneth R. Hall, 'Economic history of early Southeast Asia' (pp. 183–275) and J. G. de Casparis and J. W. Mabbett, 'Religion and popular beliefs of Southeast Asia before c. 1500' (pp. 276–339). See also Kenneth R. Hall, *Maritime Trade and State Development in Early Southeast Asia*, University of Hawaii, Honolulu, 1985.

The standard works on the Sumatera state of Srivijaya are still O. W. Wolters, *The Fall of Srivijaya in Malay History*, Oxford University Press, Kuala Lumpur, 1970, and (by the same author) *Early Indonesian Commerce: A Study of the Origins of Srivijaya*, Cornell University Press, Ithaca, 1967. See also Pierre-Yves, Manguin, 'Palembang and Sriwijaya: an early Malay harbour-city rediscovered', *Journal of the Malaysian Branch, Royal Asiatic Society*, 66, part 1, no. 264, 1993, pp. 23–46.

The art and architecture of the Javanese state of Majapahit are discussed in John Miksic and Endang Sri Hardiati Soekatno (eds), *The

Legacy of Majapahit, National Heritage Board, Singapore, 1995. Indonesian sculpture of this period is well analysed and illustrated in Jan Fontein, *The Sculpture of Indonesia*, Harry N. Abrams Inc, New York, 1990; produced to accompany a major exhibition of Indonesian sculpture at the National Art Gallery, Washington, DC, from 1 July to 4 November 1990, apart from superb illustrations it also contains very useful essays by Fontein ('Introduction: The sculpture of Indonesia'), R. Soekmono ('Indonesian architecture of the classical period: a brief survey') and Edi Sedyawati ('The making of Indonesian art').

On the Buddhist Borobudur temple in central Java, it is hard to go past John Miksic's *Borobudur: Golden Tales of the Buddhas*, Bamboo Publishing, London, 1990, for its combination of scholarly analysis and eye for the beauty of the building. The best scholarly treatment of the Borobudur is still A. J. Bernet Kempers, *Ageless Borobudur*, Servire, Wassenaar, 1976.

On the China trade, Wang Gungwu's *The Nanhai Trade: The Early History of Chinese Trade in the South China Sea*, Times Academic Press, Singapore, 1998, remains important, although it was originally published in 1958. Pierre-Yves Manguin is an expert on shipping through Southeast Asia. For those interested in this subject, his 'Trading ships of the South China Sea', *Journal of the Social and Economic History of the Orient*, 36, 3, 1993, pp. 253–80, is an excellent starting point.

Jan Wisseman Christie has written extensively on the economic history of Indonesia, and Southeast Asia more generally, for the period covered by this chapter. Among her works are 'Javanese markets and the Asian sea trade boom of the tenth to thirteenth centuries AD', *Journal of the Economic and Social History of the Orient*, 41, 3, August 1998, pp. 344–81; 'Money and its uses in the Javanese states of the ninth to fifteenth centuries AD', *Journal of the Social and Economic History of the Orient*, 39, 3, August 1996, pp. 243–86; 'Trade and state formation in the Malay Peninsula and Sumatra, 300 BC–AD 700', in J. Kathirithamby-Wells and John Villiers (eds), *The Southeast Asian*

Port and Polity: Rise and Demise, Singapore University Press, Singapore, 1990, pp. 39–60, and 'Raja and Rama: the classical state in early Java' in Lorraine Gesick (ed.), *Centers, Symbols and Hierarchies: Essays on the Classical States of Southeast Asia*, Yale University Press, New Haven, 1983.

Chapter 3

The standard work on this period of Southeast Asian history is Anthony Reid's two volumes: *Southeast Asia in the Age of Commerce 1450–1680*, published by Yale University Press in 1988 (Vol. 1: *The Lands Below the Winds*) and 1993 (Vol. 2: *Expansion and Crisis*). The richness of detail in Reid's discussions of social, economic and political life in Indonesia, and other parts of Southeast Asia, during the age of commerce makes these books essential reading for anyone interested in the history of this period.

For statistical data on Southeast Asia's exports, see David Bulbeck et al. (compilers), *Southeast Asia Exports Since the 14th Century: Cloves, Pepper, Coffee, and Sugar*, ISEAS, Singapore, 1988.

Developments outside Java are discussed in John Villiers, 'Makassar: The rise and fall of an East Indonesian maritime trading state, 1512–1669', in J. Kathirithamby-Wells and John Villiers (eds), *The Southeast Asian Port and Polity: Rise and Demise*, Singapore University Press, Singapore, 1990, pp. 143–59; Leonard Andaya, *The World of Maluku: Eastern Indonesia in the Early Modern period*, University of Hawaii Press, Honolulu, 1993, and (by the same author) *The Heritage of Arung Palakka: A History of South Sulawesi (Celebes) in the Seventeenth Century*, Nijhoff, The Hague, 1981; M. J. C. Schouten, *Leadership and Social Mobility in a Southeast Asian Society: Minahasa, 1677–1983*, KITLV Press, Leiden, 1998.

The Chinese trade in the region is covered by Leonard Blussé et al., 'Chinese trade with Batavia in the seventeenth and eighteenth centuries: A preliminary report', in Karl Reinhold Haellquist (ed.), *Asian Trade Routes: Continental and Maritime*, Curzon, London, 1991, pp. 231–45.

Chapter 4

The end of the age of commerce is discussed in Anthony Reid, 'The crisis of the seventeenth-century in Southeast Asia', in Geoffrey Parker and Lesley Smith (eds), *The General Crisis of the Seventeenth Century*, Routledge, London, 1997, pp. 206–34.

Susan Abeyasekere discusses the origins of the city of Jakarta in her book *Jakarta: A History*, Oxford University Press, Singapore, 1989.

A very interesting, and at times chilling, discussion of the early British and Dutch competition for the spice trade is Giles Milton's *Nathaniel's Nutmeg*, Farrar, Strauss & Giroux, New York, 1999.

For discussions of the VOC (Dutch East India Company), see Leonard Blussé, *Strange Company: Chinese Settlers, Mestizo Women and the Dutch in VOC Batavia*, Foris, Dordrecht, 1986; Heather Sutherland, 'Eastern emporium and company town: trade and society in eighteenth-century Makasar', in Frank Broeze (ed.), *Brides of the Sea: Port Cities of Asia from the 16th–20th Centuries*, New South Wales University Press, Sydney, 1989, pp. 97–128, and Reinout Vos, *Gentle Janus, Merchant Prince: The VOC and the Tightrope of Diplomacy in the Malay World, 1740–1800*, Beverley Jackson (trans.), KITLV Press, Leiden, 1993.

The political organisation of Mataram is discussed by Soemarsaid Moertono, *State and Statecraft in Old Java: A Study of the Later Mataram Period, 16th to 19th Centuries*, Cornell Modern Indonesia Project, Ithaca, 1981. For a major non-Javanese society see M. J. C. Schouten, *Leadership and Social Mobility in a Southeast Asian Society: Minahasa, 1677–1983*, KITLV Press, Leiden, 1998.

Chapter 5

For long the standard work on Dutch colonial history in Indonesia was J. S. Furnivall's *Netherlands India*, Cambridge University Press, Cambridge, 1967 (originally published in 1939). The book is now outdated in its interpretations, but is still a useful source. No single book has replaced it.

Peter Carey has provided a translated and annotated version of the *Babad Dipanagara*, a Javanese account of the Java War, in *Babad Dipanagara: An Account of the Outbreak of the Java War (1825–30)*, Malaysian Branch of the Royal Asiatic Society, Kuala Lumpur, 1981. For other regional accounts of resistance to colonialism, see Karl Pelzer, *Planter and Peasant: Colonial Policy and the Agrarian Struggle in East Sumatra 1863–1947*, Nijhoff, The Hague, 1978; Elizabeth Graves, *The Minangkabau Response to Dutch Colonial Rule in the Nineteenth Century*, Cornell Modern Indonesia Project, Ithaca, 1981; Ann Stoler, *Capitalism and Confrontation in Sumatra's Plantation Belt*, Yale University Press, New Haven, 1985, and Alfons van der Kraan, *Lombok: Conquest, Colonization, and Underdevelopment, 1870–1940*, Heinemann, Singapore, 1980. The best discussion of the impact of the Cultivation System on the Javanese is R. E. Elson, *Village Java under the Cultivation System, 1830–1870*, Allen & Unwin for the ASAA, Sydney, 1994.

C. L. M. Penders, *Indonesia: Selected Documents*, University of Queensland Press, St Lucia, 1977, contains a large number of useful documents translated from the Dutch.

Anne Booth et al. (eds), *Indonesian Economic History in the Dutch Colonial Era*, Yale University Southeast Asian Studies Monograph Series No. 35, New Haven, 1990, is an excellent source of analyses of the colonial economy.

Chapter 6

On various aspects of the nationalist movement see Deliar Noer, *The Modernist Muslim Movement in Indonesia 1900–1942*, Oxford University Press, Kuala Lumpur, 1973; John Ingleson, *Road to Exile*, Heinemann for the ASAA, Singapore, 1979; Bernhard Dahm, *Sukarno and the Struggle for Indonesian Independence*, (trans.) Mary Somers Heidhues, Cornell University Press, Ithaca, 1969; Ruth McVey, *The Rise of Indonesian Communism*, Cornell Modern Indonesia Project, Ithaca, 1965, and George Kahin, *Nationalism and Revolution in*

Indonesia, Cornell University Press, Ithaca, 1952.

Leo Suryadinata (ed.), *Political Thinking of the Indonesian Chinese, 1900–1995*, Singapore University Press, Singapore, 1999, is excellent on the ethnic Chinese minority.

John Legge, *Sukarno: A Political Biography*, Allen Lane/Penguin, London, 1972, is a fine biography of Indonesia's first president. The nation's first vice-president, Mohammad Hatta, is dealt with sympathetically by Mavis Rose in *Indonesia Free: A Political Biography of Mohammad Hatta*, Cornell Modern Indonesia Project, Ithaca, 1987.

On aspects of Indonesia's social, and especially literary, history in the first half of the twentieth century, see Heather Sutherland, 'Pudjangga Baru: aspects of Indonesian intellectual life in the 1930s', *Indonesia*, 6, October 1968, pp. 106–27. The emergence of the Indonesian language is charted in Khaidir Anwar, *Indonesian: Development of a National Language*, Gadjah Mada University Press, Yogyakarta, 1979. See also Joost Coté (trans.), *Letters from Kartini: An Indonesian Feminist, 1900–1904*, Monash Asia Institute, Clayton, 1992. Shiraishi Takashi, *An Age in Motion: Popular Radicalism in Java, 1912–1926*, Cornell University Press, Ithaca, 1990, is a very sophisticated account of social change in Indonesia in the early twentieth century.

On the Japanese occupation, Harry J. Benda, *The Crescent and the Rising Sun: Indonesian Islam under the Japanese Occupation*, van Hoeve, The Hague, 1958, is still very valuable. See also Harry J. Benda, James K. Irikura and Koichi Kishi (eds), *Japanese Military Administration in Indonesia: Selected Documents*, Yale University Press, New Haven, 1965.

Chapter 7

For long the standard work on the revolution was George Kahin's *Nationalism and Revolution in Indonesia*, Cornell University Press, Ithaca, 1952. Many of its basic precepts were challenged by Benedict Anderson in his *Java in a Time of Revolution*, Cornell University Press, Ithaca, 1972.

An excellent shorter work on the revolution is Anthony Reid, *Indonesian National Revolution, 1945*, Longman, Hawthorn, 1974. The often-neglected regional aspects of the revolution are dealt with in Audrey Kahin (ed.), *Regional Dynamics of the Indonesian Revolution: Unity from Diversity*, University of Hawaii Press, Honolulu, 1985. An excellent selection of first-hand accounts of the revolution is reproduced in Colin Wild and Peter Carey, *Born in Fire: The Indonesian Struggle for Independence: An Anthology*, Ohio University Press, Athens, 1988.

The standard work on the politics of the 1950s is Herbert Feith, *The Decline of Constitutional Democracy in Indonesia*, Cornell University Press, Ithaca, 1962. An excellent collection of documents from the period is Herbert Feith and Lance Castles (eds), *Indonesian Political Thinking 1945–1965*, Cornell University Press, Ithaca, 1970.

Several of the leading political and bureaucratic figures of the 1950s have written their memoirs, including Ali Sastroamijoyo, *Milestones on my Journey*, C. L. M. Penders (ed.), University of Queensland Press, St Lucia, 1979; Mohammad Hatta, *Memoirs*, C. L. M. Penders (ed.), Gunung Agung, Singapore, 1981. Sukarno's *Autobiography, As Told to Cindy Adams*, Bobbs Merrill, Indianapolis, 1965, deserves a reading, but more as a novel than as history.

Ulf Sundhaussen, *The Road to Power: Indonesian Military Politics 1945–1967*, OUP, Kuala Lumpur, 1982, is an excellent discussion of military politics in the first two decades after the proclamation of independence. The rise of the Communist Party is detailed in Donald Hindley, *The Communist Party of Indonesia 1951–1963*, University of California Press, Berkeley, 1966.

Chapter 8

The Sukarno years—roughly 1957 to 1966—have not been dealt with as exhaustively as the Suharto years that followed. All general works on post-war Indonesia cover the period, as do the biographies of Sukarno. The military politics of the time are dealt with in Sundhaussen, *The Road to Power*, cited above. The best account of the rise of Golkar is David Reeve, *Golkar of Indonesia: An Alternative to the Party System*, Oxford University Press, Singapore, 1985. The history of Indonesia's confrontation of Malaysia is dealt with exhaustively in Jamie Mackie, *Konfrontasi: The Indonesia–Malaysia Dispute, 1963–1966*, Oxford University Press, London, 1974. Charles Coppel has provided the definitive coverage of the position of Indonesia's ethnic Chinese minority during the Sukarno and early Suharto eras in his *Indonesian Chinese in Crisis*, Oxford University Press, Kuala Lumpur, 1983. See also Jamie Mackie (ed.), *The Chinese in Indonesia*, Thomas Nelson, Melbourne, 1976.

The best and most detailed study of the Suharto era is Adam Schwarz, *A Nation in Waiting*, 2nd edn, Allen & Unwin, Sydney, 1999. A good discussion of Islamic politics (and politics more generally) is Douglas E. Ramage, *Politics in Indonesia: Democracy, Islam and the Ideology of Tolerance*, Routledge, New York, 1995. See also Michael Vatikiotis, *Indonesian Politics under Suharto*, Routledge, London 1993; Hal Hill (ed.), *Indonesia's New Order: The Dynamics of Socio-Economic Transformation*, Allen & Unwin, Sydney, 1993, and Virginia Hooker (ed.), *Culture and Society in New Order Indonesia*, Oxford University Press, Kuala Lumpur, 1993.

On the military during this period see David Jenkins, *Soeharto and his Generals: Indonesian Military Politics 1975–1983*, Cornell Modern Indonesia Project, Ithaca, 1984; Harold Crouch, *The Army and Politics in Indonesia*, Cornell University Press, Ithaca, 1988; Robert Lowry, *The Armed Forces of Indonesia*, Allen & Unwin, Sydney, 1996; Salim Said, 'Suharto's armed forces: building a power base in new order Indonesia, 1966–1998', *Asian Survey*, 38, no. 6, June 1998, pp. 535–52, and Douglas Anton Kammen, *A Tour of Duty: Changing Patterns of Military Politics in Indonesia in the 1990s*, Cornell Modern Indonesia Project, Ithaca, 1999.

The best studies of the Indonesian economy during the Suharto period are Richard Robison, *Indonesia: The Rise of Capital*, Allen & Unwin, Sydney, 1986; Anne Booth, *The Oil Boom and After: Indonesian*

Economic Policy and Performance in the Soeharto Era, Oxford University Press, Singapore, 1992; and Hal Hill, *The Indonesian Economy Since 1966: Southeast Asia's Emerging Giant*, Cambridge University Press, Cambridge, 1993. See also Jamie Mackie, 'Indonesia: Economic growth and depolitization' in James W. Morley (ed.), *Driven by Growth*, M. E. Sharpe, Armonk, 1999, pp. 123–41, and Andrew MacIntyre, *Business and Politics in Indonesia*, Allen & Unwin, Sydney, 1991.

Suharto's autobiography is *My Thoughts, Words and Deeds: An Autobiography*, Citra Lamtoro Gung Persada, Jakarta, 1991. By far the best biography is R. E. Elson, *Suharto*, Cambridge University Press, Cambridge, 2001.

Susan Blackburn, 'Women and citizenship in Indonesia', *Australian Journal of Political Science*, July 1999, is an important contribution to understanding the political status of women in New Order Indonesia.

The role of the press is covered very well in David Hill, *The Press in New Order Indonesia*, University of Western Australia Press, Perth, 1994. See also Krishna Sen, *Indonesian Cinema: Framing the New Order*, Zed Books, London, 1994, and David Hill and Krishna Sen, *Media, Culture and Politics in Indonesia*, Oxford University Press, Melbourne, 2000. For discussions of law and the legal system, see Tim Lindsey (ed.), *Indonesia: Law and Society*, Federation Press, Sydney, 1999.

The Timor issue is discussed, from positions critical of the Indonesian government, in James Dunn's *Timor: A People Betrayed*, Jacaranda, Brisbane, 1983, and John Taylor, *Indonesia's Forgotten War: The Hidden History of East Timor*, Zed Books, London, 1991. For a different perspective, see Bill Nicol, *Timor: The Stillborn Nation*, Visa, Melbourne, 1978.

Two interesting discussions of student politics are Ed Aspinall, 'Students and the military: regime friction and civilian dissent in the late Suharto period', *Indonesia*, no. 59, April 1995, pp. 21–44, and Robin Madrid, 'Islamic students in the Indonesian student movement

1998–1999: Forces for moderation', *Bulletin of Concerned Asian Scholars*, 31, 3, July–September 1999, pp. 7–32.

Chapter 9

Many of the sources for this period are of necessity in the form of journals and magazines, and World Wide Web sites. The *Far Eastern Economic Review* is still the best of the weekly newsmagazines, though *Asiaweek* is a useful supplement. The Jakarta daily *Jakarta Post*, available on the Web at <www.thejakartapost.com> as well as in hard copy, provides a good English-language coverage of Indonesian contemporary politics, often from a critical viewpoint. Other Indonesian news sources available on the Web in English include *Kompas* <www.kompas.com>, *Tempo* <www.temponews.com> and *Antara News Agency* <www.antara-online.com>

Websites of value include the Central Bureau of Statistics <www.bps.go.id>, the National Commission on Human Rights <www.komnas.go.id/english/>, the Social Monitoring Early Response Unit <www.smeru.or.id> and International Crisis Group <www.crisisweb.org>: the latter is a particularly valuable source of up-to-date analyses of developments in Indonesia. The World Bank <www.worldbank.org> and International Monetary Fund <www.imf.org> maintain useful archives of material relating to contemporary Indonesia. See also the very useful website Building Human Security in Indonesia at <www.preventconflict.org/portal/main/portalhome.php> maintained by the Conflict Prevention Initiative of Harvard University.

The best of the books covering this period are Geoff Forrester and R. J. May, *The Fall of Soeharto*, Crawford, Bathurst, 1998; Ed Aspinall et al. (eds), *The Last Days of President Suharto*, Monash Asia Institute, Melbourne, 1999; Arief Budiman et al. (eds), *Reformasi: Crisis and Change in Indonesia*, Monash Asia Institute, Melbourne, 1999; Adam Schwarz and Jonathan Paris (eds), *The Politics of Post-Suharto Indonesia*, Council on Foreign Relations, New York, 1999; Chris Manning and Peter van Dierman (eds), *Indonesia in Transition:*

Social Aspects of Reformasi and Crisis, ISEAS, Singapore, 2000, and Kees van Dijk, *A Country in Despair: Indonesia between 1997 and 2000*, KITLV Press, Leiden, 2001.

The 1999 Presidential election is discussed in *The 1999 Presidential Election and Post-Election Developments in Indonesia: A Post-Election Assessment Report*, National Democratic Institute for International Affairs, Washington, November 28, 1999, available at <www.ndi.org/indonesia99.htm>

Two excellent studies of the violence in Maluku are David Mearns, 'Urban kampongs in Ambon: Whose domain? Whose desa?', *The Australian Journal of Anthropology*, April 1999, Vol. 10, no. 1, pp. 15–33, and *Indonesia: Overcoming Murder and Chaos in Maluku*, International Crisis Group, Jakarta/Brussels, 19 December 2000. Developments in Aceh are covered in *Aceh: Escalating Tension*, International Crisis Group, Banda Aceh/Jakarta/Brussels, 7 December 2000.

B. J. Habibie's pre-Presidential life is covered, after a fashion, in A. Makmur Makka, *Bacharuddin Jusuf Habibie: His Life and Career*, Cipta Kreatif, Jakarta, 1994. Indonesia's current President, Megawati Sukarnoputri, has not yet been the subject of substantial critical biography. The best source—whose title is particularly apposite—is Angus McIntyre, *In Search of Megawati Sukarnoputri*, Monash Asia Institute, Clayton, 1997.

NOTES

Chapter 1

1   During the twentieth century, at least four terms were used to refer to the western half of the island of New Guinea. The Dutch called it Netherlands New Guinea. After 1945, and especially after disposition of the territory came into dispute between Indonesia and the Netherlands, the Indonesians called it first Irian Barat, and then Irian Jaya. President Abdurrahman Wahid, in early 2000, gave support to renaming the territory Papua, although Parliament did not give formal recognition to this term until October 2001. The independence movement in the region has never used the word 'Irian', preferring 'Papua' or 'Papua Barat/West Papua'.

2   The more culturally inclusive terms 'Current Era' (CE) and 'Before Current Era' (BCE) are used here in place of the more established AD and BC.

Chapter 3

1   At the time the Chineseness of the 'saints' was obviously not seen as any impediment to the acceptance of Islam. In the 1970s, however, a book by a well-known Indonesian scholar arguing that Islam might have been brought to Java not from the west but from China was banned by the Indonesian government. Four centuries on, attitude toward both ethnicity and religion had changed substantially.

Chapter 5

1   One of the most famous of modern Indonesian paintings is that by Raden Saleh, which depicts Diponegoro's capture. He is

portrayed standing on the steps of the Residency House in Magelang, surrounded by his followers; the Dutch commander de Kock is on his left, pointing to the coach that is to take him into exile.

2   Report by L. Vitalis to the Resident of Priangan, West Java, as quoted in C. L. M. Penders, ed. and trans., *Indonesia: Selected Documents on Colonialism and Nationalism, 1830–1942*, University of Queensland Press, St Lucia, 1977, p. 24.

Chapter 6

1   The other two elements recognised one nation, Indonesia, and one homeland, Indonesia.

2   Then known as Suwardi Suryaningrat.

3   'De Indische Partij, haar wezen en doel' (The Indies Party, its nature and objectives) as quoted in C. L. M. Penders, ed. and trans., *Indonesia: Selected Documents on Colonialism and Nationalism, 1830–1942*, University of Queensland Press, St Lucia, 1977, p. 228.

4   The camp was also known by its Dutch name, Boven Digul.

5   'Emerging government: an interview with Syafruddin Prawiranegara' in Colin Wild and Peter Carey, eds, *Born in Fire: The Indonesian Struggle for Independence*, Ohio University Press, Athens, 1998, p. 193.

6   See Burton Raffel, ed., *The Complete Poetry and Prose of Chairil Anwar*, State University of New York Press, Albany, NY, 1970, pp. 7–8.

7   Harry J. Benda, James K. Irikura and Koichi Kishi, eds, *Japanese Military Administration in Indonesia: Selected Documents*, Translation Series No. 6, Southeast Asian Studies, Yale University, New Haven, CT, 1965, p. 136.

8   Quoted in Harry J. Benda et al., eds, *Japanese Military Administration*, p. 136.

Chapter 7

1   Ali Sastroamijoyo, *Milestones on My Journey*, ed. C. L. M. Penders, University of Queensland Press, St Lucia, 1979, p. 268.

Chapter 8

1   'Let us bury the parties', quoted in Herbert Feith and Lance Castles, eds, *Indonesian Political Thinking 1945–1965*, Cornell University Press, Ithaca, NY, 1970, p. 82.

2   Quoted in Ulf Sundhaussen, *The Road to Power: Indonesian Military Politics 1945–1967*, Oxford University Press, Kuala Lumpur, 1982, p. 126.

3   'Dr Subandrio announces confrontation, 20 January 1963', quoted in Peter Boyce, *Malaysia and Singapore in International Diplomacy: Documents and Commentaries*, Sydney University Press, Sydney, 1968, pp. 69–70.

4   Earlier attempts to resolve the nationality question had foundered on the problem of dual nationality. Indonesian law required that its citizens could not hold the nationality of another country, while Chinese law granted Chinese citizenship to all who were of Chinese ethnicity, and made no provision for any citizen to renounce that citizenship.

5   The word 'Sekber' was dropped from the name of the organisation at this time.

6   Abdul Latif, Minister for Labour, quoted in Maggie Macrae, 'Reforms to entice more foreign investment', *Asian Business Review*, March 1995, p. 37.

INDEX